Hindustani Sangeet
Some Perspectives, Some Performers

BY THE SAME AUTHOR

Studies in the Metaphysics of Bradley
George Allen & Unwin, London
and Humanities Press, New York, 1967
(Muirhead Library)

The Winged Form: Aesthetical Essays on Hindustani Rhythm
Sangeet Natak Akademi, New Delhi, 1979

Aesthetical Essays
Chanakya Publications, Delhi, 1981

Ever Unto God: Essays on Gandhi and Religion
Indian Council of Philosophical Research, New Delhi, 1988

Swinging Syllables: Aesthetics of Kathak Dance
Sangeet Natak Akademi, New Delhi, 1991

Art and Philosophy: Seven Aestheticians
Indian Council of Philosophical Research, New Delhi, 1994

Hindustani Sangeet and a Philosopher of Art:
Music, Rhythm, and Kathak Dance
vis-à-vis Aesthetics of Susanne K. Langer
D.K. Printworld (P) Ltd., New Delhi, 2001

Hindustani Music and Aesthetics Today:
A Selective Study
Sangeet Natak Akademi, New Delhi,
and Hope India Publications, Gurgaon, 2009

Avenues to Beauty:
Eight Essays in Aesthetics
Sangeet Natak Akademi
and D.K. Printworld (P) Ltd., New Delhi, 2009

Hindustani Sangeet

Some Perspectives, Some Performers

S.K. Saxena
Formerly Professor of Philosophy
University of Delhi

Sangeet Natak Akademi
New Delhi

D.K. Printworld (P) Ltd.
New Delhi

Cataloguing in Publication Data — DK
[Courtsey: D.K. Agencies (P) Ltd. <docinfo@dkagencies.com>]

Saxena, Sushil Kumar, 1921-
Hindustani sangeet : some perspectives, some performers / S.K. Saxena.
p. cm.
Essays; previously published.
Includes bibliographical references (p.).
ISBN 13: 9788124605394
ISBN 10: 8124605394

1. Hindustani music — Philosophy and aesthetics. 2. Hindustani music — History and criticism. 3. Musicians — India. I. Title.

DDC 780.954 22

ISBN 13: 978-81-246-0539-4 **ISBN 10:** 81-246-0539-4
First published in India in 2010

Published by:
Sangeet Natak Akademi
National Academy of Music, Dance and Drama, India
Regd. office : Rabindra Bhavan, Feroze Shah Road
New Delhi - 110 001
Phones : (011) 2338 7246; 2338 7248; *Fax* : (011) 2338 2659
E-mail : sangeetnatakak@bol.net.in

and

D.K. Printworld (P) Ltd.
Regd. office : '*Srikunj*,' F-52, Bali Nagar
New Delhi - 110 015
Phones : (011) 2545 3975; 2546 6019; *Fax* : (011) 2546 5926
E-mail: indology@dkprintworld.com
Web: www.dkprintworld.com

To

Mr Jayant Kastuar

Preface

I value this book because it serves three clear ends. First, it enables me to look at Hindustani Sangeet in relation to some Western philosophers' writings on art. Second, it gives me a chance to record my impressions not only of the artistic attainments of some of our eminent classical vocalists, but of their prersonal qualities and attitudes, of which their very commitment to music is importantly one. And, third, it provides an opportunity to me to express my warm regard for Mr Jayant Kastuar who has been very helpful to me throughout his long tenure as Secretary of Sangeet Natak Akademi.

As for the content of this book, it is an intentional amalgam of essays not only on four masters of classical singing, but on some abstract matters of aesthetic theory as they relate to a few select philosophers on the one hand, and to Hindustani music, rhythm and Kathak dance, on the other. So far as I know, this book is the first to speak of Croce, Kant, and Hegel in relation to *sangeet*, and to attempt full-length essays on Ustads Altaf Hussain Khan and Rahimuddin Khan Dagar who deserve fuller attention than they have so far received in print. As for its essays on Kathak dance and the traditionally emphasized spirituality of our music, they should please readers generally because of the very novelty of their approach to, and treatment of, the subjects.

At the same time, however, I am painly conscious of what will perhaps strike some watchful readers as a serious defect of the book. Though they occur in only one or two chapters, repetitions of whole verbal collocations, ways of arguing, and perhaps even illustrations are likely to ruffle the relish of reading. I very much wish I could somehow remove this blemish. But when I finally handed over the manuscript to my publishers the strain of repeated proof-checking had left me with very little energy to do the needful. What yet serves to steady me somewhat is the thought that the work is replete with clear and serious thinking along some quite unwonted ways.

As for the overall look of the book, I feel deeply beholden to the following: Mr A.N. Sharma, for his meticulous typing; Mr Avinash Pasricha to whom I owe the gift of the visual that dignifies the book's jacket; Mr Vinay Jain who has designed it all with his customary care, and at short notice; and Mr Susheel K. Mittal of D.K. Printworld not only for his patience with my insistence on repeated proof-checking, but for his kindness in submitting them to me in an enlarged print which was easy on my ageing eyes.

S.K. Saxena

Contents

1

Essentials of Hindustānī Music[1]

MY purpose in this article is to bring out the basic features of Hindustānī music — the music[2] of north India. Carnatic music, or the music of the south, is different. Fortunately, however, some basic concepts are common to both styles. The more important of these are: *svara, ālāpa, rāga* and *tāla*.[3] So, a treatment of Hindustānī music is not to be regarded as throwing no light at all on its Carnatic parallel. The bases of my attempt are provided essentially by my own experience as a listener. But I have also drawn, at times, on established musicology; and, what is equally important, on some aesthetic insights gleaned from some of our consummate musicians' often quite obscure way of talking about music with those who not only admire but revere them.

1. This article first appeared in *Diogene*, 45, Paris, January–March 1964. Here it is reproduced with some very slight, but needful changes. Though about forty-five years have passed since its first publication, I still regard it as worthy of notice, for it is not only a simple but truthful account of the basic concepts and some genres of Hindustānī music, *and* also of the traditional way of looking at the whole of our *sangeet*.

2. Today, we freely identify *music* with *sangeet*; but, as traditionally understood, *sangeet* covers choral singing too, and has also been generally taken to mean the art and science of music and dance.

3. *Tāla* is rhythm. *Ālāpa*, which precedes a *dhruvapad* song, is singing without the help of words and rhythmic accompaniment. *Rāga* is a specific melodic scheme which admits of many compositions. *Svara* is our word for a musical note. All these terms have been explained later in the essay.

In their conception of the ulitmate aim of music, the two systems of our music, Hindustānī and Carnatic, agree entirely. Traditional Indian aesthetics conceives of every art as a pathway to the Ultimate. Music is no exception to this. Only its approach is specific — the disciplined cultivation of sound. The Absolute as Sound is spoken of as *Nād Brahma*.[4] It is admittedly difficult to think out the possibility of actually realizing the Ultimate through the practice and contemplation of music. Yet the conception cannot be dismissed summarily. Tradition has it that both Saint Tyāgarāja in the south and Swāmī Haridās in the north attained salvation through the worship of *Nād Brahma*. Their compositions, frankly devotional in character, are revered all over the country even today. I know of a *dhruvapad*[5] song which describes the way in which the vital breath can be made to pass (in singing) through the six psychic centres, leading ultimately to the *sādhak*'s liberation.[6]

A bit too exalted though it may look to casual notice, this conception of the ultimate aim of music would not appear quite without significance if we realized that it serves as the basis of

4. *Brahma* stands for the Absolute. *Nād* means sound, heard and unheard or *āhat* and *anāhat*. So *Nād Brahma* may be taken to mean the Absolute as all-pervading sound, heard and unheard. Sound becomes manifest in and through the human body too. This perhaps explains why in *Sangeet Ratnākar*, which is a classical work on music, care has been taken to describe the human body too. See *Sangeet Ratnākar*, English tr. Dr C. Kunhan Raja, The Adyar Library, 1945, vol. I, chapter 1, p. 10.

5. The word *dhruvapad* means not only a specific genre of our classical vocal music, but also a composition in this genre.

6. I owe this bit of knowledge to the late Ustad A. Rahimuddin Khan Dagar. The song here referred to is a composition which outlines, in brief, the way to success in *yoga*, a system of psycho-ethical discipline to which the concept of six psychic centres is pivotal. The composition in question is also a part of the repertoire of the maestro's own son, Ustad Fahimuddin Dagar, the eldest living member of the Dagar family, who has won almost every significant award meant for our top classical vocalists.

many key concepts and stylistic features of Hindustānī classical music. Devotional and contemplative effects are even today regarded as the hallmark of great music by our seasoned *rasikas*, though the average listener still prefers to be tickled with light and frolicsome flourishes. Now, an important device by which a contemplative look can be evoked in music is the use of such melodic passages as traverse the region between adjacent *svaras* very slowly and quite unbrokenly, yet without the slightest fading of tonal colour.[7] An attentive listener is thereby enabled to follow the melodic run very closely, in perfect attunement (or *tādātmya*); and the very diminution of self-awareness in such moments produces a relish of contemplation serene. The adjacence of two *mādhyams* in *Kedār* or of two *nishāds* in *Mian ki Malhār* easily admit of the device I have just spoken of. The blissful gradualness I here visualize should also make it clear why so much importance has been given by our musicology to the use of *śrutis*[8] or microtones in Indian music.

Again, if music is conductive to God-realization it should (at least) serve to steady the mind. This at once gives us a clue to the Indian conception of *svara*[9] or the musical note as the beautiful-in-itself[10] (*svameva rājate*). In other words, according to the Indian point of view, the ideal rendering of a note is that which makes it appear winsome without a support. Here, I may add, the word *rājate* is noteworthy. It means *shines*. Now, to shine is not the same thing as to *glimmer*. A glimmer is a mere momentary twinkle. So, taken as one, *svameva rājate* may

7. A consummate *ālāpiyā* can do this with ease, partly because he is free from the trammels of beat-measured rhythm.

8. A *śruti* is an interval smaller than the semi-tone, not necessarily an equal division of the latter.

9. A *svara* is one of the seven notes of the gamut.

10. I have actually heard a *dhruvapad* from Ustad Rahimuddin Khan Dagar the text of which includes the plea; *digambar svara rākh re*, that is, "keep the *svara* quite open to the four sides" or "do not let it (the *svara*) nestle closely together with other notes."

be taken to mean that which remains manifest for a while (and winsomely). The *momentary* appeal of a sweet note is one thing; its keeping us charmed *for a while*, quite another. The latter effect is possible only where the singing is leisurely. So, the *vilambit* idiom is practically necessary not only because it makes it easy for the listener to follow the run of music patiently, and so to establish *tādātmya* without which *rasa* cannot arise,[11] but also because it alone can meet what the standard definition of a *svara* demands. In our *drut khayāl*-singing, however, it is only as woven into the patterned setting provided by other notes that an individual *svara* appears beautiful. This, however, only shows that our practice has moved a little away from the ideal. It does nothing to detract from the practicability of the norm; for, even today, if only at the *taar shadj*, our singers are occasionally seen to put their all, so to say, into the utterance of the single *svara*, making it look self-dependent in its charm.

But, one may ask, *can* any note in fact *be* independent of all context? We may not at once say, yes. Grammatically, the correctness of a note depends on the rightness of its intervallic distance from its adjacent notes. A *rishabh* is truly (or correctly) itself only if it is rightly *related to* its immediate neighbours on either side, namely, *shadj* and *gandhār*. This is true also of a *svara*'s aesthetic look taken in the simple sense of sweetness as heard. A note which is surounded by some other sounds or *svaras* will appear differently sweet (if at all) from the one which just punctuates enveloping silence and is then no more.[12] To say so, however, is to think of a *svara* only as an object for a (more or less) detached listener, other than the singer himself. What about the singer himself as involved in the act of singing

11. I say so on the basis of my understanding of Bharata's theory of *rasa*.

12. As for the relation of *svaras* (or music taken generally) to silence, see my essay, "Music and Silence", *Journal of Indian Council of Philosophical Research*, vol. XX no. 3, July–September 2003, pp. 224-34.

the *svara* and a *rasika* who may be very well equipped (and keen) to listen to music knowledgeably? Now, in respect of the latter (that is, the *rasika*) we can safely say that, whatever be the extent to which a note's heard character is *in fact* determined by the silence around it or by the other notes that immediately precede or follow it, it will *appear* sweet *in itself* (if it *is* correct grammatically) simply because the listener is here intensely absorbed and quite undisturbed by whatever may be there beside (or external to) the note in question. But the singer himself is not a mere listener. He is also actively creating what he listens; and whereas the *sāmājika* (or the listener as a member of the audience) is for a while released from preoccupation with self in the act of listening concentratively, the singer, on the other hand, may put one of his own cherished thoughts, feelings, or attitudes into the utterance of a sweet, but single phrase or note. To illustrate, if the vocalist is also a devout person, and if what is to be uttered musically is the word पार as it occurs in the following words of fervent yearning in a Sūrdas *bhajan*, चाहो तो पार करो, at *taar rishabh* and in *rāga Sohnī*, the note may be purposely thinned and elongated, yet sweetly and steadfastly, to chime with the thought of transcendence or going beyond. When this acutally happens, the felt sweetness of the note will be as much a matter of expressiveness as of mere auditory appeal. Such a *svara* will be (for the singer) captivating in itself not merely by *excluding* all that is strictly non-musical but by *incorporating* a vital detail of his own incidental prayerful state. Here the beautiful-in-itself is so also because of its significance. I feel like adding, at this point, that Swāmī Haridās, the patron-saint of Hindustānī music, is said to have been eminently capable of losing himself in the unwavering contemplation (*samādhi*) of one single *svara*, making it a veritable symbol of his own devout aspirations.

But, one may ask, does a single *svara* at all admit of *indwelling*? I believe, it does; and in such cases, the singer looks like exploring the *svara*'s very interior, so to say. The net effect evoked in such cases is that of contemplation in the very moment of creation. The possibility of this aesthetic device is borne out not only by the actual singing of some of our masterly vocalists of living memory, but can even be *argued*, say, as follows. The sweet singing of a note can be done in a broad, full-throated way *or*, quite as well, in a thin voice which may look like illuminating the very core of the *svara* daintily. In point of effect the alternatives would provide a case of majesty as against quintessential fineness. For theory, on the other hand, the implication here would be that, as actually sung, a note of music is no mere point, but is ever possessed of an invisible inner extent, and is therefore open to creative indwelling.

Be it noted, however, that our traditional definition of *svara* does not only need to be supported by the kind of thinking we have just done, but is itself of help in understanding a key feature of Indian music. If a note is to appear beautiful *in itself* it is obvious that it should not be swamped in the simultaneous playing of other notes, however concordant it may thereby look. This is probably why in Hindustānī music we have little use of harmony.[13] Yet it would be wrong to think that there is no harmony at all in Hindustānī music. The *tānpūrā*[14] provides a continuous sounding of some of the important notes of the *rāga* as the musician goes on performing. Moreover, the right drum is tuned carefully (generally) with the tonic of the main performer or with a key note of the *rāga* chosen for treatment; and this sound, as the drum is played, repeatedly occurs *along with* the other notes of the *saptak* as the main performer traverses them.

---

13. Some scholars insist that in ancient India we used harmony too in our music. But the dominant feature of Indian music *today* is clearly melody rather than harmony.

14. It is a musical instrument which is used in every performance of classical music to provide a kind of ceaseless "accompanying" drone built upon some important notes of the *rāga*.

All this is common knowledge; but what does deserve explicit mention, because it is likely to be missed in the present climate of excessive liking for *taan*s of varying pace and design, is the fact that though he may not voice it openly, the orthodox Hindustānī musician certainly cherishes the faith that the lesser the orbit of the object of attention, the greater is the necessity, or possibility, of creative penetration. While singing all alone or to a coterie of trained and friendly listeners, our best vocalists even today take delight in trying and appearing to reveal ever newer charm in or around what is commonly regarded as one simple note; and the attempt not only transports, but tends to overawe them with a deeper awareness of how much beauty is implicit in the basic particles that go to make the varicoloured fabric of music. It is important to note that such concepts as "contemplation" and "meditation" are to be found not only in India's ethico-religious thought but also in our musicology, though they are not quite clearly expressed in the talk of our orthodox musicians. I may also mention in passing that such eminent Hindustānī musicians of the past as Tānsen have confessed to it in some of their compositions that the span of a single human life is hardly enough for the mastery of even a single *svara*. Be that as it may, it is unquestionable that the more seasoned of our listeners often keep waiting eagerly to see if the performer is able to sing some select notes in the chosen *rāga* immaculately. Here the note that is most likely to come to the mind of those who know Indian music is the *gandhār* of *rāga Darbārī*.[15]

Further, if a note is to be regarded as something which is beautiful in itself, it is obvious that due attention is to be given to how it is actually sung. Whether it is to be thrust full-blown into the listener's consiousness or whispered gently into the setting of silence; whether it is rendered long enough to be

15. Grammatically, this note is *atikomal*, that is one *śruti* lower than *komal*.

satisfying or cut short in the mid, leaving our aesthetic sensitivity "half-fed," as some orthodox *ustāds*[16] may say; again, whether it is to be presented clearly and steadfastly, or merely hinted at, *not marked,* as the stilling of a luminous flow, — all this receives, as a rule, due care at the hands of the orthodox Hindustānī singer even today. This should become clear as we turn, a little later, to speak of *ālāpa* as a distinct genre of Hindustānī vocal music.

Yet, at this point too, because it is demanded by the context provided by what we have been talking about (that is, the value of the single note) one point relating to *ālāpa* may be made forthwith. Whether the note is winsome or not, and what exact shade of aesthetic suggestiveness it possesses, all this depends, in a measure, also on the length of time for which it is sung or played. Always the element of time enters into a musical note, contributing vitally to its net look and impact. A simple example will here serve. If we sing a particular note briefly and then immediately pass on *without* a break or jerk to a nearby note, the aesthetic effect would be one of continuity *which is straight,* but if the transition from the first to, say, the third note is accomplished in a *leisurely,* yet unbroken manner, the look evoked would be not of mere continuity, but of a convex run which appears to describe a little graceful dive, so to say, before rising up to touch the third *svara.*[17]

We often forget this while trying to understand the concept

16. An *Ustād* is a Muslim master musician of the orthodox variety.

17. It is certainly true that, for the classical Hindustānī musician, "the passage from one note to the next [often] becomes an adventure in subtle portamento, gliding and vacillating variants in microtonality." H.A. Popley, *The Music of India,* The Heritage of India Press, 1950, p. 87.

It is, however, not only such adroit transitions, but due emphases on, and immaculate singing of a *rāga*'s keynotes that constitute (a part of) the test of a Hindustānī singer's skill.

of *rāga*, which is basic to Indian classical music. Today, every *rāga* is identified (partly) by its *vādī* or dominant note, and the other notes are expected to contribute to its beauty noticeably. The aesthetic centrality of this *svara* also requires that, like all the other notes, it is sung (or played) tunefully and may be, *unlike* everyone of them — steadfastly, that is, *long enough* to become quite manifest. The truth that an element of time is implicit even in those concepts that relate to the *melodic* aspect of Hindustānī music is often ignored, though it is common knowledge that here even a slightly exaggerated stay of voice at a particular *svara* can mean a clear outrage upon the grammatical character of the *rāga* being presented.

A *rāga* is indeed nothing very easy to handle or understand. First, singing a *rāga* properly is, as a rule, very different from merely traversing its constituent notes in the simple ascent-descent manner. The *svaras* are to be rendered in a particular way, different from their given manner of existence in the scale.[18] Not the same notes may be used in both ascent and descent; and they may be used in varying sequences. Again, not every constituent note of the *rāga* is to be given equal importance. What is more, many *rāgas* employ intervals subtler than whole-steps and half-steps. At the same time, they all share some common features. First, every *rāga* is a *specific melodic matrix*. It is *melodic* in the sense that the *svaras* it comprises all follow a before-after order; and it is *specific* in the sense that because of the distinct disposition and accentuation of its notes, every *rāga* strikes the ear differently from other *rāgas*. Its being a *matrix* is another fascinating feature of a *rāga*. The meaning is, first, that every *rāga* is fecund or aesthetically productive in the sense that it admits of numberless compositions; and secondly that, being a complex of musical sounds itself it also functions as the very material of

18. The Hindustānī scale, in its sol-fa initials, is as follows;

Sā, re, gā, mā, pā, dhā, ni, sā.

these compostions, if in different ways. Like a concept, a *rāga* subsumes many particulars (or different compositions), but is not exhausted by them. Different musicians may sing the same *rāga* in the same session of music; and yet no individual exposition may appear a mere imitation of the others. Grammatically, of course, they will conform to the same pattern (of the *rāga*), but their aesthetic look and impact could vary profoundly. Yet a *rāga* is not itself a mere concept or type; only our understanding of it is so. Itself, it is an actual object of auditory perception, not only initially, but all along. What is more, quite a few *rāga*s are supposed to have a specific emotive look, and many more are believed to suit a specific hour (or season, in some cases). The general principle is that a grave or plaintive *rāga* is to be sung in *vilambit laya* or "adagio," and a sportive one in *drut* or "allegro."[19] But whatever be the character of their dominant individual look, serious or light-hearted, because of their auditory uniqueness most *rāga*s can be easily distinguished from one another by a trained listener. Today, it is common to distinguish *rāga*s by marking their *vādī* and *samvādī svara*s, that is, their pivotal and acoustically concordant notes. The ability to keep a *rāga*'s grammatical (and so auditory) uniqueness clear throughout a recital is a key criterion of evaluation for the critic. In fact, the concept of *rāga* determines both creation and criticism in the field of Indian music.

At the same time, the individual *svara*'s value is by no means bedimmed by the *vādī-samvādī relation* in a *rāga*. In fact, a *rāga* only adds to the charm of the individual note by providing to it an eleborate melodic setting. Indeed, this is how a *rāga* comes to appear what it is (by definition) required to, that is, something which can charm people in general. It certainly comprises quite a few *svara*s, very rarely less than five. But, whatever be their number, they are not to look like a mere

19. "Moderato," on the other hand, comes *between vilambit* and *drut*. So it is called *madhya laya*.

aggregate. The truth indeed is that in the singing of a great vocalist a *rāga* can appear as an original unity, and here it would not be improper if we spoke of it as an *euphorganism*. Some of the best Hindustānī musicians living today are wedded to the view that a *rāga* is like a living entity and that it is to be handled with the same reverent care as is demanded by a living organism.

Ordinarily, a deviation from the grammatical character of a *rāga* is not permitted. Some great singers, however, occasionally take the rare liberty of incorporating a (grammatically) dissonant note [20] in the rendering of a particular *rāga, thereby heightening the total effect perceptibly*. This is naturally possible not in the very beginning of a recital but only when a spell has been worked up after some solid performance of sustained effectiveness. Such a deviation from norms cannot only make for added beauty, but can even be justified theoretically, say, as follows. The grammatical structure of a *rāga* is itself based on *samvāda* which is a matter of aesthetic or factual consistency. Theoretical consistency is agreement in respect of meaning. Thus, if the word *absolute* is taken to mean "without limits," as is indeed one of its acknowledged meanings, it would be theoretically (self-)inconsistent to speak of *two* absolutes, because so to speak of them is necessarily to mean that they *delimit* each other, whereupon neither truly remains *absolute* which they have been said to be. Aesthetic consistency, on the other hand, is agreement or accord in respect of mere *fact*. Thus, we freely speak thus: "This colour goes well with that one." Here, no question of *meaning* is involved. So, because *samvāda*, which is a basic essential of *rāga*, is itself a matter of factual agreement, where the insertion of a *vivādī svara* does not *in fact* displease the ear, it may be said to

---

20. To be precise, the reference here is to what is called a *vivādī svara*, that is, a note which, though it is not expressly forbidden (or *varjit*) is not generally used in a *rāga*.

be warranted even theoretically, that is, as a matter of argument. Our music does admit of an occasional transcendence of mere grammar for the sake of an extra touch of beauty. This will be further confirmed by our analysis of the Indian system of rhythm.

On its rhythmic side, the main concepts of our Hindustānī music are *laya, mātrā, bol, tāla, ṭhekā,* and *layakārī. Laya* has been spoken of in some of our ancient texts as the interval of flow of time between (two) time-beats.[21] What it means in the actual practice of Hindustānī music has, however, to be thought out. During the course of a recital the interval *between* two time-beats is not kept intact by the singer *calculatively*. Yet, he has got to keep the time-gap between any two beats absolutely even. So the steadying which *laya* demands is done essentially by the musician himself, that is, by means of his own mental attunement. It is like holding on to the flow of time in utter imdependence of a watch. An accomplished Hindustānī musician (or Kathak dancer) may not look at the drummer for a pretty long time without for a moment losing his subconscious grip over the precise flow of *laya*. And a listener too, if he is duly saturated with a sense of *laya*, can quickly show his disapproval where he perceives even the slightest lapse in the pace of the *laya* between any two beats (or segments) as marked by the drummer.

So far, however, our analysis has not revealed anything very aesthetic about *laya*. Keeping the flow of time even certainly makes for a look of orderliness; but even a watch does that. Aesthetic creativity makes its distinct appearance only when one variegates (without disrupting) the regular pace of *laya* (as marked by the *ṭhekā*) with patterns of diverse filling and design.

---

21. For a detailed discussion of the basic concepts of Hindustānī rhythm, see my book, *The Winged Form — Aesthetical Essays on Hindustani Rhythm*, Sangeet Natak Akademi, New Delhi, 1979.

But the clearest mark of the ascendancy of *laya* (as imaginatively apprehended and aesthetically regulated) over the normal practice of keeping to it with the help of beats is seen in *ālāpa* of the *dhruvapad* variety. Here, there is no drumming as "accompaniment," no assistance of beat-measured segments (*vibhāgs*); and the vocalist regulates the time taken in singing one *svara* or in traversing a tonal phrase simply by means of his own aesthetic sense and solely with an eye to the evocation of some winsome effects. Today, however, what dominates the practice and presentation of Hindustānī music is *laya* as beat-measured rhythm. Now, considering this music as a whole, *laya* may be taken to mean that the musician at work identifies himself imaginatively with the flow of (musical) time with a view to steadying it, or to transmuting it into the material of variform beauty, with *or without* leaning on to the beats of the rhythmic cycle. As we turn (in thought) from *laya* to *tāla* we pass from *what is ideally and personally taken to be proper* to *what is mathematically and objectively accurate*, from that which is appropriated freely to the artiste's aesthetic needs of the moment to something objective, namely, the cycle of rhythm with its fixed *vibhāgs* or segments.

How *laya* is related to *tāla* should be easy to see. *Tāla* is to *laya* what a yard is to distance; that is, the one is a measure of the other. That which makes this measurement possible is the unitary timing-beat or the *mātrā*. The measured, segmented and cyclic passage of *laya* as played on the drum by way of "accompainment," throughout a musical recital is the rhythm or the matrix of rhythm chosen. All this is common knowledge. Yet, the following reflections seem necessary. Where a cycle comprises sixteen beats, the thought that a *mātrā* is 1/16 of the whole complex seizes only the grammatical,[22] not the aesthetic significance of the *mātrā*. As we *experience* it, the *mātrā* has a

22. Grammatically, a *mātrā* here means that which measures a segment of the *laya*-flow.

distinct psycho-aesthetic setting, which really gives it the value it has. First, it serves as distinction which thought everywhere needs for its working. To think of something is at once to hold on to, or to interject a distinction therein. A *mātrā* is the recognition of this primal need of thought while dealing with a flow. It gives the mind a foothold, as it were, into the being of *laya*. Secondly, the *experience* of a *mātrā* is at once one of an accent *as articulating or diversifying the laya-flow*, and not merely of a sequence of numerals that simply follow a before-after order and are not related to anything else. A flow which all along steadies the marks by which it itself keeps to the proper course, and remains quite seamless — this is the basic form of how we experience the rhythmic charm of Hindustānī music; and I call it *aesthetic* (or relating to beauty) because it is common to define beauty as unity in diversity. Our patterns of rhythm, which are numberless in principle, all alike heighten this semblance of an articulate, yet undivided flow.

What steadies them all is, however, their relation to the *ṭhekā*, that is, the basic rhythm-cycle as played on the drums. As the steadfast ground of all *layakārī*,[23] it does not only hold on to a chosen pace but has a character its own as well. It is, in fact, a structural unity with a distinctive centre. It has its quota of *mātrās*, its off-beat which is called the *khālī*,[24] and, of course, its very first beat (as the centre of its cyclic flow) which is called the *sama*. Quite a few subtleties of Hindustānī rhythm consist in highlighting, in a regular recital, anyone of these elements of the *ṭhekā*. However, the first beat (or the *sama*) receives the greatest emphasis here; it is indeed the focal beat, and is always taken to remain here as such, though it may not be played emphatically. But, be it noted, the *sama* is important

23. *Layakārī* means variations of aesthetic pace and creation of rhythmic patterns of different range, pace and design.

24. *Khālī* is the offbeat, a beat which is not actually marked on the drums, but is only (yet necessarily) kept in mind.

not merely as the centre of a cycle, but aesthetically too; it is a fount of value. It does not merely have a specific location in the cycle, *but must appear as determining the beauty (or at least wholeness) of that which encompasses it*. Indeed, if the *sama* is to be true to its requisite character as an aesthetic centre, it must not only appear as a distinct accent, but also as a manifest determinant. First, it must have an unmistakable sharpness and (or at least definiteness) about it, though this look can be brought about variously, say, through an emphatic stroke of the plectrum in the case of *sitār/sarod* playing; or, in dance, through a sharp culminating turn of the neck or decisive stroke of a foot. Secondly, it should appear not merely as the last stroke or *mātrā* of the *ṭhekā* or of a rhythmic pattern, but as the natural high point, more or less restful, of a self-evolving movement.[25] Putting the two together, we say that the *sama* should appear not only to arrive but to *emerge* as the natural end-point of an oriented flow. Musicians and dancers in India revel in working up well-designed accesses to the *sama* from the most unsuspected recesses in the fabric of the *ṭhekā*. Sometimes, indeed, a pattern of rhythm is seen to bestir itself even from the unmarked interval between two adjacent *mātrā*s or beats. What is, however, a basic requirement throughout the course of a recital is the fact that the performing musician has to keep the round of the cycle — its manner and speed — unceasingly in mind. At the same time, he is expected to flow freely along with patterns which flit across the basic rhythm, sometimes at a wayward angle; and, what is more, to return to the *sama*, at suitable intervals, with split second accuracy. Here a listener who is trained in the subtleties of Hindustānī rhythm enjoys every detail of this rhythmic play, that is, the unwavering steadiness of the *ṭhekā*; the intricacy and design of the rhythm pattern; the abandon of the angle at which it may

25. It would here be relevant to note that the word *sama* literally means "composure after agitation."

be made to deviate from the normal flow of the *ṭhekā*; and, finally, the immaculateness of the musician's (or drummer's) periodical return to the cycle which remains the aesthetic matrix of all rhythmic exercise in the region of Hindustānī music.

The subtlety of our rhythmic patterns can be truly amazing. Some of them reveal, as they unwind themselves, moments of intentional slowing or raising of pace. The challenge of purposive waywardness is, in such cases, powerful; and the listener who tries to keep to the cycle, in spite of the deviation, delights in the very act of making the effort. Specially skilful are those collocations of rhythmic syllables (or *bols*) which designedly end "away" from the *sama* and which are, therefore, called *visham* or "displaced." They provide us with another good example of transcendence, in our music, of the merely grammatical in the interest of beauty. If the pattern is so designed that it ends a little before the normal location of the *sama* in the *ṭhekā*, it is said to belong to the *anāgat* sub-class; that is, here, when the movement has ended, the real *sama* is still to come, an instant later. And if the last accent of the pattern comes slightly *after* the normal *sama* has come and gone, we have a pattern of the *ateet* sub-class, *ateet* meaning "past" or "has-been," the reference again being to the focal point *of the timing-cycle*. Here, it is important to note that the mere isolated act of pausing this side of the *sama*, or just nodding meaningfully a little after it, is by no means enough, because so to behave is simply to show that one remembers where the *sama* is. The stopping-short and overstepping both become aesthetic *only when they terminate a perceptible dynamic design*.

I suspect that a fair part of our music presented so far to the West has been of the merely obvious kind. This may well have secured for it a ready acceptance and a larger sympathy, but the best, in this process, has only been held back. Consider, for instance, what is today a popular item at our Festivals of Culture: a drums ensemble, presenting drummers from different countries. With a view to heightening congruence, our men have to replicate the rhythmic work of others only in respect of the extent and run of the rhythmic phrase. How is notice here invited to the fact that we have *bol*s and recitation (पढ़न्त) corresponding to the drum-beats, *or* to a pattern's shapely and evolving access to its *sama*? Unless they spend some time in getting used to the Indian scale and to the more popular rhythmic cycles of Hindustānī music, our friends in the West cannot be expected to admire discriminatingly what is truly of value. And this, the very best in our music, is essentially *formal*:[26] that is, *ālāpa* which uses no words, and *tāla* or the rhythmic criss-cross which, though it is surely heard, can be truly relished only through imaginative self-identification with both the rhythm-cycle which keeps itself unwavering and the patterns which frolic sportively against it. Once this ideal oneness with the basic pace as marked by the cycle is achieved, whatever be the point at which the drummer chooses to peck it emphatically, and whatever be this accent's angle of deviation from the basic flow, one does not only stay undisturbed, but may even be bewitched, as by a look of love that is sweetened by its sheer slant.

Not many people in the West know that in India a very elaborate and effective attempt has been made to identify the various sounds produced by the drums when their different (skin-covered) parts are struck in specific ways. These sounds have been given names, in terms of mnemonic syllables or *bol*s. The latter are supposed to resemble, not to describe or explain, the character of the sounds produced by the drummer. The sonant variety of *bol*s is truly fascinating. Some of them such as *dir, dir* have about them a repetitive and tremulous fluency. Others are weighty and elongated, such as "dhar*anna*," in articulating which the italicized portion is prolonged noticeably.

---

26. "Formal" not in the sense of having no content but as being aesthetically effective *quite without the use of language*.

The suggestion of radiation from a common centre is provided by such fragment of a *bol* as *trā* (in त्राम) where the *r* follows immediately upon, not loosely after the त (or *t*) sound. Not every drum is regarded as suitable for producing every kind of *bol*. The *tablā*, which dominates the field of classical Hindustānī music today, comprises two pieces named literally after the manner in which they are placed alongside the drummer — the right one and the left one. The right one is expected to contribute sound-syllables which are crisp, fluent, successive, light and sliced. The left one supplies syllables of weight, a little depth, continuity and resonance. Perhaps its most likeable contribution is the effect of (what may be called) a breathing depth (or सांस, *sāṅs*). When the two are played properly together, some of the lighter effects of the right one tend to acquire a shapely roundness within the depth of the left one; and then, if what is being played rightly is the basic rhythm-cycle, it would appear not as a mere series of independent strokes, but as an internally diverse, yet unbroken wholeness. Not any two syllables (or *bol*s) can be put side by side. Only such of them can be juxtaposed as admit of playing in quick succession without straining the hands overmuch. An important mark of a drummer's efficiency is his ability to insert, where the rhythmic pace is a little leisurely, as many syllables as possible *between* two beats, without of course damaging the shapeliness of the whole pattern. Sometimes, during the recitation or actual drumming of a pattern, a short and sparkling syllable is so put within an intense tuft of *bol*s that by *its very sonant character* it appears to couple them *apart*; and I really wonder if there is any better way to diversify the flow of time aesthetically.

The Hindustānī rhythmic system is indeed a fascinating subject of study. Here, we may note, a virtually infinite amount of creative thinking is done *without the use of language*. The very sound of individual letters or of their bunches is studied in its aspects of heard character, pace, accentuation or sheer onward flow; and the *bols* are woven into patterns, recited and played with an unremitting care for all these details. Thus, if in articulating the syllable *tak* the letter *k* (क) is made to come stiffly and sharply *along with*, rather than loosely *after*, the त (or *t*-sound), it would be regarded as a quite distinct *bol* from तक् and तका where the same letter — that is, *k* (respectively) describes a little droop and upturn, though (apart from these details) the constituent letters remain the same. The *given* material of rhythm is rather colourless. We only have some meaningless sounds or *aksharas*, which are surely not sweet in the *graded* way of music and which are just interjected, though never randomly, into motion that is not actually seen but is only apprehended ideally. These sounds (or *bols*) are christened and grouped; and they are made to shuffle, flit across, and variegate the flow of *laya* in numberless ways. The flow of time, so treated creatively, becomes a veritable locus of exhaustless charm. It should now be clear that *layakārī* or creative manipulation of rhythm is not a matter of mere calculation. Variety of flow and design, relief of a ground with a figure, gentility or vigour of impact, and moments of intentional or adroit waywardness — these are here the finer sources of appeal.

From the basic concepts of Hindustānī music we may turn now to the more important forms that its actual presentation takes. Here *ālāpa* comes first. It is such a vocal treatment of a *rāga* as is done quite without the help of language and rhythmic accompaniment. Yet, where it is properly done it can enthral the listeners. The chief effects which good *ālāpa* can evoke are those of leisureliness or repose, dignity, inwardness and even sublimity, besides, of course, the semblance of a veritable canopy, so to say, of the *rūpa of the rāga* chosen.[27] I say so in the light of my personal experience. Some lovers of music may

27. Here, I have specially in mind the *dhruvapad*-singing of the elder pair of Dagar Brothers, Ustads Nasir Moinuddin and Aminuddin Dagar.

well disagree with my apotheosis of *ālāpa*. But, be that as it may, *it* would be patently wrong to believe that singing without language cannot work up any winsome effects. The truth rather is that language not only conveys meaning but may also, *when spoken*, broaden and so damage a dainty breath of sound. Thus, if a musical passage is intended to run as just a sweet sinuous line, the simultaneous use of a word will surely counter the requisite effect of quintessential fineness and uninterrupted fluidity. The diversity of letters will ruffle the needed singleness of look, and their varying volume, as spoken, will inhibit the fineness aimed at. *Ālāpa* may perhaps be said to be grounded in the faith that the use of language does not quite square with the finest effects that pure music can evoke. Like our rhythm, *ālāpa* celebrates the aesthetic potential of sheer, wordless sound.

As already pointed out, one important determinant of the charm of *ālāpa* is *laya*, that is, the flow of time as regulated with an eye to some effects of beauty,[28] rather than with the help of beats. How this is in fact done by an *ālāpiyā* may be brought out as follows, with the help of a very simple example. Suppose the vocalist sings the tonic for a mere instant and then immediately provides a steady, *elongated* utterance of the next note, say, *komal rishabh* before returning to the tonic. The effect in this case is very likely to be one of emergence, essentially because of the *vilambit laya* of *rishabh;* but nothing of the kind would happen if one returned to the first *svara* promptly, that is, at a quicker *laya*. The consummate *ālāpiyā*, Ustad Rahimuddin Khan Dagar, would freely speak of some skilfully sung *svaras* (in *ālāpa* in specific *rāgas*) as *lajjit* or coy, or as *sanyastha*, that is, suggestive of detachment. The *rishabh* of *rāga Puriyā* does not assert itself against — rather, it gently yields to — the recoil of

---

28. It is definitely wrong to say, as has actually been said by at least one writer on Indian music, that in *ālāpa* the notes of the *rāga* are sung in a loose kind of rhythm, regulated simply by convenience. See, here, H.A. Popley's *The Music of India*, p. 88.

the *ne, re, ni* passage, and may therefore appear *lajjit* to a sensitive imagination. It may even be said to be *pavitra* in the sense that even a slightly exaggerated stay of voice at it would, so to say, *defile* its (grammatical) identity. The *taar* notes of *jogiyā*, on the other hand, may suggest to some specially *sahṛdaya rasika* a pining for release from mundane ties. Be that as it may, the point here simply is that just as a poem is truly read not if we only grasp the literal meaning of the words it comprises, but also if we happily visualize the word-bound images that may dawn on us easily if our reading is intense and sympathetic, so the proper singing of a *rāga* is not merely to traverse its set notes correctly, but to live the ideal-emotional experience it *can* provide to one who sings not only with his voice, but with the inside of his being, so to say, that is, as determined by his developed aesthetic sense and his dominant attitudes towards what life has provided to him so far — attitudes, say, of gentility and sweet acceptance, resolute combativeness, or a growing disenchantment with pleasures of sense.

Along with *ālāpa, dhruvapad* (which follows it) is another very old form of vocal music which some singers still cling to assiduously. It is surely not as popular as the *khayāl*-form. Yet, even now it is looked upon as capable of working up effects of structural dignity and peaceableness. Here only such decorative devices are employed as do not detract from the requisite seriousness of music. At the same time, specially in the hands of an indifferent performer, a *dhruvapad* song can easily appear stiff, inelegant and even repulsive. The cycles of rhythm it employs are also those which do not permit light-hearted treatment. Traditionally, the word *dhruvapad* is taken to mean determinateness of the various segments of the total singing, that is, *sthāyī, antarā, sañchārī,* and *ābhoga*. As a general way of singing, however, it also stands for music which is very steadfast in its adherence to requirements of *rāga* and *tāla*. Here, it may be said to differ from the *khayāl*-form, because only the most seasoned *khayāl*-singers find it possible to keep the character of *rāga* (being sung) quite manifest and unsullied during *phirat* or the criss-cross of *taans*.

Yet, in spite of its rigidity in keeping to *rāga* and *tāla*, it would be wrong to suppose that the *dhruvapad* genre of singing just recalcitrates variety of imaginative treatment; and my argument here could run thus:

First, rhythm is here to be handled adroitly.[29] Secondly, variety of effect is here easily secured by availing of some of those formal devices which distinguish *ālāpa*, in the main. So I protest against the popular view that *dhruvapad*-singing is intrinsically deficient in using imagination for producing effects of beauty. Melodic passages are, at times, very daintily conceived here. In singing a composition in *rāga śrī*, for instance, Rahimuddin Khan would revel in linking *rishabh* with *pañcham* in a way which enabled him, in casual talk, to speak of the second note, that is, *pañcham*, as *kamalvat*. His meaning here was that, in the case in question, the voice rises from the first note to the second one with the slenderness of a stem, and then finally opens up at the second one (*pa*) like the blooming of a lotus. Further, in those *dhruvapad* songs which are called *ārādhanātmaka* (or worshipful) we have imaginative fineness at its best. Here, the complete text of the song is to be rendered in a sweet and sylphlike manner; and the whole melodic utterance gives one the impression of a sigh welling up, so to say, from the very depths of being or of incense borne aloft on the very wings of devotion, evoking an aura of quiet contemplation all around. In such *dhruvapad*s the manner of singing has to be consistently soft as dew, yet quite steadfast; and very little improvization (or *upaj*), if any, is allowed. There

29. That is, in principle. In practice, on the other hand, some members even of the famed Dagar family have been a bit too free in doing *layakārī*.

is about such songs an intentional leanness of manner; the notes are very light accents in the run of melody; and the whole singing feels closer to spirit than to sense.

Such *dhruvapad*-singing is however a rarity today, and the genre which dominates our music today is undoubtedly *khayāl*. In actual singing it permits longer spells of freedom from the trammels of rhythm than the *dhruvapad* form, though the *sama*, of course, has to be marked with absolute accuracy in either case. Another key feature of this style of singing — one which distinguishes it sharply from *ālāpa-dhruvapad* — is its liberal use of *taan*s which are such collocations of *svara*s, in varying design and at both quick and leisurely pace, as aim at keeping the run both single and yet quite articulate or internally diverse. It is this varying character of *taan*s which is, at times, seen to make the *khayāl*-singer move his hands or fingers in different ways. The diversity of notes in a *taan* keeps out monotony; and the overall unity of the pattern makes for unbroken attention. This is one major reason why *khayāl* is more popular today than the older form. Occasionally, with a view to securing some ready applause, a *khayāl*-singer resorts to such turns and twists of voice as have the lightness of fancy rather than the depth of tranquil singing. However, *vilambit* or slow-speed *khayāl* is quite capable of evoking an aura of high seriousness. *Drut* (or allegro) *khayāl* has a lighter gait; it excels in working up nimble and colourful effects. "Accompaniment" by the drummer is an integral part of both *dhruvapad* and *khayāl* singing.

A normal presentation of *instrumental* music, specially if it be one on a *sitār* or *sarod*,[30] has four clearly identifiable movements — *ālāpa, joḍ, jhālā* and *gatkārī*. The first three of these are done without the drum "accompaniment" which is

---

30. These are our more popular instruments today in the region of classical Indian music.

an important source of delight in the case of *gatkārī*, that is, playing of the basic, rhythmically organized composition, and of patterns or *taan*s that flit across it in various ways. *Ālāpa* here means slow, contemplative playing. It seeks to bring out the basic form of the *rāga* in its dimension of depth. Here the manner of playing may build occasionally on extensive glides. *Joḍ* introduces successiveness, emphatic discreteness, and a quicker speed. *Jhālā*, on the other hand, seeks to blend the look of the first two stages, and at great speed — that is, the apparent seamlessness of *ālāpa* with the diversity of *joḍ*, so that the net effect here is one of a single vibrant background against which the recurring sharpness of the plectrum looks pleasing because it not only relieves monotony but heightens, by contrast, the overall unity. The *gat* or the basic tune, which is "accompanied" by the drummer, has its own design. Its centre is the *sama*, and the instrumentalist delights the trained listener by providing such accesses to the focal beat as vary happily in speed, extent and design.

A distinct way of presenting instrumental music, made popular by the Ravi Shankar–Ali Akbar combination,[31] is the duet or *jugalbandī*. Here the two performers, duly accompanied by the drummer from the end of *ālāpa, Joḍ* and *Jhālā* onwards, try to reinforce each other's effects by matching playing in one octave with similar or simultaneous playing in the other; and by trying to articulate audibly what the partner's playing, as it ends, demands, or suggests. Occasionally, one just caps with the little singleness of but one *svara*, the suggestion or the manner of the patterns of the other. *One heaves a sigh, so to say, and the other lends just a tear to it.*

---

31. Bharat Ratna, Pandit Ravi Shankar, the sitarist, and (the late) Ustad Ali Akbar Khan, the sarod maestro, have been the most widely admired instrumentalists of modern India.

2

Hindustānī Music and Two Idioms of Aesthetic Concern[1]

A WIDELY acknowledged meaning of the word *aesthetic* is "relating to aesthetics"; and insofar as, historically, *aesthetics* has been *generally* regarded as that branch of philosophy which is concerned with the principles of beauty in *art*, all the major *ways of our aesthetic concern* — such as aesthetic attitude/experience/viewpoint, and aesthetic judgement (in exercising which we use aesthetic *predicates* like *beautiful*, *graceful*, and *sublime*) — have to be considered largely in the context of art. It is true that in contemporary thinking *beauty* and *art* are not the only concerns of aesthetics, and that artistic *meaning* (*or significance*) and *nature* are also given due thought. But just because our present concern is with the *art* of music alone, lack of frequent references to nature in this essay may well be allowed to pass. What is more, we may not find it possible all along to reflect on the ways of aesthetic concern we have distinguished in utter separateness from each other. This limitation is forced on us by the fact that instead of being concerned with the mere *concept* of, say, the aesthetic attitude or aesthetic judgement, our attempt will be to bear in mind their *actual exercise* as well. Now, when we in fact adopt the

---

1. With some necessary changes, this essay reproduces what has already appeared, under the same head, in *Sangeet Natak*, vol. XXXIX, no. 2, 2005, pp. 19-29.

aesthetic attitude in respect of a work of art we may well feel captivated by it (aesthetic *experience*) because we find it, say, beautiful (aesthetic *predicate*); and, what is more, may also *say* so (aesthetic *judgement*). At the same time, care will have to be taken to bring out the individual uniqueness of the ways in question. After all, even the most intense focusing of attention on a work — say, an epic — may not enable one to conclude definitively whether it is to be called merely grand (or majestic) *or* sublime, that is, whether it only impresses us, if overwhelmingly, or also tends to make us feel elevated for a while.

In this chapter we may deal only with aesthetic attitude and aesthetic experience, for the concepts of aesthetic viewpoint and judgement are closely related to art criticism, and so call for elaborate treatment in a separate essay. Now, to turn first to aesthetic *attitude*, we may note that — quite in consonance with the fact that the word *attitude* means *any* way of thinking or behaving, the acts of perceiving, attending, and following discriminatingly are all directly involved in the aesthetic attitude at work. This indeed is duly provided for when Stolnitz defines this attitude as that of

> . . . distinterested and sympathetic attention to and contemplation of any object of awareness whatever, for its own sake alone.[2]

However, even a casual look at some words in the second line of this quote (any object of awareness) may suggest some sceptical questions. Is it justifiable to say that the attitude in question can be adopted in respect of *any object of awareness?* It

---

2. J. Stolnitz's essay "The Aesthetic Attitude", in *Introductory Readings in Aesthetics*, ed: J. Hospers, The Free Press, 1969, p. 19.

   For a reasoned defence of this definition of the aesthetic attitude, see the debate concerning my essay "The Aesthetic Attitude", *Philosophy East and West (PEW)*, 28, no. 1, January 1978; "Reply to My Critics" (*PEW*, 29, no. 2, April 1979), and "The Aesthetic Attitude: Reply to some New Criticisms" (*PEW*, April 1980).

would surely be rash to say, *yes*. If a patient, writhing in pain, is able to give to his physicain a precise account of the nature of his discomfort, maybe because he is used to such introspective activity, will it be proper to regard it as an exercise of the aesthetic attitude simply because the pain has been very carefully attended to, and "for its own sake alone," that is, quite without any thought (presently) of what has brought it about, or of its possible curability? And would not an affirmative answer to this particular question run counter to the fact that the actual exercise of the aesthetic attitude always leaves us satisfied, or even positively happy, if not rapturously so? Further, has it actually been found that the attitude in question can be adopted in respect to any (or every) object of awareness? Even if we give no thought to what may occupy our attention in future, have we been able to consider *all* the objects that can be available to awareness in the present?

However, questions such as these need not disturb us; for, I repeat, our concern is only with the *art* of music; and even where it seems to be generally bedewed with pathetic feeling — say, because it builds on words that speak of the world as a mere dream, and so of the vanity of self-importance — classical singing, in virtue of the very semblance of feeling it is able to evoke *effectively*, does not make us sad, but only tends to satisfy us deeply and even to elicit our open applause.

Such consummate singing, however, does not only *require us to adopt* the aesthetic attitude, but may itself easily elicit it, say, after the first few moments of vocal warm-up through a round or two of *sthāyī*-singing in a mellow and plaintive voice.[3] Here, at once, another question may suggest itself. Is our aesthetic attitude to music adopted *by us* wilfully, or are we

3. I have here in mind the Sadārang composition, जगत सपना री आली, काहे करत गुमान, in *komal rishabh asāvri* as sung by Ustad Iqbal Ahmad Khan (of Delhi *gharānā*) and as recorded by me at Sangeet Natak Akademi on 22 April 1996.

just induced into it *by the power of music itself?* The question may be answered as follows, bit by bit, but strictly in the light of actual experience:

Those who enter a concert hall are neither equally interested in, nor evenly capable of, enjoying good classical music. Now, the case of those who just drop in casually and look on music as only a kind of relief from their routine jobs — or as something by appearing to care for which they can raise their status in society — may well be ignored by us, if only because they may be taken to look on music as simply a matter of agreeable sounds and not as a specific art with its own distinctive craft, structural devices, and potential to engage and refine our imagination and sensibility, nay, even our whole personality. In respect of classical music, the aesthetic attitude — even if it is taken to involve only one activity, namely, *intelligent* following — just cannot be adopted by those who are ignorant of the basic grammar of the art. This is a patent fact; yet it is precisely this which is ignored by the definition we chose for discussion at the very start — a defect which just cannot be avoided by attempts to characterize the attitude in question quite generally, that is, without relating it to any particular art. Why *such* relating is essential can be clarified easily.

Take the case of sculpture, architecture and painting. Here, what the contemplator has to start from is all given to the eye (may be, through varying slants) though its precise or full artistic significance may have to be thought out or visualized painstakingly. In music, on the other hand, aesthetic pace enters at the very outset; and this has to be held on to ideally; so attention, here, has to be vitally mental (in part) from the very beginning. Where the art object attended to is a beautiful piece of sculpture or a painting, factual details signified by such terms as *front-back, around, side by side, up and below* are all open to perception, though — as in the case of some such sculptures of Rodin as are not literally complete in their parts — sometimes the work may have to be given wholeness by the onlooker's trained and sympathetic imagination. In music, on the other hand, neither *laya* nor subtle differences of pitch which make the notes appear a little higher or lower are given to mere perception; these have all to be seized and held on to ideally, that is, by means of a mental effort; so, the "sympathetic attention" of which our definition speaks is, from the very beginning, *not quite of the same kind* here as in the case of the visual arts. There is yet another subtle difference which is likely to be missed by those who do not adopt a meticulously phenomenological approach to our experience of listening to music *and* of looking at the other arts. Where a trained contemplator of paintings finds that in a work, which he is presently looking at, a particular shade of colour does not go well with its immediate neighbour, he will surely feel *disturbed, but not necessarily shocked*, because his expectation with regard to proper colouring in the work in question has not been quite definitely predetermined by the essential character of the picture itself. In music it is different; here, because a definite *laya* has been established by the very opening line (*sthāyī*) — of course with the help of the "accompanying" *ṭhekā* — even a minuscule deviation of singing from the set pace will feel like a painful jab at the *rasika*'s heart. As a knowledgeable response to a work of art, aesthetic experience does not gladden or suffuse our being or ruffle our relish *identically* in the case of *different* arts. The *visual* images that the close reading of a good poetic line may evoke are utterly unlike the following that we freely find in good classical music: the criss-cross of rhythm within the ambit of a single cycle, or the decorative patterns against the ground of the selfsame *rāga* which are both relished (in part) *ideally* as the charm of efflorescence, so to say, of a determinate singleness.

How exactly our attention is *directed* in listening to music and how varying are the demands which it can make on the listeners is, however, yet to be brought out clearly. First, as the *rasika*s wait for the music to begin, their attitude is just a readiness to receive, not the focusing of mind on any specific object. Yet it is not wholly passive either, because it is necessarily a more or less willed, if not quite unremitting abstention from all thought except the indeterminate one of what the opening recital is going to provide. The compere's prefatory remarks at once make the attitude oriented towards the *rāga-tāla* of the opening composition "announced" — peaceably in case the *rāga* is a familiar one, and a little wonderingly if it is a rare (*aprachalit*) one. Here it should be clear that if we speak of the aesthetic attitude quite generally, as just one of sympathetic attention to the object contemplated, we only miss the little affective changes that enliven the aesthetic attitude when it is actually adopted. All along, however, what here persists as the essence of the aesthetic attitude is a quiet waiting for the music to unfold itself — passive (as patient) necessarily, but at the same time watchful; so that, if not the whole-form of the *rāga* (if it is *aprachalit*), at least the tone of the *svara*s it comprises, as also the requisite evenness of *laya*, are both all along duly checked.

It is also important to see how, barring of course what we have characterized as its abiding essence, the aesthetic attitude varies in respect of its little details in accordance with the individual genre of the music contemplated. Yet, whatever be the kind of music we are listening to, how the performer *looks related to the opening svara or svaras* — that is, merely physically or as inwardly attuned — importantly determines, as a quiet working of empathy, whether the beginning of singing will help or hinder the continuance of our aesthetic attitude. This is not quite covered by the norm of *shuddha-mudrā* which only calls for a pleasing or unconstricted facial bearing.

The determinant we have just emphasized is perhaps more pressing in the case of listening to *ālāpa* of the *dhruvapad* manner than where the object of attention is *khayāl*-singing. In the latter case, if the opening utterance does not appear to surge from within, the possible lack of its impact on listeners can be easily redressed by the rhythmically formed look of the *sthāyī*. No such alternative is open to the *ālāpiyā*. As the music moves on, the *khayāl-sthāyī* gratifies the (knowledgeable) listener with its look of self-completing wholeness; provides him with a definite object for (a more or less) *effortless* contemplation because it embraces a *diversity of svaras* (it being obvious that what is quite without inner differences cannot be easily held in attention); and is happily welcome if the *rāga* projected is not difficult to identify. On the other hand, where the music presented is *ālāpa*, the listener's attitude is not only one of feeling *interested in* (assuming that the singing is sweet) but *importantly that of looking forward to* what is to come next. There are some seasoned *rasika*s who feel so satisfied on listening to a well-structured (*khayāl*) *sthāyī-antarā* presentation that they may not feel like caring too much for what is to follow. In listening to *ālāpa*, on the other hand, as it develops by degrees, the *rasika*s' attitude is at least as much of looking forward to the next musical step as of focusing on the immediate *svara-samooha*. The attitude and the related experience are necessarily open-ended, so to say.

It is true that, in its earlier stages, *khayāl*-singing too shows a glimpse of a leisurely unfoldment of the *rāga* chosen — say, in the way of what is freely called *baṛhat*; but it is too brief, and not quite without the use of words; and so it cannot be regarded as a true parallel of the idiom of *ālāpa*. What is more, the two genres differ in what they are anchored in during actual singing. The *khayāliyā* steadies himself anew (in respect of renewing his feel of the *rāga-tāla* chosen) by returning to the rhythm-bound *sthāyī* after every few *taan*s which distinguish this genre of singing; and so what the listener here experiences is a figuration of patterns *against* a set ground which has its own determinate form. What the *ālāpiyā* returns to, off and on, is only the tonic which surely has a character (because it has to sound sweet by being grammatically immaculate), but is quite without *form* regarded as a coherent singleness of *many svaras*. Yet, in spite of the obvious sustenance it provides to the total singing, the *shadj* cannot be regarded as the *distinctive* anchor of *ālāpa*, just because it has the same sustaining role to play in *every* kind of singing. In our music as it so far is, every successive note has to relate itself rightly to the tonic which has therefore to be kept in mind all along and in *every* form of singing. The true anchor of *ālāpa* is only the *rāga-rūpa* as the individual singer visualizes it; and so, as they appear to the listener, the soothing stretches of *ālāpa* are no mere melodic lattice-work *against* a settled frame, but the flowering, so to say, of the melodic matrix itself, that is, the *rāga*-form. Here, what the listener is *finally* rewarded with is the feel of "an intense diffusion, a serene Omnipresence"[4] — determinate, to be sure, because of the *rāga*'s specific identity, but by no means circumscribed because it is just a sweet ambience and no mere object with clear-cut outlines. One here feels encompassed by or (so to say) swamped in, rather than confronted with what the *ālāpiyā* has been able to conjure up.

Yet, though our actual experience of music and the intenseness of our attention to it naturally vary with the precise quality (which is itself changeable) of what we listen to, there *are* some features of *the aesthetic attitude* which (are required to) persist in our concern with every work of art. This becomes clear when we focus on the following words in the definition we have been reflecting on: *disinterested and sympathetic attention to and contemplation of*. It is obvious that the first of these words, *disinterested*, cannot be taken in the merely negative sense of "lack of interest in"; for such interpretation will clearly clash with the words that follow, that is, *sympathetic attention to*. The word has rather to be taken to mean, first, that (as Kant pointed out long ago) our attention here is not determined by

4. P.B. Shelley's *Epipsychidion*, lines 94, 95.

considerations of reality or actual existence (or occurrence) in space and time; and secondly, not even by purely personal considerations which can easily take the following forms: "this is truly the music of the *gharānā* to which *I* am proud to belong"; or "listening to it watchfully is essential, for it can give *me* some relevant material for the project *I* am presently working on." Similarly, my attitude will be quite non-aesthetic if I began listening with the insistent expectation that, insofar as it is going to be an essay in classical singing, the imminent recital must last at least two hours. Again, the listening will be just as clear a deviation from the aesthetic attitude if it began with the preconception that the music expected is very likely to be good because its venue is the prestigious Kamani Auditorium, or because the performing artist is going to be my own mentor in music. It may seem unnecessary to project such negations to which no one would object: but the fact is that, as in life, so in art contemplation, it is difficult to be impersonal in judging the value of objects (or persons) we have to deal with.

Anyway, the word *disinterested*, as used in the definition in question, is to be taken to stand for an impartial way of looking at the art object; and therefore it is quite as true to hold that the aesthetic attitude *has to be adopted by us* as to say that it is often elicited by the winsomeness of good music itself. Both sides of the matter are supported by the actual experience of listening.

But there are two other details of the way we have proceeded so far which are yet to be put together acceptably. If, as is unchallengeable, how music appears to a listener depends (in part) on *his* (a) uniquely trained imagination and sensibility, how can we say, at the same time, that the aesthetic attitude calls for (b) non-subservience to purely personal factors? The answer here is that whereas what we have put as "a" directly makes for discriminating attention to what is actually there in the music contemplated, the considerations we have listed as "b" call for abstention from those factors (namely, emphases such as *my gharānā, my mentor,*) which are likely to divert listeners' attention from music's own character to his own individual interests; and that therefore "b" only (indirectly) supports, instead of colliding with "a."

If there is still some vagueness in our understanding of what the aesthetic attitude really is, the following should dispel it:

Consider how we contemplate a beauteous object of nature, say, a rainbow. We just keep looking at it delightedly, quite without wondering if it *really* exists as it seems to. In fact, we will only feel disturbed if someone began to *explain* what really conjures up this (mere) appearance of the rainbow as overhanging the sky. Here, the sheer delight of the experience is enough for us.[5] We do not wish to *understand* the phenomenon. At the same time, we do not keep looking at the rainbow explicitly *for the sake of* becoming happy; the delight is incidental. In other words, our attitude here is neither scientific (or theoretic), nor practical; it is aesthetic, the attitude of just contemplating what meets the eye. No extraneous consideration here determines our attention.

It is also obvious that to register the beauty of (raw) nature we do not need any prior training. Nor do we raise any question of moral rightness here. Contemplation of works of art is not so simple. Indeed, as incidental to it, the aesthetic attitude calls for a fuller account, say, as follows:

a. We may roughly say that, in its wider sense, an *aesthetic*

5. The referemce here is to the following well-known poem of Wordsworth:

My heart leaps up when I behold
A rainbow in the sky:
So was it when my life began;
So is it now I am a man:
So be it when I shall grow old,
Or let me die!

attitude is adopted whenever an object is apprehended or judged without reference to its utility, actual (spatio-temporal) existence *or moral rightness:* in other words, when it is merely contemplated.[6]

b. "This is the attitude of *perception*, the *activity of the spectator pure and simple*, the mental stance and the posture of attention *which are habitual in those who have developed a trained skill to appreciate*."[7]

Looking at these quotes in the context of our music we can make some points of value:

1. The aesthetic attitude (of discriminating perception) cannot be adopted by those who have not trained themselves for the purpose; and those who *have* become so eligible, look at music habitually as an intelligent and intelligible structure of *svaras* (and as making a specific *rāga*) and not as a mere medley of sounds, however sweet they may be. This is indeed why genuine *rasikas* look for much more in a recital of classical vocal music than mere agreeableness to the ear. They do not register the *svaras* simply as several impressions of sweetness, but as ordered in a specific way and as making a whole of intelligible identity, that is, the *rāga* chosen for rendering. Naturally, they see much more in music that mere *kanarasiyās;* and *their* attitude alone is at once an incipient sensing of aesthetic value, if not an explicit and worded assessment of it.

2. However, it would not be proper to speak of the attitude in question as that of a mere "spectator, pure and simple" where the object contemplated is an

6. C.W. Valentine, *The Experimental Psychology of Beauty*, 1962. Emphases added.

7. Harold Osborne, *The Art of Appreciation*, OUP, 1970, p. 24. Emphases added.

absorbing music recital *and* where the contemplator is a *rasika*. A spectator only looks at, but does not get into the spirit of (or identify himself imaginatively with) what is looked at. To such a way of attending to works of art our traditional emphases on *tādātmya* and *tanmayī bhāvanā* would be simply irrelevant; but quite apart from such semantic considerations, is it not a fact that a top class vocal recital, which is not only grammatically correct but also deeply moving, often leaves us feeling enwrapped, so to say, in willing surrender to the music's lingering sweetness? How otherwise could music be said to be capable of refining, in a way, our entire personality, as it surely can, though not without the aid of some helpful qualities in our own personalities? The impact of a work of art as properly contemplated does not end with the overt act of attending; and it is not for nothing that, in respect of the completion of listening to good music, aestheticians have spoken emphatically as follows:

> When music relapses . . . definitively into silence, that silence is not nothingness or privation, but possession and fulfilment. When real sonority fades away, then is born the remembered sonority of thought.[8]

It may be added, in passing, that as in Wordsworth's communion with the daffodils, the delighted contemplation even of an object of natural beauty may not only keep reverberating, but abide in one's memory, and serve as a recurring source of delight.[9]

---

8. Gisele Brelet's essay "Music and Silence", in *Reflections on Art*, ed. S.K. Langer, Baltimore: The John Hopkins Press, 2nd printing, p. 118.

9. Here, I have in mind the following lines of Wordsworth's poem, "I Wandered Lonely as a Cloud":

→

3. Yet, there is a good deal of sense in the first of the two quotes (a) I have cited, I mean in its emphasis that the aesthetic attitude is free from determination by considerations of utility and morality. A fervent lover of music will only feel amused or irritated if a hard-headed person tried to wean him from the "addiction" with the argument that listening to music does not serve any practical purpose. Nor will he buy the argument that the *dhruvapad* form is to be preferred to *khayāl*-singing simply because its thematic content is often far richer in respect of ethico-religious significance than that of *khayāl* compositions. However, this is not to deny that situtations may arise when we are forced to determine the comparative importance of the moral and aesthetic values, say, *from the viewpoint of social welfare taken generally*, and so may have to raise the question of the possible moral impact of some kinds of compositions of vocal music. But when we are actually engaged in listening to some music, the wonder if the act is going to be of some *moral help to us* is just not there. What is more, in respect of our classical *instrumental* music, it clearly does not make sense to ask if our attention to it, and its effect on us square with the demands of morality.

→ I wandered lonely as a cloud
. . .
When all at once I saw a crowd,
A host, of golden daffodils;
. . .
I gazed — and gazed — but little thought
What wealth the show to me had brought;
. . .
For oft, when on my couch I lie
In vacant or in pensive mood,
They flash upon that inward eye
Which is the bliss of solitude;
And then my heart with pleasure fills,
And dances with the daffodils.

Indeed, so long as our attitude to music remains truly aesthetic, no purely personal or public consideration is allowed to influence it. If I focus attention on a *sthāyī* simply because it is a part of the repertoire of the *gharānā* to which I belong — or because (by virtue of its being a *sadārang* composition) it has been acclaimed by many a maestro — and not essentially because of its own character, my attitude will be non-aesthetic (because it is not *disinterested* or objective as impartial). Further, to be truly aesthetic, our attitude here has to be one of "sympathetic attention." The word *sympathetic* in this context obviously does not mean "being inclined in favour of" (because such an interpretation would clash with what the word *distinterested* signifies), but only *understanding* or *intelligent*. In other words, the overall structure and inner details of the object, here a *sthāyī*, are to be properly registered. The aesthetic attitude is surely no casual or indeterminate concern; and it is very clearly not so where the object is a work of art. The word *contemplation* reinforces the emphasis.

What art *contemplation* really is has, however, to be brought out. In its secular uses, the word generally means: "to go over something mentally," or "to look thoughtfully at something." Now, where the object looked at *thoughtfully* is a recital of classical music, the "looking" in question can only mean discriminating listening, that is, a listening which registers *everything* that the music has to offer. By "everything," I mean here not only the sensed (or merely heard) character of the melody and its constituent notes, but its grammatical identity — which is an object of understanding because, if only implicitly, it is realized on the basis of its distinctive "approach phrase" (*pakaṛ*) and/or *vādī-saṁvādī* relation — and so is also quietly distinguished from other "neighbouring" *rāga*s. Further, its basic pace and the variations within or across this pace; and, above all, the various melodic figurations which make the inner filling of the music, as also its general evocativeness, that is, its ability to produce semblances of some feeling, or of height or depth, or sheer exuberance. Now, all these requirements of fruitful listening cannot be met unless the listener has acquired the ability to do so, *and* unless the object — the ongoing music — is somehow *isolated* for attention not only from its immediate surroundings, but (I repeat) from all non-aesthetic — that is, practical, theoretical, and moral — considerations. Now, the fact that the aesthetic attitude which is "paradigmatic for aesthetic experience"[10] has to be cultivated is common knowledge; and as for the *isolation* we have spoken of, it may be understood in the light of the following from Osborne's *The Art of Appreciation:*

> Music is a structure built-up of artificial sounds which do not occur in nature[,] and concentration within the world of structure which they create is ordinarily so intense that the listener is no longer fully aware of his surroundings[,] and [hence] the intrusion of an alien sound impinging willy-nilly on the attention — such as the blare of a motor-horn — causes disproportionate shock.[11]

We may add that *our* music is "framed apart" for attention also by the cyclic quality of the rhythm as marked on the "accompanying" drums. However, for a fuller understanding of how exactly the aesthetic attitude *differs from our attitudes in real life* we have to turn to the following pointed words:

> The greater part of our waking life . . . is lived in such a way that present experience is coloured by expectations for the future and associations from the past. This happens not only when we . . . are planning ahead . . . [but] in our most ordinary and everyday perceptions. Whenever we are expectant . . . apprehensive, hopeful, confident, or exultant, . . . [:] whenever we become aware of something as suspect, dangerous or

10. Harold Osborne, *The Art of Appreciation,* p. 26.

11. Ibid.

> innocuous — in all such situations as these we are moulding the present experience in the light of its implications for the future. . . . [Similarly,] when we are surprised, disappointed, moved by regret or self-congratulation, soothed by a comfortable feeling of familiarity, or disturbed by a sense of the unfamiliar, we are experiencing the present in the context . . . of a selected past. All such attitudes and emotions are foreign to aesthetic contemplation. . . .[12]

Now, it is noteworthy that this elaborate account of how aesthetic contemplation is not coloured by anything extraneous is all covered by just two of the many qualifications that Bharata has used to distinguish *rasa*-experience: *vedyāntarasparśaśūnyo* (or being void of contact with any other thing) and "non-determination" by *nijasukhaduḥkhādiviveśibhāva* (or preccupation with one's joys and sorrows). Be that as it may, there is an unmistakable air of freshness about the aesthetic attitude and the experience it generates. Both indeed differ qualitatively from our everyday attitudes and experiences.

Yet, merely to distinguish *our experience of listening to music* from our everyday experiences is not the same thing as to see what it positively is; and to provide the needed supplement it is by no means enough to consider all that the music itself offers. We have also to take account of its *varying relatedness to the listener* — in a fuller way than we have done so far. The need is heightened by the fact that some aestheticians of note, like Clive Bell and Pepita Haezrahi, look on aesthetic experience as the only true starting-point of aesthetics. Quite a few other philosophers of art maintain that aesthetic discourse (or our talk about art) makes sense only if it is somehow done in the light of actual aesthetic experience.[13] So, partly on the basis of

12. The view of Stanislaw Ossowski as cited by Osborne, ibid., pp. 29, 30.

13. See, here, the essay "What makes an Experience Aesthetic" by Michael H. Mitias, in *Journal of Aesthetics and Art Criticism*, Winter 1982, p. 169.

the points already made, a succinct account of aesthetic experience (of music, in particular) may here be given, say, as follows:

Throughout its run, aesthetic experience is importantly an exercise in *perceptiveness,* not in the simple sense of ordinary seeing or hearing, but as discernment or comprehension, that is, as a making out. Where the object is a music recital the listener may or may not find any emotion in the music, for this depends as much on the quality of what strikes his ears as on his own perceptiveness; but he must be able to grasp the grammatical and aesthetic character of the *rāga* and its constituent *svara*s, as also of the rhythm to which the singing is set. Acuity of both listening to and identifying (though not of active analyzing) what music presents is indeed the prime requirement here. Such listening, however, is not brought about merely by an immediate effort of the will. It calls for a trained ear and a cultivated ability to focus on even such melodic details as he may not be familiar with as yet. Such equipment arises from long and repeated direct exposure to music, and willing reminiscence of the more striking melodic details or overall impact of recitals, maybe even well after the end of actual listening; and it itself gains in quality after every exercise. As a result, the *rasika* is able to register not merely such obvious details as the composure of a seasoned singer and his abstention from *striving* after effects, or the due projection of pivotal notes like the *darbārī gandhār,* but to see, partly on the basis of recall after overt listening, how the *wondrous delight* produced by Bade Ghulam Ali's meteoric arrivals at the *sama* — by way of *taan*s of three clear but very close segments — differs from (so to say) the *sucking of sheer melodic sweetness* (रस के से घूंट पीना) provided by his blissful sustainment of some individual higher (*taar*) *svara*s, or how two neighbouring *svara*s appear markedly soothing when their adjacence is projected as a glide and not as a mere succession of two individual accents. Such advances in meticulous listening are actually cherished by a *rasika*; and though he cannot show them off to others, he quietly revels in his growing perceptiveness, and feels enriched on the inside. Riches of aesthetic sensitiveness, we may note, are quite as definite as spiritual ones (*daivī sampadā*), and though they may not elevate one morally, they certainly provide a sense of inner fullness and contentment. This partly explains why quite a few of our *gharānedār* musicians, in whose families music has been the sole commitment for many generations, find it possible to bear "*the slings and arrows* of outrageous fortune"[14] and neglect, without for a moment thinking of resorting to another means of livelihood. This inner, abiding gain in respect of imperturbability of commitment to aesthetic values — which results from the cumulative experience of dealing with music for years — is however not so easy to verify as what the *rasika* experiences during the course of actually listening to Hindustānī music. In this context, as distinguished from that of aesthetic experience taken generally, we may finally say the following:

Except in the case of reading literary works, where attention to the very sound of words (as in reading poetry) is never of considerable importance, the starting-point of an aesthetic experience is always some pointed attention to the perceptual details of the object. Yet, however subtle and trained it be, mere perception is never the whole of aesthetic experience. A measure of felt collectedness, arising in part from temporary freedom from worldly worries and preoccupation with the self, is also always there. Nor is sheer vividness of preoccupation, along with the ability to make out what is seen or heard, ever without a sense of satisfaction. What is more, in emphasizing the role of perception alone, we do not provide for the following actual features of aesthetic experience:

---

14. Shakespeare's *Hamlet*, Act III, Scene I.

. . . say, its many felt movements; the sense of flowing with, or of following, the course of the art-work [as it unfolds its meaning or form]; the exchanges of being, so to say, between self and the object — for instance, the radiation of being with wonder and delight on seeing a resplendent sunrise; or the suck of the [moving] sweetness of a musical *svara* or phrase that seems to yearn for something far away. Aesthetic experience is indeed pretty often a very rich mass of organized sensations . . . [cognate thinking], half-blown impulses to visualize what may come next, and occasional uneasiness at the thought that . . . say, the *taar shadj* has not been duly "fed" — that is, its aesthetic potential has not been quite brought out —, or that the *sthāyī* has not been . . . [effectively] established. What is more, when we admire the expressiveness of a song, aesthetic experience often includes the recognition — and sometimes the actual experience [, if only as a passing whiff] of the emotion projected by, or rather in the work.[15]

15. Anjali Mittal, *Hindustānī Music and the Aesthetic Concept of Form*, D.K. Printworld, 2001. Emphases and bracketed words added.

3

Some Aesthetic Predicates and Hegel on the Sublime[1]

Introduction

THE need of this essay is easy to bring out. Hegel's philosophy is being reviewed today. The sublime, on the other hand, is hardly ever discussed in present-day aesthetics. But if the concept of beauty can still engage serious philosophic attention,[2] and if it be borne in mind that in the past the beautiful has often been discussed along with *the sublime*, it should seem proper also to turn anew to this concept which has been written on freely by both philosophers and literary critics from Longinus onwards. Current interest in phenomenology too demands that we reckon with experiences which we tend to call sublime and which seem unnameable otherwise.

Now, the sublime has been generally put at the top of an ascending array of aesthetic concepts. So it may be of help to open by marking it off from some of these — and also by distinguishing them mutually — quite simply, as follows:

---

1. This essay is an abridged version of my article: "Hegel on the Sublime" published in *Religious Studies*, England, no. 10, pp. 153-72.
2. A recent evidence of such interest is the essay "Kant's Unified Theory of Beauty" by M.L. Johnson in *The Journal of Aesthetics and Art Criticism*, Winter 1979.

Consider the pretty, to begin with. It means "pleasing in a moderate way, but not deeply." An object which is pretty is one of superficial charm, and it is never called dignified. We speak of a baby as pretty, or of a kitten playing with a ball of wool as a pretty sight. The object is here small, and in finding it pretty we incur no strain. The negative aspect is here essential; for, smallness by itself does not make for prettiness. A small but intense poem, like Nirala's *Juhī ki Kalī*, the artistry of which has to be unknit with care, cannot be called pretty.

The beautiful, on the other hand, is not so tied up with smallness. Nor is it so easily registered as what is pretty, especially where the object attended to is a literary masterpiece or an architectural marvel. Nobody speaks of the Taj as being merely pretty; it is an impressive edifice of ravishing beauty. The joyous reaction it elicits, because of its perfect symmetry, is not without a touch of wonder, and its charm is not quite sucked by the very first peck of attention. We feel captivated, and the total experience is quite unlike the easy titillation of sense by things that we find pretty in everyday life.

Yet there are features that the pretty may be said to share with the beautiful. One of these is sensuous appeal. Barring literature where the sweet sound of words is rarely, if ever, given pre-eminent value, the beautiful in art is generally some bewitchment of sense as well. Again, the likeable feeling is in both cases disinterested — in the sense that it does not issue from the thought that the object in question can be practically useful. When we speak of *the graceful* we have in mind some manner of movement, literal or merely apparent. Thus, a cricketer's batting is said to be graceful if it is free from jerky, discontinuous movements; and appears to be fairly effortless. It is not that his strokes do not involve any actual effort; some effort *is* there; only it does not surface because of mastery born of long practice. Similarly, when we compliment a dancer on her grace, the meaning (in the main) is not that her own figure is graceful, but that (while dancing) she just appears to float or glide quite without effort;[3] and that her movements are nowhere jerky or disjointed. I may add that even in the aesthetics of sport gracefulness is explained as "perfection of controlled physical behaviour."[4]

Fluency and effortlessness are, however, not quite enough to make a movement *appear* graceful. There is another requirement too. The movement should not be too quick; it should rather seem a little leisurely, so that one can *follow* it without much effort. This is why the *ati drut taan*s of the late Ustad Bade Ghulam Ali Khan cannot be called graceful, though they are invariably flawless in *sur*[5] and articulateness of notes. On the other hand, the relaxed, little flourishes in which the singing of some vocalists (like Pandit Jasraj) abounds at its very inception[6] are quite apt instances of grace. But if, as in the early stages of *ālāpa* of the *dhruvapad* singer, the passage of music is *very* slow and looks contemplative, it cannot be said to be *graceful*, for the word *grace* implies gentility as against seriousness or profundity of temper. On the other hand, the musical passage known as *dagar* in *ālāpa* may well be called graceful because it is a gentle, sinuous flow, and followable with ease because its pace can never be too quick. In the literary arts as well, grace is a matter of easy flowing rhythm and such winsome meaning as is not difficult to get at. An apt instance here is the following Urdu couplet:

मुअत्तर मुअत्तर, ख़रामा ख़रामा
नसीब आ रही है कि वो आ रहे हैं

---

3. It may here be noted that grace in religion means such a descent of His mercy as cannot be said to be *determined* by any merit of ours.

4. Benjamin Lowe, *The Beauty of Sport*, New Jersey: Prentice-Hall, Inc., 1977, p. 179.

5. Or musicality.

6. Or within the *vilambit sthāyī*.

However, whether it be bodily (*āṅgika*) or as rhythm, it is not *actual* movement alone which can be graceful. What only *suggests* movement can also appear to be so. Graceful indeed are the long, flowing lines that distinguish the work of the well-known Florentine painter, illustrator, and engraver, Botticelli. They do not move in fact, but they sure enliven the pictures with a semblance of movement, in part because they are curvaceous.

The predicate *beautiful* is, on the other hand, just as usable in respect of what is shapely *and moveless* as for that which *is* moving or just appears to be so. Thus, we speak not only of beautiful melodies, but sometimes of the wondrous beauty of a landscape; and far more freely, of the beauty of both rhythmic flow and quiet postures as they distinguish a good dance recital.

Again, beauty may be said to be neutral also in the sense that it neither goes with *greatness* invariably nor tends, like prettiness and grace, to exclude the (italicized) quality firmly. It is common to be struck by the *beauty* of a well designed *chhotā khayāl;* but, however appealing it be, we never call it *great*. Conversely, the *impressive* proportions of the Taj surely do not detract from its beauty which is irresistible. The impact of beauty is indeed often more powerful than the easy, fleeting charm of grace. Again, quite unlike grace, beauty can even go with situations that are sorrowful. Which lover of Indian films does not know that the patently tragic character of a role would would only add to the beauty of a Nargis or a Meena Kumari? To say that here they look only *graceful* would be simply to miss the gravity of our actual experience. Tragedies are often called beautiful, but never graceful. Generally, indeed, where the impact of art is one of high seriousness nobody thinks of calling the work graceful.

Yet, contemplation of the beautiful is not as great a strain on our powers of apprehension as that of the sublime. Only those things and experiences are said to be sublime which are felt to be overwhelmingly serious. What is more, the object here can be not merely lacking in such qualities as formal symmetry, balance and sensuous charm, but even marked by positive deformity. What is more, objects that appear sublime are sometimes possessed of intense power and commotion, as is generally the case with a storm-tossed ocean, providing (what Kant would prefer to call) a clear case of dynamical sublimity. Some such cases of sublimity as are accessible generally, because they have been put in words (which abide), are provided by the following: the storm scenes in Shakespeare's *King Lear* where not only the "nature's moulds" but the bounds of Lear's very being appear to crack;[7] and [I may add] some events and attitudes (relating to Gandhi's closing days) movingly portrayed in Pyarelal's *The Last Phase* where the writing often seems sublime because of the *very greatness of* what it portrays: *vast insurmountable problems, intensely* prayerful and anguished self-searching, and an *overall loftiness of manner and motive*:

> Is our independence going to end in such a fratricide? . . . Only the force of arms is keeping the trouble under check. . . . What an ordeal for a votary of *ahimsā* like me. . . . I am in a furnace. There is a raging fire all around. We are trampling humanity under foot. The ordeal this time is going to be much more severe. I am straining my ear to catch the whispering of the inner voice. I have been brooding over it [the fast] for the last three days. The final conclusion has flashed upon me and it makes me happy. *No man, if he is pure, has anything more precious to give than his life*. Behind this [decision] is my four days' heart-churning and prayer.[8]

7. The reference here is to King Lear's opening speech in Scene II of Act 3, Shakespeare's *King Lear*.

8. Pyarelal, *The Last Phase*, Ahmedabad: Navajivan Publishing House, 1958, pp. 696-704. The original order of words has here been changed with an eye to making the meaning more easily seizable. Bracketed words and italics have all been added.

However, the commonest feature of what seems sublime is its greatness, which may be taken to cover bigness of size, largeness of vision *and* superlative quality which may not be ethico-religious at all. The point becomes clear when we think of situations like the following: standing at the foot of, and gazing wonderingly a lofty, snow-clad mountain range; surveying a massive temple or the wide expanse of (say) the Brahmaputra, gently alight with the last few vaporous sun-rays; and steeping oneself in the depth and profundity of *ālāpa* as done by a masterly *dhurpadīyā* or *veeṇā* player.

Subjectively, therefore, a clear element[9] in the experience of sublimity is the feeling of one's own relative smallness. Like soulful prayer, the sublime makes us feel a little subdued, but it also tends to elevate and satisfy us very deeply. The impact is here powerful and one feels as if the very core of one's being is gripped. All this should become clearer after we have gone through Hegel's account of the matter.

However, before we do so, a question may be faced. Is the sublime an *aesthetic concept* at all? The question is by no means unnecessary. The eminent Italian philosopher, Croce, contends that it is the business of psychology, not of aesthetics, to deal with the sublime; and that, insofar as it stands for an uncommon expression of surpassing moral *and immoral* force, it is difficult to give the concept in question a self-consistent meaning. Now, Croce's importance as a philosopher of art is unquestionable; but this particular protest of his does not seem to be so, and I think we can meet it as follows:

If psychology is taken, as it here seems to be, as a concern with the essentially subjective, we could readily point out that the first known writer on the subject we are dealing with — namely, Longinus — specifies *objective* structure as the most

9. But only an element in, not the overall look of, sublime experiences.

important of the factors that make for an experience of sublimity.[10] As for the charge of self-inconsistency, it is true that even the portrayal of Satan in *Paradise Lost* has at times been called sublime. But, we may note, this is so because he seems possessed of surpassing will power in "refusing to accept defeat from an omnipotent foe";[11] and because this particular quality — of being surpassing, illimitable or overwhelming — is shared by both "good" and "bad" instances of the sublime, the concept is clearly not without a common core of meaning to build itself on.

Nor would it be proper to think that the sublime is never discussed in relation to art today. Consider, for instance, the following from an essay on architecture:

> Nothing in nature is more sublime than centred space and for the architect this kind of space is for safekeeping. As he tries to protect and preserve centred space, its power tends to lead him to iconic and conventional symbolizations. The rolling roof of Le Corbusier's Chapel of Notre Dame du Haut . . . at Ronchamp,[12] which twists up as if in agony and sweeping appeal, suggests ultimate concern; the dim flickering luminosity of the perfectly balanced interior of Saarinen's Chapel of M.I.T. suggests reverence; and the fresh radiant simplicity of Matisse's Chapel of the Rosary at Venice[13] bespeaks peace.[14]

---

10. Thus see "The fifth cause of sublimity, which embraces all those preceding, is majesty and elevation of *structure*." "On the Sublime", tr. of *Peri Hupsous* of Longinus, by H.L. Havell, Everyman's Library, 1963, p. 144.

11. A.C. Bradley, *Oxford Lectures on Poetry*, MacMillan, 1965, p. 46.

12. In France.

13. Ibid.

14. "Architecture and Sublimity" in F. David Martin's *Art and the Religious Experience: The "Language" of the Sacred*, Lewisburg: Bucknell University Press, 1972, p. 256.

Towards Hegel

Anyway, now we may turn to Hegel's treatment of the Sublime which is, in my view, both detailed and sensible. He not only defines sublimity, but distinguishes and evaluates its types or stages from one select point of view, namely, the viewpoint of God-world relation;[15] and the way he does this, on the one hand, distinguishes him from many others who have also contributed to an understanding of the concept; and, on the other hand, enables him to suggest, if but implicitly, a criterion for distinguishing the sublime from allied concepts. What is more, he discusses the matter in the context of diverse cultures, making quite a few insightful references to Eastern literature; and, consistently with his own view of philosophy, also from the viewpoint of historical necessity, so that *the sublime* appears, in his *Aesthetik*, as a specific stage which the evolving story of art has got to traverse. The limits of this essay do not permit such a comprehensive look at the subject and so we may turn straight to see what lends distinction to Hegel's conception of the sublime.

Now one particular emphasis of his is here unmistakable. Hegel is convinced that it is the *religious conceptions*[16] of the Hebrew race and their sacred poetry that provide the original and truest specimen of the sublime. It is in fact the Old Testament, the Psalms in particular, that enable him to fix the basic ideas implicit in genuine sublimity as follows:

---

15. We must . . . deduce our classification of the art-type of the sublime from this . . . relation of the substantive unity (regarded as significance) to the phenomenal world. Hegel, *The Philosophy of Fine Art*, tr. by F.P.B. Osmaston, London: G. Bell & Sons, 1920, vol. II, p. 87.

16. This may perhaps be taken to suggest that Hegel admits the sublime also to the region of religious *ideas*, as distinguished from that of religious *poetry*.

(a) An unmistakable recognition of the nullity of objective fact;

(b) A corresponding "exaltation and extolment" of God; and

(c) Consequently — insofar as he is made in the image of God[17] — a spiritual exultation also on the part of Man who finds in the first two emphases (if indirectly) the source of his own self-respect.

Let us now see how these ideas interrelate. A sublime work of art (according to Hegel) aims at representing the One *absolute* substance or God. Extolment of God is here the prime requirement. But what exactly is the way to meet this requirement artistically? The answer may not be easy, for "in his own seclusion," God is without form. His own "positive essence . . . is incapable of being expressed by aught that is of the world and finite." From this it follows, first, that no plastic image can really be true to Him — so that we have to look for the sublime only in the region of poetry; secondly, that a re-presentation of His nature can therefore be attempted only by building on *His relation* to the world;[18] and not on anything that is merely worldly; and thirdly, that — insofar as the supreme purpose of this representation is to extol His *transcendent greatness* — the God-world relation here does not only show *the Lord* as actively creating and sustaining the world, but also, as a logical sequel, *the whole of phenomenal existence* as having no reality or value apart from the sustenance[19] provided by Him.

> We must . . . look for the real sublime in the fact that under this view the entire created world is limited in time and space with [a] no independent stability or consistency, and as such

17. This is my attempt to *explain* what follows immediately.

18. Hegel, *The Philosophy of Fine Art*, vol. II, p. 100.

19. If this account of the sublime is accepted, it at once becomes impossible to confuse it with the graceful, the pretty, or the merely pleasant.

> an adventitious product which exists solely [b] to celebrate the praise of Almighty God."[20]

Hegel distinguishes these two aspects of the relation in question as positive and negative; and maintains that as art grows increasingly sublime in the genuine sense, the negative aspect (a) gains complete ascendancy over the positive one (b).[21] What is more, in respect of the positive aspect, we are repeatedly reminded that *creation* by God has to be conceived not as any natural process of generation, but as achieved instantaneously by a spiritual fiat. This, *we* may add, is only demanded by the basic requirement of the sublime; for it would be clearly inconsistent with the absoluteness of God to suggest that He brings the world into being in a piecemeal, laboured way with the help of some material *provided* to Him.

It should now be easy to see the distinctiveness of Hegel's view. He does not follow Longinus in regarding sublimity as a quality of "elevation" in writing, or of intensity or eloquence, though he certainly regards the opening words of the Hebrew Law-giver's *Genesis*:

> "God said" — what? "Let there be light, and there was light; let there be land, and there was land,"

as an ideal instance of sublimity.[22] Again, though he cannot be said to totally ignore the subjective aspect of our experience of the sublime — because he actually hails the "genuine" sublimity of the Psalms partly on the ground that they give eloquent utterance to Man's *spiritual exultation*[23] — he also does not favour Kant's thesis that the *source* of sublimity is wholly subjective,

---

20. Hegel, *The Philosophy of Fine Art*, vol. II, p. 102.
21. Ibid., pp. 87, 98.
22. The reason why Hegel regards this as sublime is simply because it represents God's act of creation as utterly spiritual, that is, quite free from dependence on the material.
23. Hegel, *The Philosophy of Fine Art*, vol. II, p. 103.

or "*that* nature which is peculiar to ourselves" as human beings.[24] In Hegel's view, the "fundamental source" of the concept in question is rather "the *absolute* substance"; and this emphasis also distinguishes him not only from Croce who looks upon the sublime as a merely psychological concept, but from Burke who regards practical fear as the foundation of our experience of the sublime (and distinguishes sublimity from beauty on the basis of such perceptual features as obscurity and darkness); and also from Winckelmann who regards the vastness of the sea as a typical source of sublime feeling. A.C. Bradley, it is true, gives us a comprehensive account of the matter, with perhaps even emphasis on the objective and subjective aspects of our experience of sublimity. But he too does not discuss the sublime *primarily* with reference to the Absolute. Further, what Bradley *emphasizes* as being necessarily present in *every* experience of sublimity — that is, our felt impulse to "go out to the sublime thing, identify ourselves ideally with it, and share its immense greatness[25] — is not a point of such major importance in Hegel's account of genuine sublimity. Finally, to speak generally, whereas other interpreters of the sublime tend *to proceed from* objective bigness or immensity — and then turn to regard sublimity as that consciousness of an infinite or absolute which is awakened in us by the objective "through the shock it gives to our finitude,"[26] — Hegel's *very starting-point is the Absolute.*[27] This indeed is what, in a measure,

24. See here the following: "We have therefore not, as we found to be the view of Kant, to refer the sublime exclusively to the subjective content of the soul, and the ideas of reason which belong to it." Ibid, p. 87.

25. A.C. Bradley, *Oxford Lectures on Poetry*, p. 52.

26. Ibid., p. 53.

27. In the context of Hegel's treatment of the sublime, "absolute" may be taken to stand for God. Where he discusses "the (true) art of sublimity," significance is said to consist entirely in: "the One

→

enables him to distinguish the sublime from the merely symbolic.[28]

Whereas a symbol is a *specific* object, however big, the sublime emphasizes the divine as "interpenetrating the *entire* extension of the visible world."[29] Secondly, unlike genuine symbolism which builds upon some basic affinity between the spiritual and the natural, sublime art extols the divine as sovereign and represents the phenomenal as being utterly subject. In addition to these basic grounds of contrast, Hegel marks the following differences too between the sublime and the symbolic:

(a) In symbolic art, the mode of the external form is the main point of interest. Content is here but obscure. In art which is truly sublime, on the other hand, there is a full recognition of "*significance in the absolute sense of the term.*"[30]

(b) A work that is sublime *deliberately affirms* the incompatibility of form to significance — a suggestion which is but *implicit* in the region of symbolism.[31]

(c) "Insofar as it accepts the divine as comprised in the content of its productions," symbolic art may, in general, be said to be *sacred*. But, in its complete sense, the epithet (put in italics) is applicable only to the art of sublime; for, it is here alone that God receives all honour.[32]

→ substance," "God as absolutely spiritual," "intuitive vision of the essence of God", *The Philosophy of Fine Art*, p. 973; or again in "the self-subsistence of One" (p. 98), "God" (p. 99), "His pure unity" (p. 100), and the "Absolute," (p. 104).

28. Hegel, *The Philosophy of Fine Art*, vol. II, p. 31.

29. Ibid.

30. Ibid., p. 99.

31. Ibid.

32. Ibid.

(d) In the case of sublime works of art, the content is relatively restricted and definite in nature. It is, in the main, the surpassing excellence or power of God. Genuine symbolism, on the other hand, does not thus delimit its content. As in the case of Egyptian architecture, it may seize as its significance the enumerability of the planets or of lunar revolutions[33] or even the persistence of life through death. That is why symbolic art is much freer than the art of sublimity in choosing facets of the natural for expressing the spiritual. Again, insofar as the nature of Spirit, as also its relation to the world are here but imperfectly conceived, symbolic art permits what the sublime just cannot, that is, a *facile* transformation "of that which is spiritual into natural images, or of that which is essentially material under accordant fusion with Spirit."[34]

(e) Again, unlike the symbolic, the sublime is recalcitrant to plastic representation; and is to be found only in the region of poetry. The sublime has as its content "the substantive One," in contrast to the totality of the phenomenal. In its absolute purity this One can be present only in thought.[35] This is why it is not possible to present this substance in any mode of externality; and therefore, to that extent, all real symbolical character disappears. It is a necessary assumption of the sublime that "no magic whatever is adequate to express the nature of the divine."

---

33. Thus, the twelve steps or seven pillars of Egyptian architecture are symbolical. 7 stands for the planets, and 12 for the lunar revolutions. These numbers are here sacred, because they are present as determinants "in the great elementary relations." Ibid., p. 72.

34. Ibid., p. 99.

35. Ibid., pp. 86-87.

The content of the sublime is a wondrous vision or experience of the absolute substance; and here external existence which seeks to embody substance for sense is at once seen to be utterly inferior to, and dependent on that substance,

> such deposition and vassalage constituting *the only mode*, by means of which the God who is in His own seclusion without form, and in His positive essence incapable of being expressed by aught that is of the world and finite, can be . . . [visualized] by artistic means.[36]

Hegel shares with Kant the view that "the Sublime is, in short, generally the attempt to express the infinite, without being able to find in the realm of phenomenal existence such as is clearly fitted for its representation."[37] In the case of the beautiful, on the other hand, "the inward transpierces external reality,"[38] appearing as the inward essence of the specific sensuous medium. Content and form are here adequate to each other, and so look perfectly fused. Hence, the distinctness of the sublime from the beautiful is, in Hegel's view, unmistakable.

GENUINE SUBLIMITY AND THE PSALMS

Our concern, however, in this essay is with what sublimity positively is, according to Hegel. Now, the first noteworthy point here is that his view does not fail to emphasize the *subjective aspect of experience* in genuine sublimity. Nor is such sublimity deficient in an open recongition of God's *transcendent greatness*. These (italicized) elements are both here vital; but in true sublimity, they are so dominated by what Hegel calls "the negative aspect" or emphasis on the nullity of objective fact that the realization of God's sovereignty comes not so much as a positive and intellectual enumeration of attributes like

---

36. Hegel, *The Philosophy of Fine Art*, vol. II, p. 98.

37. Ibid., p. 86.

38. Ibid., p. 98.

omnipotence and omnipresence — which it does in the *Gītā*, generally — as a felt recoil from the finite, in faith, prayer and humility; and His greatness is here adored *by the self* not merely as the source of bliss, as in the pantheistic raptures of the Persian, but with "lament and groaning unutterable" over "the sense of its (own) nothingness" — in the form of *confessions* that at once gnaw at and nourish the self. Hegel's own writing is here quite clear:

> . . . *Man* is *[here] conceived in his absolute unworthiness* before God; *his exaltation consists in the fear of the Lord,* in trembling before his scorn over and over again, [and this] with a directness which tears aside every veil and opens the very depths. *We have* [here, in the psalms] *the cry of the soul to God depicted,* the sorrow over the sense of its [own] nothingness, *increasing lament and groaning unutterable.*[39]

Hegel nowhere directly refers to the sublimity of *confessions*. But the idea has a warrant in his own words just cited. And even generally, if in its relation to the self sublimity be regarded as a blend of adoration and self-abasement, it seems quite proper to speak of the sublimity of an enormous confession extorted, as a reflex, by an overwhelming vision of the Good. Some of the confessions of St. Augustine are cases in point. And, to turn to the Indian saint, Sūrdās, where he bemoans "his vileness unparalleled,"[40] it is no mere cognitive exaggeration of a fact, not even a simple act of comparative assessment, but a consummate confession where the evil in man is heightened beyond measure by its sheer contrast with the absolute glory of God.[41]

---

39. *The Philosophy of Fine Art*, p. 104.

40. The reference here is to his well-known cry of anguish:
    मो सम कौन कुटिल खल कामी

41. Cf. also: "I desire to record *all* my past vileness and the carnal corruption of my soul: not that I love retrospect, *but that I may love*
→

We may now indicate, following Hegel, the main marks of the sublime as manifest in the Psalms:

(a) To begin with, what is emphasized here is not "the positive immanence of the absolute in the created phenomena," but the independence of the one substance "affirmed as sovereign Lord of the world." The substance, here, is a pure inwardness. "As absolutely spiritual and apart from all image," God in the Psalms is "opposed to the things of the world and nature . . . and [completely] delivered from determinate existence in the finite." This opposition, however, is no complete disjunction; and it certainly does not make for a dualism of God and the world.[42] It only signifies that God here appears wholly sovereign, and the finite, utterly dependent on, and thus related to His power and will.

(b) Again, though a representation of the power and wisdom of God is certainly secured here (in the Psalms), this is done not through that exaggeration of the dimensions of a finite object which characterises the "fantastic symbolism" of the ancient Hindus, but

---

→ *Thee*, O God."

The Confessions of St. Augustine, tr. C. Bigg, London: Methuen & Co., 1929, 69. Emphases mine.

A spiritual confession is not a matter of ordinary discomfort. Quite a feature of it is an experience of "earthquake mutterings and menaces of a violated conscience"; and its expression in words is often characterized by a fair measure of the qualities called "hupsos," "schemata," "phrasis" and "sunthesis." See the description of his "spiritual condition" by Henry James in H.W. Schneider's *A History of Americal Philosophy*, New York: The Liberal Arts Press, 1946, p. 162.

42. "For that which has been brought into being is his work, possesses no consistency as apart from his." Hegel, *The Philosophy of Fine Art*, p. 101.

indirectly, by emphasizing the evanescent powerlessness of the phenomenal as estranged (in thought) from His sustenance.

As already pointed out, it is the negative aspect of the God-world relation that is highlighted here. On the one hand, the phenomenal is shown as having "a purely negative subsistence, (as) a creation of God, subject to His power and service." On the other hand, the very representation of the finite as "a loyal accident in His service" or as "a show that vanishes before the divine essence . . . " brings out the sublimity of God's transcendent sovereignty.

The fact that the finite *is* there is of course not denied; but

> its claim to existence is exhibited as a part of the goodness of the Creator, which not only veritably affirms the impotence of that which is essentially nothing apart from Himself, but thereby asserts His substance as the source of all power.[43]

It would here be pertinent to add that these requirements of true sublimity are (in Hegel's view) ideally met by the following thoughts and images in the Psalms:

1. The light is Thy mantle which thou wearest; thou spreadest out the heavens like a carpet, etc.[44]
2. Thou hidest Thy face, and they are affrighted; thou taketh their breath away and they are gone and become again as dust. (90th Psalm, *The Prayer of Moses*).

---

43. Hegel, *The Philosophy of Fine Art*, p. 98.

44. A further development of this idea, "that light, heavens and clouds . . . are . . . merely an external vesture . . . in the service of God" is the extolment of His wisdom "which has ordained all things. The springs which leap from their sources, the waters, which flow between the hills . . .; all these the Lord hath made." Ibid. p. 103.

> 3. Thou sufferest them to pass away like a brook; they are like a sleep, even as the grass which is soon withered, and in the evening is cut down and dried up. Thy scorn makes us to pass away; Thou showest thine anger and we are gone. (90th Psalm, *The Prayer of Moses*).

(c) From the viewpoint of its relation to the human soul, the sublime may be said to emphasize not only the finiteness of man, but "the insurmountable aloofness of God."[45] By virtue of the first emphasis, the sublime becomes recalcitrant to belief in immortality of the soul; and the second simply heightens God's qualitative otherness from the world:

> In religion of the Sublime it is only the One that is apprehended as imperishable; *opposed to* that all else merely subsists and passes away, is neither essentially free nor infinite.[46]

It may be added in passing that, insofar as it emphasizes the God-world relation negatively, the art of the sublime appears based on a contradiction. On the one hand, "it assumes the One substance to be the significance of the external world"; and, on the other hand, it represents this significance as being what it is mainly by virtue of *transcending* the world.

(d) Finally, the Psalms appear sublime by virtue of the idea of *spiritual* creation that they emphasize. How such a conception is demanded by the very self-sufficiency of God has already been brought out; but it would be no mere repetition if Hegel's own account of the matter were given here, as follows:

> The Lord of all, the one substance, proceeds, it is true, under the mode of self-expression; but the type of this

---

45. Hegel, *The Philosophy of Fine Art*, p. 103.
46. Ibid., p. 104.

> bringing forth is the purest, nay, a mode of expression ethereal, so to speak, and without material form [that is], the word [and with thought alone] as the ideal power, *in conjunction with whose mandate that it shall exist, the existing thing is veritably and immediately posted under the relation of tacit obedience.*[47]

Concluding Remarks

This, then, is what Hegel means by the sublime. Whether his view is on the whole tenable is, however, quite another matter. I find it difficult to accept his insistence that true sublimity is intrinsically recalcitrant to plastic or visual representation; and my objection could develop thus, by organising some of Hegel's own views and remarks:

(a) Hegel argues that God is (in his essence) formless, and that this is why no shape or visual representation can be really true to God. But it may be noted that all the Psalms which he cites as perfect instances of sublimity — that is, those which *also* emphasize the *absolute* dependence of the created world on God — owe their expressiveness to the employment of *visual* imagery. Consider, for instance, the following:

> The light is thy mantle which thou wearest;
> Thou spreadest out the heavens like a carpet

Here, it would be perfectly fair to protest that, from the viewpoint of representation, there is hardly any basic difference between a visual image and a physical shape, and that what is expressible in terms of visual imagery evoked by an adroit use of language can in principle be expressed through those arts as well the immediate appeal of which is to the eye.

47. Hegel, *The Philosophy of Fine Art*, p. 100.

(b) Again, Hegel himself seems to hold that the sublime *mode of expression* is that which seems surpassed by the content it seeks to express, or that the sublime calls for a significant leanness or austerity of styles.[48] Now, the Bible, as we know, abounds in images of such intense simplicity. "Incline thy ear to the Lord"; this is, to be sure, no lecture on the value of silence, faith and intimate prayer. It is simple in form, and rich in significance; hence, it is sublime too, upon Hegel's own conception of the sublime mode of expression. What is more — and *this* is what I here wish to emphasize — the image lends itself beautifully to plastic or graphic presentation.

Is it merely venturesome to think that in quite a few great paintings and works of plastic art representing Christ and his Crucifixion, the tilt in question — the inclination of the head to a side — does not merely suggest the flaccidity of a lifeless body, but a continued spiritual listening to God? The feature is of course not prominent in *Crucifixion* by Mathias Grunwald and *Descent from the Cross* by Pontormo; but it certainly catches the eye readily in the work of greater artistes — say, in *The Descent from the Cross* by Peter Paul Rubens and *Pieta* (in marble) by Michelangelo.[49]

---

48. This is how I interpret the following utterance of his: "That mode of giving form, which is annihilated by the very thing which it would set forth, so that it comes about that the exposition of content affirms itself as that which renders the exposition null and void is in fact the sublime." Hegel, *The Philosophy of Fine Art*, p. 87.

49. My suggestion here is but tentative. I see it clearly, as I did not while writing this essay, that in the Oḍissī style of Indian classical dance, the tilt is frequently employed, as *atibhang*, only for a *decorative* purpose.

4

Hindustānī Music and The Philosophy of Art[1]

MUSIC has for long been an object of serious reflection in India.[2] Quite a few attempts have been made in the past to define its basic concepts, such as *rāga* (melodic matrix) and *tāla* (rhythm), and to determine the real purpose of this art. Even today our talk about music abounds in phenomenological insights and aesthetic predicates, some of them being fit to be used even with respect to a single *svara* (or note).[3] Yet if philosophy be regarded as a serious attempt to clarify, distinguish, and interlink the meanings of concepts relating to a particular subject, or as phenomenological *analysis* — or, quite generally, as a resolute attempt to think ever more clearly — it would be difficult to say that a *philosophy* of contemporary Hindustānī (or north Indian) music is really there at present. We have no

---

1. This article is an abridged version of the way it appeared in *Sangeet Natak*, nos. 105-106, July–December 1992, pp. 3-21.

2. In India, music is freely spoken of as *sangeet*; and, traditionally, this word has been interpreted as follows: a song sung by many voices with instrumental music; chorus; a concert; any song or music; and *the art and science of music and dancing*. — M. Monier-Williams, *A Sanskrit–English Dictionary*, p. 1120, New improved edition, Motilal Banarsidass, Delhi, 2002.

3. The *gandhār* of *rāga Darbārī*, for instance, is said to be *atikomal*.

properly thought out book on the subject, and even the number of essays on music written in the way of philosophical aesthetics is quite limited.[4] This partly explains why I have not worded the subject of this essay directly as philosophy of Hindustānī music.

I am mindful of the constraints to which this article is subject. Those who happen to read it cannot all be expected to be conversant with the philosophy of art as it is being done in relation to music in the West today. Therefore, I have to put everything so clearly that the lack of foreknowledge may inhibit understanding but minimally. I must also bear in mind the pragmatic thesis that "ideas must be expressible in living and behaviour or they are merely verbal;"[5] for otherwise, besides some other points which this essay seeks to make, my writing on the traditional Indian conception of the aim of music, which is frankly *metaphysical*, will not seem to make any sense. Above all, to elicit and hold the attention of readers I have to relate my treatment of the subject, wherever I fairly can, to our music *today*. At the same time I see it clearly that our understanding of the music of India stands to gain in clarity from the way people in the West are philosophizing about *their* music, and that they too may be expected to get some stimulus or corrective from a thoughtful look at *our* music. In the present chapter, however, I propose to focus only on the following three

4. Most of these articles, written by me, have appeared in different issues of *Sangeet Natak*, official journal of Sangeet Natak Akademi, New Delhi. The substance of quite a few of these essays has been provided, if differently orgainzed, in my book *Hindustani Music and Aesthetics Today*, brought out by Sangeet Natak Akademi and Hope India Publications, early in 2009. So it is no longer true to say that there is no properly thought out book on the philosophy of contemporary Hindustani music.

5. L.E. Hahn, *The Philosophy of Charles Hartshorne* (vol. XX in The Library of Living Philosophers), La Salle, Illinois, Open Court, 1991, p. 531.

concepts: music's ultimate objective, *ālāpa* and *rāga*. Rhythm will be left out because it has already been discussed, at fair length, in the fourth and sixth essays of my earlier book *Avenues to Beauty*. Other concepts and problems which may be expected to receive some incidental attention are: music and metaphysics; the pure and the profound in music; music and expression; and form as organic or "living."

Music's Metaphysical Aim

Metaphysics has been understood variously, and the word metaphysical too admits of different meanings, one of these being "relating to the supernatural or supersensible realities." It is in this sense that the aim of music is metaphysical, according to the ancient Indian view. Music, we are told, is not a matter of mere entertainment, but essentially a way to spiritual emancipation[6] — an experience that is said to relate to the innermost depths of our being, and not to the senses that provide our everyday experience. Now, this is bound to repel the majority of contemporary philosophers of art. But I find it possible to plead for a patient consideration — though not of course for the positive acceptance — of this view; and my arguments here would roughly run as under:

a. If, as a more or less determinate view of reality as a whole, metaphysics may be *in*separable from such a no-nonsense subject as science — I have here in mind the view (of Popper and Einstein) that "to try to purify science of all metaphysics is to hamper or cripple it"[7] — it would be clearly dogmatic to hold (without due enquiry) that, in its other sense of an earnest concern with supersensible realities, metaphysics has *nothing* to

6. The Sanskrit text here is *muktidāyakam na tu rañjakam*: Music does not merely entertain but conduces to the attainment of liberation.

7. *The Philosophy of Charles Hartshorne*, p. 570.

do with the art of music *which is so freely used in prayer and worship.*

b. Further, it is widely believed in India that some of those saints who are now a part of our settled religious history, in fact realized their spiritual destiny through the pursuit of music. Three such saints are Swāmī Haridās, Mīrā Bāī, and Tyāgarāja who is widely revered in south India as a classical composer of the highest quality. What is more, I know of a *dhruvapad*[8] song the text of which opens with the emphatic declaration that a knowledge of the essential or ideal significance of a *svara* — or how it can make for elevation of one's being — comes only as a sequel to the direction of one's whole life towards the goal of spiritual liberation; and then proceeds to speak of the way in which *prāṇa* (or the vital force) is to be made to pass through the six psychic centres (*chakra*s) and to lead to liberation[9] ultimately.

But, I hasten to admit, all this does nothing to prove that the relation of the discipline of music to spiritual exaltation is a *necessary* one. Even a casual look at our masters of music today will bear out the point. As for the *saints* who are generally believed to be positive evidence for the relation in question, how can we be sure that they attained to the end supreme *primarily* because of their commitment to music rather than in virtue of their own inherent spiritual fineness and fervour? Nor is this uncertainty dispelled by the

8. *Dhruvapad* is the oldest living form of Hindustani classical vocal music.

9. I owe my knowledge of this composition to my mentor in music, Ustad A. Rahimuddin Khan Dagar. For (a part) of the text of this composition, entitled *Yogasiddhi kā Dhruvapad*, see the essay "Aesthetics of Hindustānī Music" in my book *Aesthetical Essays*, Delhi: Chanakya Publications, 1981, p. 123.

composition I have referred to. A religious orientation may perhaps well be said to heighten sensitiveness to the deeper values of music, such as introvertive depth, serenity and sublimity; but if the secret of a *svara* (whatever it may be) can be had only after an orientation of our whole life towards the goal of *mukti*, and if such orientation is to take the form of a kind of *yogic*[10] discipline — which is what the ascending progression of *prāṇa* through the six psychic centres really is — how can *music* be regarded as the major way to our spiritual goal?

c. At this point a traditional Indian, who may be thoroughly conversant with *dhruvapad*-singing too, would perhaps rejoin that we have not yet reckoned with those *ārādhanātmaka dhruvapad*s which are not only distinguished by a patently devout text, but also by the very manner of singing which has about it an unmistakably ethereal look. But here the sceptic may come out with the protest that, in the case of the specific compositions just referred to, it is the devotional import of the language used which importantly determines (where it does) one's orientation towards God; that, as is the actual evidence of vocal (*dhruvapad-*)*ālāpa* and of the whole of our instrumental music, language cannot be regarded as the essence of music; and that, therefore, the question remains open if music *alone* can take us closer to our religious goal. That kind of singing which works quite without language (and so is *pure* in the sense of being free from admixture with anything which is not merely musical) is *ālāpa*. Could *it* be said to have the potential of taking us inevitably towards *mukti*? Let us see.

10. *Yogic* is adjective from *yoga*, the latter being the Indian word for a number of systems of physical and psycho-ethical disciplines by which the end of spiritual emancipation may be achieved.

Of Music as "pure": Ālāpa

What is *pure* music or music *alone*? Lovers of Indian music would at once say: it is *ālāpa*[11] or singing which eschews both language and beats organized as rhythm-cycles,[12] and which can yet be very expressive and generally winsome. Such a view of *purity* in art, we may note, is very different from Clive Bell's view of the same. I say so because none of the appraisal words that are commonly used in respect of good *ālāpa* — say, *deep, dignified, orderly, serene* — is intelligible except in the light of our adult experience of life which Bell's formalism labours hard to eschew, and which is precisely the reason why *ālāpa* (of the *dhruvapad* kind) does not generally appeal to the very young. Nor would it be correct to say that *ālāpa* is "pure" in the sense that what it expresses — sadness, joy or sheer serenity — is utterly different from what or how such affective states feel in real life, for if the singer straight away sets out to sing a sad *rāga* (or melody-type[13]) at a *nimble* pace, the procedure would strike the knowledgeable as improper for the simple reason that, as a rule, sadness in *real life* recalcitrates alacrity. The typically *Indian* answer to the question how exactly *ālāpa* is "pure" would be that just as milk is pure when it is not adulterated with water,[14] so is music "pure" when it is free from admixture with what is

11. *Ālāpa,* to be sure, but of the *dhruvapad* singer. Exponents of the *khayāl* style of singing also often resort to *ālāpa*, that is, singing without *words*; but they never lose sight of the beats of the *rhythm-cycle* which accompanies the singing.

12. How Hindustānī rhythm is cyclic has been briefly explained in the first essay of this book; and in greater detail in the fourth and sixth essays of my earlier book, *Avenues to Beauty* (Sangeet Natak Akademi and D.K. Printworld, 2009.)

13. My translation of *rāga* as melody-*type* is here but tentative. It *is* the usual translation; but it is, in my view, questionable. Why I say so should become clear when I turn to discuss this concept later in this chapter.

14. Such adulteration has for long been a common practice in India.

not absolutely essential to this art, that is, language and beat-measured rhythm (or *tāla*). But, one may wonder, how can a mere melodic run, quite without language and cyclic rhythm, be expressive at all? Our answer, here, would be a dual appeal to the evidence of fact. Either listen to an actual singing of *ālāpa* by a good *dhruvapadiyā*;[15] or look at the way we talk in daily life. Are we not able to express our thoughts and feelings duly quite without the aid of cyclic rhythm? And must a woebegone face resort to doleful verse with measured end-rhymes for impressing us with its sadness?

All this should become clearer as we turn to dwell a little longer on the nature and significance of *ālāpa*. The aesthetic resources of *ālāpa* (as sung), I repeat, do not include a pre-fixed and concurrent rhythm.[16] Nor do they cover language as ordinarily understood. The materials of *ālāpa* are only the following: tones, tonal passages, and some alphabets of the Hindi language which may well be used in rapid succession, but are never so put together as to make a (meaningful) word. It is true that in the past a Sanskrit text, having a clearly religious meaning, was regarded as an essential preface to the actual beginning of *ālāpa*. But in current practice hardly anyone cares about that text — many even do not remember it correctly; and the focus of the singer's attention is all along on tunefulness and evocation of variform effects within the technical confines of the *rāga* chosen for treatment, so that the singing is, on the whole, necessarily a projection of the *rāga*'s own aesthetic potential. For production of effects, certain set ways of singing individual notes and traversing their linkages are empolyed.

---

15. That is, an exponent of the *dhruvapad* style of vocal music.

16. *Concurrent* rhythm — that is, a rhythm-cycle as played by the drummer by way of support and accompaniment to (or along with) the singing — is an essential feature of *dhruvapad* and *khayāl* songs which all avail of both meaningful text and rhythm, though in varying ways and measure.

Thus, the device commonly known as *gamak* suggests depth and power; and *dyut, āndolan, dagar,* and the *anuraṇātmaka* way of utterance work up, respectively, the effects of a twinkle, oscillation or swing, an upgoing meander, and a kind of nasal resonance which can be so regulated as to sound very similar to the tinkling temple-bells as they sway and appear to approach and recede alternately.[17] Yet it would be wrong to believe that the effects worked up by *ālāpa* are only euphonic, for they can also relate to the life of feeling and desire, say, by creating (in the *taar* notes) the tonal analogue of a longing for what is far off and is yet earnestly desired.[18]

On the whole, however, the true aesthetic (and verifiable) warrant of *ālāpa* is its unmatched power to produce effects of grandeur, serenity, continuity and limitlessness; and to evoke an intense yet identifiable *rāga*-atmosphere. It is indeed this dual power, and clearly no such meaningful relevance to the major issues of life as may distinguish a good tragedy,[19] that makes for profundity in *ālāpa*. But though it is true that the *rāga*-atmosphere, or the overall look of the *rāga*, as built up by *ālāpa*, is felt to be *seamless*, our response here is by no means undiscriminating. The *rāga*'s individual character, and its

---

17. Here, however, we may note that — except where he may seek to interest lay listeners by *explaining* the effect to them — the singer himself does not seek to represent any object or happening in real life. Presently, *I* am explaining the effect in question with the help of an analogy. The *singer's* own aim is all along at investing the singing with ever newer effects of beauty.

18. An easy way to produce this effect is to touch the upper tonic with the brevity of an instant, but of course sweetly; and then to project for a while the adjoining *komal rishabh* without a jerk, yet quickly, in the way of a thin ray of light.

19. I have here in mind Peter Kivy's approach to the question of profundity in music. The reference is to his well-known work: *Music Alone — Philosophical Reflections on the Purely Musical Experience*, Cornell University Press, 1990.

differences from other (neighbouring) *rāgas* are never lost sight of by knowledgeable listeners. Should it appear a little self-discrepant to speak thus, and so questionable, I would rejoin by pointing to an experience that is in no way out of the ordinary, say, the experience of walking through a flower-laden avenue and of feeling wooed by a breeze that seems to be blowing *everywhere* and is also the bearer of a *distinct* fragrance.

Here, at once, a question may be put. If in listening to *ālāpa* the *rāga* being sung is distinguished from some other *rāgas*, can a particular exposition of *ālāpa*-singing be said to have (or to be) a form? Yes, I would readily say, in case "form" is taken to mean a skilful and aesthetically significant interlacement of all that has gone into the total singing. Great care has to be lavished in *ālāpa*, not only on the articulation of individual notes, but on the manner, both euphonic and temporal, of interlinking them. What strikes almost every knowledgeable listener as the singer commences *ālāpa* is the contemplative and often reverential way in which the very opening notes are sung. A really good *ālāpiyā* rarely seems to be singing *for* an audience. In intense attunement with the *rāga*'s growing form, he rather appears to be seeking and securing a foothold for moving ahead, not only marking the *svaras* accurately, but, so to say, *feeling for their melodic insides*; and the introvertive look recurs freely at many a place in the course of *ālāpa*. The point to be noted here is that *ālāpa*-singing provides a clear illustration of the truth (which Coleridge emphasized) that actual art-making is a rhythm of the alternating impulses to create *and to contemplate*.[20] Further, insofar as every presentation of *ālāpa* is done in a *rāga* regarded as a matrix — that is, not only within the limits of a specific

20. Coleridge's own way of putting the matter is, however, a little different. He says that the mind of a composer at work suffers alternate pulses of active and passive motion. — Owen Barfield, *What Coleridge Thought*, London: OUP, 1972, p. 78.

melodic scheme, but also as a heuristic concern with the creative possibilities that the scheme in question offers — on completing a well-done *ālāpa* the singer feels not merely satisfied but, at times, even a little overawed at the immense aesthetic potential of a single *rāga*. And, to a knowledgeable listener, it is not uncommon for a good *ālāpa* recital to look profound. I say so in the light of my own experience as a *rasika*.

The Profound in Music

Profundity as experienced by the singer of *ālāpa* and his listeners derives from the following factors: a tranquil and regulated build-up of the melodic fabric which captures attention partly by virtue of the very attitudes it requires us to adopt, that is, not merely sympathetic attention to the present *svara* or tonal phrase, but patience in waiting for what is to come next, *and* a creative imaginativeness to bridge the many intervals of literal silence that punctuate the course of singing, an act which is helped by our own knowledge of the *rāga*-form; abounding moments of manifestly absorbed, and not merely tuneful singing; the seemingly endless capacity of the *rāga* to admit of ever newer effects of depth, height and beauty; and the melodic atmosphere which, once it has come to establish itself, appears to be all around us, and steeps us (so to say) in a feeling of happy subservience. Phenomenologically, profundity is here a sheer immensity of satisfied feeling which comes as a sequel to a blend of some purely musical values in what meets the ear, and undivided yet discriminating, but not analytic attention of the listeners, including the singer himself.

It is, I believe, improper to start our search for profundity in music by using great literature as the paradigm. For whereas literature, at its best, generally builds upon a subject-matter of high seriousness, and may well be said to be *about* matters of general and abiding interest, such as the vicissitudes of life, what we call *profound* in the region of Hindustānī music —

whether it occurs in the course of *ālāpa* or in *khayāl*-singing (which uses both language and rhythm) — is never importantly related to references to the course or content of life. The *ālāpa* that I have been trying to focus on is not *about* anything at all. In spite of its vast canvas, it is just itself; a clear vindiction of the power of the merely euphonic as against the verbal, of *laya* (or tempo, aesthetic pace) in opposition to *tāla*, and of the *rāga*-form as distinguished from the individual notes it builds upon.

I suggest that even in respect of literature a distinction may be made between a work's actually looking profound presently and *a rational account*, a little later, of what makes it appear so. At the level of immediate appearance — that is, when it has just cast its spell on us — the work only seems to be infinite in significance, and to engulf us, happily; it touches us deeply — of this we are sure; but our being quickened into reflection over what it deals with — that is, the criss-cross of human foibles, attitudes, and actions — is a subsequent happening. This perhaps explains, if in part, why after the seizure of a work's profound significance one is not straight away willing or able to talk about it explanatorily. It seems to me that if the primary phenomenal level is kept in mind — that is, if profundity be regarded as the felt and immediate impact of the seemingly fathomless significance of a work — it would help us in seeing the likeness of profundity in music and literature without losing sight of unlikeness of the ways which make the quality in question appear in the two arts.

Be that as it may, artists and critics in India do not generally talk of the *meaning* of music; they only speak of the presence or absence of some aesthetic qualities such a shapeliness, sweetness, creative variety and abandon, and a moving or spellbinding quality. From the Indian point of view, the characterization of the value or charm of music as its *meaning* is rather glib. Where a musical continuation is said to make sense the meaning simply is that the succeeding notes quite accord with the preceding ones, or that the passage in question clearly meets the technical demands of the *rāga;* and just as neither a perfectly proportioned figure nor a finely drawn triangle is said to be *meaningful*, so too a melodic passage that is not internally discordant or patently off-key may only be said to be agreeable or acceptable in itself rather than meaningful.

But does this mean that what we call pure music has nothing to do with real life? The answer cannot be given forthwith. We have to make some distinctions. *Ālāpa*, our paradigm of pure music, is surely not *quite* unrelated to real life. It is, in every case, the work of a particular singer, a product of the sense of musical excellence he has come to develop; and so his personal experience of the life of feeling cannot but determine, directly or otherwise, the music he produces. Yet, however manifest be the effects of, say, repose and unboundedness in his music generally, when he sets out to do *ālāpa*, or during the course of it, he is surely not guided by the image of a tranquil lake or that of the heaven's vast spread. Nor does the trained listener *directly experience* the variform effects of *ālāpa* as likenesses of things and happenings in real life, though when he is asked to *describe* the effects in question he may well have to refer to some contents of the actual world by way of illustration. The insistence that aesthetic *form* (as contemplated) and worldly significance seem to be ultimately inseparable cannot be taken unreservedly.[21]

What is Rāga?

What, however, may well be said categorically is that if *personality* be taken to mean an organized whole with a variform inner content and a distinct character of its own, *ālāpa* is a clearer

21. Cf. Nick Mcadoo's essay "Can Art Ever be Just About Itself?" in *JAAC*, Spring 1992, p. 137.

witness to the aesthetic personality of a *rāga* (as against its merely grammatical identity) than anything else in our music. So I take it as an important task of the philosophy of Hindustānī music to pick and integrate the elements of truth in our various traditional definitions of *rāga*; and further, to so enlarge our understanding of the concept that not merely the components of a *rāga* but *the very dynamics of the way it is created and experienced may be duly covered*. With this larger end in view I propose to define a *rāga* as follows:

> A *rāga* is a specific melodic form which serves to permit and determine, as a matrix, the creation and contemplation of music on the basis of the quality, emphases and relatedness of tones and rhythmic abidance or passage, with an eye to evoking (in listeners) either the appropriate *rasa*[22] and/or (at least) a sweet apprehension of the *rāga*'s own whole-form, the listeners' actual responses to and experience of the melody varying necessarily, *in respect of detail*, in accordance with their individual capacities for technical grasp, and aesthetic sensitiveness.[23]

Let me now explain this definition by commenting on its key ideas.

To begin with, a *rāga* is a specific melodic form. This means, first, that it is a form, or an integration of its constituent *svaras*. It is an integration — not a mere putting together — of notes because, though none of them can be allowed to suffer in respect of grammatical accuracy and sweetness, they are all to be so

22. See essay no. 8 in my book *Avenues to Beauty* for a detailed account of the *rasa* theory.

23. This definition first appeared in my essay "The Concept of *Rāga* — An Essay in Understanding" in the May 1991 issue of *Śruti*, Chennai. I am grateful to the former Editor-in-Chief, the late N. Pattabhi Raman, for permission to use it here. The whole article, I may add, was reprinted in *Sangeet Natak*, nos. 101-02, July–December 1991, pp. 32-46.

built on that they may not seem to usurp the requisite aesthetic dominance of the relation of the focal (*vādī*) and consonant (*saṁvādī*) notes. It is indeed important to remember that a *rāga* does not attach *equal* importance to the *svaras* it comprises. Some of them are indeed to receive less emphasis than others. No note can of course be allowed to appear off-key; but, on the other hand, prominence cannot be equally given to every note of the *rāga*. In other words, the *rāga*-form is a unity of *varying* emphases; it is not to be regarded as a rosary of *identical* beads; and where, as in ordinary *khayāl*-singing, a fluent pattern (*taan*) seems to treat every note evenly, the question may indeed be put if it is able to preserve the proper character of the *rāga* being sung.

Secondly, the suggestion that a *rāga* is a *melodic* form means that its different notes follow a definite (before-after) order. This order in the region of music is necessarily a series of the higher and the lower; therefore, progression and descension (or *āroha* and *avaroha*) are integral movements in the being of a *rāga*.

Thirdly, by saying that a *rāga* is a *specific* melodic form we only mean that every *rāga* has a distinct and identifiable perceptual character. It strikes the ear differently from another *rāga*. But insofar as two different *rāga*s may employ exactly the same notes, if in dissimilar ways, the perception of the precise character of a *rāga* may call for a finely trained ear and adequate knowledge of *rāga*s and *rāginī*s on the part of the *rasika*. In other words, a *rāga* as heard is not merely received passively, but is generally at once an exercise in due discrimination by the listener.

Further, I have chosen to speak of a *rāga* as a *matrix* of melody, and not as a melodic *type*. (This is important because, in quite a few presentations of Hindustānī music to Western audiences, the word *rāga* has been translated as melody-*type*.) A type is the *concept* of a class. It certainly covers or is applicable to all things of the same kind; but it obviously does not make or enter into the substance of these things. A *rāga,* on the other hand, is the substance or material of the melodic whole which it is developed into by the singer in a particular recital. So it may be said to be a matrix in the sense of being a melodic ground-plan which is *at once the necessary and pervasive condition, the material, and the regulative and individuating principle,* of musical creation. Further, though it is true that whatever is seen to appear in the treatment of a *rāga* must not transgress its grammatical character, and that one cannot here draw upon anything which lies beyond the technical bounds of the *rāga,* yet (within these ultimate limits), there is such infinite room for the creation of ever newer beauty and effects that no one, not even all the musicians of India taken together, can claim to have exhausted the aesthetic possibilities of even a single *rāga.* From this point of view, a *rāga* is limitless in spite of its being possessed of a specific individuality.

It would be interesting to see, at some length, how the *rāga*-matrix functions. Here, an analogy would be of help. Just as the bed and banks of a river facilitate, determine and contain the seamless flow of its waters, similarly — by virtue of its compass and character — a *rāga* provides both freedom and direction to the contemplation and creation of music. Again like the river bed which leaves the waters free to ripple or to eddy, or to simply flow noiselessly, a *rāga* too, apart from the norm of accordance with its grammatical structure and the classical idiom generally, offers infinite freedom for musical expression and embellishment. But, of course, the analogy is by no mean absolute. The bed of the river is clearly not a constituent of its billows and ripples; but a *rāga,* on the other hand, by virtue of the notes it comprises and builds upon, is the very material of its musical filling. But, one may protest, all this is a bit too general. What are the specific elements which a *rāga* utilizes? The answer is: quality, emphases and relatedness of tones, and rhythmic abidance or passage.

However, to say so is to mean a great deal, and the implications must be distinguished. The quality of a note may be taken to cover the following: its being high or low by virtue of its placement in the bass, middle or upper register; its thinness or richness, tangentiality or penetrativeness which respectively mean how dainty and caressing *or* steadfastly quintessential is the abidance of voice at a particular note; and, above all, what it expresses because of its adjacence to the other notes — may be gaiety, a sad and yearning intenseness, or a simple soulful quality. Variations of aesthetic pace can also lend a look of repose or impulsiveness to a tone; but their effect is also freely that of abandon, easy confluence, decorativeness and winsome grouping. The words "relatedness of tones" may be taken to cover the various formal graces some of which have been already listed.

It is important to see how the many forms of our present-day classical music contribute variously to the evocation of the full aesthetic character of a *rāga*. *Ālāpa* of the older kind, we have seen, brings out the spaciousness, repose and dignity that are implicit in a *rāga*; and, what is more, even its power to elevate us and to encompass us in the way of a rarefied atmosphere. A good composition (or *bandish*), be it a *khayāl* or *dhruvapad*[24] one, projects the *rāga* as a single and *easily* identifiable wholeness. The *taans* of the *khayāl*-singer manifest how a *rāga* is quite as open to a close and varied filling of vivacious and decorative patterns as to the reposeful stretches of *ālāpa*. So, to speak comprehensively, a *rāga* is neither a mere arrangement of ascent and descent (*āroha* and *avaroha*), nor a skeletal fixture to which the music has only to conform, but a rich and integrated wholeness of implicit depth, accommodativeness,

24. A *dhruvapad* song conforms more visibly and undividedly to a rhythm-cycle than a *khayāl* composition in adagio. What is more, a *dhruvapad* song has four set movements, whereas a *khayāl* composition has only two.

repose and vitality, and variform beauty and expressiveness. That is why our master musicians freely speak of a *rāga*'s *personality*. Indeed, just as a man's personality is an actualization of his determinate potentialities, so is the form of a *rāga* a realization of its aesthetic potential within the limits, and on the basis, of its grammatical structure.

In other words, if we look at it from the aesthetic point of view, a *rāga* is what or how its grammatical character comes to appear as a result of the musician's actualization of the creative possibilities that it offers. The *rasika* and the critic have to follow this process of actualization and to gather its successive moments through a constructive use of their sympathetic imagination.

Music and Expression

In my discussion of *ālāpa* and *rāga* I have spoken of effects and expressiveness pretty freely. But, as we know, "expression" in the context of art cannot be taken in the same sense in which we speak of expressing or *externalizing* our thoughts and feelings overtly in terms of language. Where we find sadness in music no pressing *out* is involved. However manifest it be, the sadness in question remains where it is; that is, in the music itself. This is why we should prefer to say: "The music is sad" or "The music *looks* sad, or *appears* or *seems* to be sad," as against 'The music *expresses* sadness, specially because the word *express* is generally taken to suggest a kind of pressing-out. Nor can we replace the sentence, "The composition *looks* [or is] very balanced" with "The composition *expresses* [or embodies!] balance." However, because of the admitted importance of the expression theory of art, and also because we quite often speak of the expressiveness *of music,* I have to give due attention to the question as to how (pure) music is related to expression. It is of course obvious that the relation is not necessary. A substiantial amount of Hindustānī music is admired simply because it is properly structured, sweet, and sparkling. But where music *is expressive*, how does it come to wear the look of what it seems to express? And what exactly is "expressed" or presented to contemplation? To turn to the second question first, what seems to be expressed by (or rather *in*) music is not merely the wide range of feelings which are commonly known as emotions, such as joy and grief, but a good deal of what Susanne Langer speaks of as the general "forms of feeling," say, the following: excitement and repose; the easy passage of a reverie; sudden activation, perhaps of an impulse or thought; a moment of intentional waywardness; "precipitate advances [and] victorious emergences";[25] "the drive and directness of desires; and above all the rhythmic continuity of our selfhood."[26] All this may be accepted. But the vital question relates to the "how" of such expressiveness or its semblance. How is all this brought about?

My answer is: in various ways. But before I explain why I say so, I must make a distinction. The question we have posed may be broken up into two. What does *the singer* have to do to invest the music with its variform look or expressiveness? And what are we, *the listeners*, required to do; or how are we to equip ourselves to register the expressiveness in question? Now the answer to the second question is clear. One has to become a *rasika* or a knowledgeable listener by acquiring a knowledge of the grammar of music *and by cultivating percipience through repeated and devoted attention at concerts*. A layman may well be able to distinguish soft from vigorous music, and a slow passage from a fluent one. But the individual moments of pathos and pain — or of cheer and abandon — which a turn or passage of

25. Albert Gehring quoted by S.K. Langer in *Mind: An Essay on Human Feeling*, vol. I, John Hopkins University Press, 2nd printing, 1975, p. 83.

26. S.K. Langer, *Problems of Art*, Routledge and Kegan Paul, 1957, p. 133.

voice traversing but two or three notes may provide, and sensitiveness to which can deepen or refine our response to the overall affective look of the melody, are accessible only to discriminating listeners because, quite unlike the lay lover of music, they are not only possessed of a foreknowledge of the *rasa* (or overall emotive look) of the *rāga* being sung, but are also all along alive to the factors which make for expressiveness, say, the regulation of tempo, the comparative duration of individual notes, and *their disposition in passages of ascent or descent*. To take a simple instance, the gentle oscillation of a note in the lower half of the middle register may express a mere *entreaty* — and a similar treatment of another note in the upper half may look like a kind of *aspiration* — to the *rasika*, *if* he knows that the rules of the *rāga* being sung often require a *descent* to follow in the first case, and the sequel of an *ascent* in the second.

But what does *the singer* have to do to make his singing expressive? A lot, I would say. The assistance of language is unavailable to pure music; and so the musician, here, has to make the most of the formal devices at his disposal. And no single one of them, such as regulation of aesthetic pace, will suffice for *every* kind of expressiveness or effect. The concept of musical movement does not trouble me. It is surely not as problematic as it has sometimes been made to appear. *What* is it, one may ask, that could here be said to move, and what exactly is the *path* traversed? My ready answer is: it is the human voice which moves, and the *way* it covers is the up-and-down stretch of the *rāga* in the scale. Some have wondered if music can ever provide a perception similar to that of "a wave moving across the sea."[27] But the kind of passage we call *dagar* in the language of *ālāpa* is a clear, if gentle, meander; and the early

---

27. Malcolm Budd's essay "Motion and Emotion in Music: How Music Sounds" in *BJA*, Summer 1983, p. 211.

stages of *ālāpa* on the *veeṇā*[28] abound in suggestions of a mighty billow (not a mere wave) arising from and receding into the depths of the melody; and enabling us to glimpse at the same time the points of its upsurge and subsidence. It is, therefore, too much to contend that in music "there is not even the appearance or illusion of something that moves between the positions."[29] But the point I wish to press rather is that the familiar device of expressing, say, intense grief in music in the same way in which the emotion manifests itself in life — that is, in terms of hushed tones *and enervated pace* — cannot account for *all* that music may be seen to express. *Where music is deep and tranquil*, the expressiveness cannot be explained on the analogy of sheer *physical* movement; and where a particular passage is meant to look soothing, some notes may have to be caressed daintily, so to say, instead of being projected. Further, the waxing and waning of feeling may have to be suggested through a slight, but perceptible regulation of vocal volume — a device which does not (seem to) have any analogue in the way we *move* about in daily life. Clearly, in investing music with expressiveness much more is involved than skill in handling aesthetic pace alone.

Yet, I may add, such skill itself can work in more ways than are commonly recognized. Thus if, during the course of *ālāpa*, the passage of the voice from the first note of the *rāga* to its third one is *leisurely* and unbroken — that is, unruffled by the discreteness of the second note — and if, what is more, the passage also involves the gentle regulation of vocal volume I have just spoken of, a kind of convex curve can be so accomplished that it may look somewhat similar to the inner

---

28. The *veeṇā* is commonly regarded as the queen of Indian musical instruments.

29. "Motion and Emotion in Music: How Music Sounds", p. 214.

kneeling implicit in an earnest entreaty.[30]

The *directness* of the way in which we see feeling in music, where it *is* there, is a matter of experience; and it would be a clear travesty of fact to suggest that when a piece of music appears sad to us the sadness is somehow first evoked in us and only then read into the music. However, the question if we *ourselves* become sad where the *music* seems sad to us is not so easy to settle. Much would depend on how manifest and pervasive the sadness (in the music) is. But a few remarks may be safely made. Where the music we are listening to is "classical" — by which we generally mean the quality of being doubly framed, that is, in a particular *rāga* and in a specific rhythm-cycle — there is an unrelaxing (yet effortless) cognitive awareness of the technical requirements of the dual setting; and this does not allow our sensitiveness to the pathos in music to turn our total experience into one of *overall* sadness. I do not deny that authentic musical awareness is always a case of "knowing-this";[31] but where we listen knowledgeably to classical Indian music, the "this," whether it be a tuft of notes or just a *single svara*, is generally, if implicitly, viewed *in relation to* the technical requirements of *rāga* (and generally also of *tāla*). At the same time, as *rasika*s, we do not fail to notice anything in the ongoing music, and so the look of some *specially sad moment*s in it may be so specifically registered by us that we ourselves may feel a little moved in fact.

---

30. The look of supplication may well be clear here, but whether it will be the supplication of a sorrowful entreaty *or* of a grateful prayer is undecidable. I see, here, the point in Susanne Langer's emphasis on the *forms* of feeling rather than on specific emotions and emotional situations.

31. L.A. Reid's essay "Art: Knowledge-That and Knowing-This", in *BJA*, Autmn 1980.

I think it necessary here to develop how much is involved in a genuine or direct understanding of music. It may not be wrong, but it is hardly very enlightening, to suggest that the understanding in question is "essentially a description of the course of the music and of the experience of its connectedness";[32] and we have to guard ourselves here against some possible misunderstandings. We have to avoid over-emphasis on the course or passage of music; for the steadfast and tuneful singing of even a single note can satisfy us deeply with its lingering look of warmth or tranquillity. (It may be noted, in passing, that if the tarrying in question is overdone, the determinate character of the *rāga* being sung may be seriously upset, bringing it dangerously close to another *rāga* from which it is expected to be kept distinct. This, incidentally, is a pointer to two truths: first, that a *rāga* is an organic unity, insofar as its overall look depends upon the specific character of its parts; and, second, that duration enters as a determinant into the very constitution of a *rāga*.) Further, the coupling of "course" with "connectedness" (see the quote in inverted commas) is not to be taken to suggest that features like literal *dis*continuity or occasional pauses, and variform turns and emphases do not contribute anything to the expressiveness of music. Finally, especially where we listen to an excellent live exposition of Hindustānī classical vocal music, the look and impact of the course of music cannot be abstracted from the singer's own manifest absorption in the singing. However questionable be the *theory* that music is a kind of direct self-expression, the *fact* unquestionably is that the most moving moments in our classical singing are those which seem to give visible utterance to the singer's innermost being.

---

32. Stephen Davies, "Is Music a Language of the Emotions?" in *BJA*, Summer 1983, p. 223.

Conclusion

I may now close the chapter by listing its main points as follows:

a. The metaphysical Indian conception of the ultimate purpose of music is of little relevance to our present-day practice and understanding of this art. But *if* it is borne in mind, it can surely make us a little keener than we presently are for effects of high seriousness in music, and may also be of some help to those who want to deepen their own religiousness through this art.

b. It is a fallacy to believe that only instrumental music can be *pure*. What is called *ālāpa* (as a form of *vocal* music) in India is clearly pur*er*, for it bewitches us, where it does, *also* without the help of beat-measured rhythm. Representation is quite foreign to *ālāpa* done seriously; but some expressive moments do seem to be essential to good *ālāpa*. However, when the *ālāpa* singer seeks to express some feeling, if only because he has to invest the *rāga* being sung with its requisite overall emotive look, what guides him *directly* is not any image of expressiveness in real life, but simply the professional employment of those formal devices, both melodic and temporal, in which he has been trained, and which are, in his own judgement, essential to good singing.

c. Profundity in (Hindustānī) music is not a merely objective quality. It is rather the intenseness and depth of — and our own felt suffusion with — the impact of some purely musical values.

d. A *rāga* is not a mere melody-*type*, but a determinate *matrix* which is at once the material and regulative norm of a recital of classical music; and also a chartered region for the exercise of freedom to produce ever newer effects of beauty out of a specific number and disposition of notes.

5

The Aesthetic Viewpoint

Kant and Some Indian Art[1]

I PROPOSE in this essay to discuss a particular account of the aesthetic point of view; and to bring out, in this context, the relevance of Kant. For illustration I will refer, in the main, to some forms and features of the music of India.

I

In all our talk about the aesthetic point of view two ideas are implicit: first, that it is a *point of view*; and secondly, that it is a *particular* point of view. These two ideas, specially the second, may now be developed.

(a) To begin with, the aesthetic point of view is not a mere vantage point. The latter is a spot from where we get a good or full view of an object. The word "viewpoint" too may be taken to mean a selected *position*, say, for admiring scenery. But when we speak of the *aesthetic* point of view, the reference is to a particular *way of regarding* the object. Here we have in mind some criteria, more or less implicit, in relation to which we consider the given. Specificity of regard, and not mere fullness of view, is here the main concern. I realize that in the

---

1. This is an enlarged form of my essay: "Kant, Aesthetical Theory and some Indian Art" which first appeared in *Kant Studien*, vol. II, 1978, Berlin and New York: Walter de Gruyter, pp. 194-204.

case of some visual arts it is often necessary to take a vantage point as well in looking at the works. Thus, we may have to stand at a place from where the painting being contemplated is clearly visible; and to vary the places to ensure that nothing in the work escapes our notice. But looking *aesthetically* here means mainly that we consider the work in respect of, say, its structure or expressiveness. And, of course, where what engages attention is a literary work, the question of a vantage point just does not arise.

The aesthetic point of view is also to be distinguished from the aesthetic *attitude*. An attitude is the way in which a *person* is disposed towards the object. A viewpoint, on the other hand, is a particular angle from which *the object* is considered. An attitude can, in a way, be closer to the subject than a viewpoint. Thus, we speak of a sympathetic attitude, not viewpoint. On the other hand, the seven viewpoints of Jaina philosophy are objective positions from which a thing may be judged. There is perhaps a simpler way to bring out the difference in question. An attitude may well be a disposition to feel. So is, for instance, the sympathetic attitude. A viewpoint, on the other hand, determines how we perceive or think about an object.

This should not however be taken to mean that the aesthetic attitude and point of view are antithetical to each other. The truth rather is that the selfsame *rasika* may first feel lost in a music recital, consciously revel in its accents of beauty, put no question as to how it can benefit him or whether it is real, thus adopting the proper aesthetic attitude; *and then* may also point discriminatingly to the well-knit structure of the *bandish* and the visible self-activation of the *āmad* as it appears to make for the *sama*,[2] from a particular point of the melodic flow, registering at once the unity of form and a regional quality.

(b) The word "point" too is here noteworthy. It means that a viewpoint is determinate, specific. Indeed, every individual viewpoint is different from the others, because of its own immanent criteria. The aesthetic viewpoint too is clearly distinct from the viewpoints of utility and theoretical coherence which (respectively) determine our conduct in life and our intellectual pursuits. To look at a painting aesthetically is surely not to care for such matters as the price it can fetch or its safe preservation. What is more, in adopting the aesthetic point of view we decide to care for some select features. What these features are should become clear presently, as we turn to discuss Beardsley's account of the matter. Before however we do so, a distinction may be made. Concern for a work's inner cohesion is a necessary part of *the* aesthetic viewpoint. Judgements like the following (say, in respect of a painting) are indeed paradigmatic of the aesthetic viewpoint: "The composition was coherent — not a single irrelevant stroke."[3] Similarly, when during the course of dealing with a poem, we judge that in the words of a particular line sound and sense have been made to chime perfectly, the viewpoint adopted is clearly aesthetic.

---

2. *Sama*, in Hindustānī music, is the first (or focal) beat of the cycle. *Āmad* is that part of the first line (or *sthāyī*) of the song which may seem to so activate and direct itself (at a particular point in its run) as to look moving towards the *sama* in a well designed way. For a fuller understanding of the point, see my essay: "The Fabric of Amad: A study of Form and Flow in Hindustānī Music", *Sangeet Natak*, official journal of Sangeet Natak Akademi, New Delhi no. 16, April–June 1970, pp. 38-44.

3. F.J. Coleman, *Contemporary Studies in Aesthetics*, New York: Mc Graw-Hill Book Company, 1968, p. 16.

II

We may now turn to Beardsley's view. Briefly, it runs thus:

> To adopt the aesthetic point of view is to care only for the aesthetic value of the object. Such value lies in the satisfaction which the work of art in question gives (or can give) us by virtue of its formal unity and (or) regional qualities.[4] This means, first, that value is inseparable from, though not identical with satisfaction; and secondly that, however various be the ways in which they occur in the different arts, *formal unity* and *regional qualities* admit of fairly clear identification.

The two concepts which have been put in italics may now be discussed at some length:

Formal Unity

Formal unity is the unity of form. The word "form" may either be taken to mean shape, which it does in ordinary discourse; or uniqueness in the organization of a work of art, which it is commonly taken to signify in aesthetics. As for the *unity* of a work of art, we have to remember that it means no mere singleness but a complex unity that includes and transcends differences. A single note or pigment, however appealing, is not as such a work of art. The question, whether an art work's parts have any self-existence, may be difficult to answer. But this can hardly be questioned that they are not here rubbed indiscriminately into oneness. Taking both words together, *formal unity* may be taken to mean the completeness and coherence of a work of art.

COMPLETENESS

To adopt the aesthetic point of view in respect of art is at once

---

4. The reference here is to Monroe C. Beardsley's essay "The Aesthetic Point of View" in *Metaphilosophy*, vol. I, no. 1, January 1970, pp. 43-46.

to seek to ascertain whether or not the particular work is (or appears) complete. But what is *completeness?* Here it is important to mark that the word does not convey identical meaning in respect of different arts. It may make sense to say that dramatic plays — or music and dance recitals — appear complete as we can easily mark their beginning and end. But we cannot, it is plain, speak of completeness *so regarded* in respect of painting, sculpture and architecture. With this note of caution, let us now turn to the various arts:

(a) In a rather superficial way, a painting may be said to be complete if it has a definite frame, and seems to stand out against the colour of the wall. Such seeming will be hampered if the colours of the work appear to run out into the wall's (similar) colouring. This risk is however minimal where the work being contemplated is an "assembly" of such diverse material as tin and wooden blocks.

(b) In the case of plays, a beginning is not the mere occurrence of one part before others. The opening scene here may also readily convey a feel of the essential spirit of all that is to follow. This *is* true of many of the opening scenes of Shakespeare's plays. Thus, in *Twelfth Night,* the relaxed and effusive manner of the very first speech[5] may make us prefigure that the play highlights those who make a mere show of deep feeling, say, love or grief — which it certainly does. In Macbeth, on the other hand, what is captured by the opening scene is the eerie character of a good deal of what happens in the play. It rightly develops thus:

An Open Place

Thunder and lightning. Enter three witches

---

5. The speech opens thus: "If music be the food of love, play on . . ."

1. Witch : When shall we three meet again?
in thunder, lightning, or in rain?

The point to be noted here is that when the opening of a play has impressed us as something singular, we do not, as we move on, cease to care if it goes well with the play's essential spirit. In other words, coherence is also given a measure of attention all along, if not quite explicitly.

(c) In the region of Hindustānī classical music the completeness of a recital is determined by distinguishing the four stages of aesthetic pace or *laya*, namely, *vilambit, madya, drut* and *atidrut*. But here too a remark may be made to reinforce the idea that the question of the work's completeness cannot (in principle) be kept altogether apart from that of its coherence:

At the *atidrut* (or very fast) stage, the inner accents of the fabric of both *gat*[6] and *ṭhekā*[7] are, as a rule, blurred. In other words, pace here does not cohere or go well with form as aesthetic. What we here have, as a rule, is mere speed and loudness, no articulated form; and those who admire just this kind of music react to sheer fluency and force rather than to musical form. Their response is mere excitement, bereft of aesthetic quality, because it is undiscriminating.

(d) Here it at once seems needful to mark off completeness from two allied features: *self*-comple*tion* and *self*-complete*ness*. A figurative statue, no limb of which is broken, is a simple case of literal wholeness. Here, if the inner design too is good, completeness will not seem a merely outer quality of unbroken outline. But

6. *Gat* is the basis composition in the region of our classical instrumental music.

7. *Ṭhekā* is the rhythm-cycle as played.

completeness in the sense of mere termination can also appear externally imposed, as when a danseuse has to cut short her last number just because the audience seems to be getting a little bored. This also is freely seen in the case of (instrumental) music recitals. Thus, when the *atidrut* stage becomes unmanageable — and music, a mere flowing lump — the performers may *have to* bring it to a close, and (what is more) to *show* that they are doing so, by openly patting their instruments to signal the end.[8] On the other hand, when a *sthāyī* attains to the *sama* in a well designed way, it may seem to be comple*ting itself*.

It is to be remembered, however, that the two suggestions of self-comple*tion* and simple completeness that an artist may work up are not necessarily opposed to each other. They may in fact occur as a kind of mutual supplement. Thus, when a well-designed rhythmic pattern is *completed* the danseuse may herself pause for a while, assume a moveless posture, and so actively add to the seeming *self-completion* of the pattern. It may here be added that the suggestion that an art-work is comple*ting* itself is easier to secure in the case of occurrent arts, such as music and dance, where we see the art-work *being* made, than in the region of arts like sculpture, architecture and painting where we (as a rule) contemplate works that are already complete. In the case of the non-occurrent arts just listed the suggestion in question is possible only if the inner disposition of the work is so dynamic that every part may seem to clearly make for the import of the total work.

8. This suggestion of *imposed* completeness can be replaced with that of *self-completion* if, after a spell of fast playing, the instrumentalist returns gradually, though not tardily, to the original speed of play. This would convey the suggestion that a plan (or a pattern) has been completed. No one, however, does this at present.

(e) That *self*-completeness is essentially a matter of the dynamics of internal design may be brought out by considering some works which are in fact incomplete, but which do not yet disturb us with their literal incompleteness. Rodin's well-known statue, "The Inner Voice," does not have arms. The artist himself justifies the absence of arms on the ground that insofar as the title of the work is "The Inner Voice" — which means the contemplative life — arms which signify action would not have gone well with the purpose of the work. For us, however, the point to be noted here is that the incompleteness is not really felt by the onlooker, probably because the expression which the work has been able to capture seems interesting in itself. Or, perhaps because of the coercive quality of the (measure of) form secured in the work, a *rasika* (that is, a knowledgeable contemplator) is able to put in the supplement himself, as an act of "concretion"[9] and may even feel happy in doing so. Technically, the device (of leaving a work incomplete purposely) may enable the artist to overcome some inherent limitation of his material. See, here, the following remarks of Walter Pater on a detail of Michelangelo's art:

> In a way quite . . . peculiar to himself . . . he secured for his work individuality and intensity of expression while he avoided a too hard realism, that tendency to harden into caricature which the representation of feeling in sculpture must always have . . . Michelangelo gains by leaving nearly all his scultpure in a puzzing sort of incompleteness, which *suggests rather than realizes, actual form*. . . That incompleteness is Michelangelo's . . . way of etherealizing pure form, of relieving its hard realism,

---

9. As Roman Ingarden would say.

and communicating to it breath, pulsation, the effect of life.[10]

COHERENCE

Completeness, however, is not all that we mean by unity of form. We have to consider coherence too. Only that work of art can be said to be a formal unity — or to have aesthetic value — the details of which seem to go well together. The materials it builds upon may well be diverse; but within the whole work they should seem to belong to, or even demanded by one another.

(a) The coherence we here speak of is obviously *aesthetic*. It means that two (or more) details *in fact* make an agreeable unity. Theoretical coherence, on the other hand, is a matter of *meaning*. Thus, in music, a *svara* which pleases the ear when played along with, or quickly after another note, is *aesthetically* concordant (*saṁvādī*), not logically coherent. No question of meaning or logic is here involved. We go only by the evidence of fact. The difference we speak of may be brought out thus. Theoretically — or in respect of meaning — "sound," it is clear, disagrees with "silence." But in the art of music, or aesthetically, pauses of silence are often seen to add to the effect of a complete music recital or of its segments.

(b) One cannot say, however, that only some select *materials* can be properly blended in art. There is no real limit to the artist's creative powers. Painters of class have often beautifully blended many such colours as were earlier thought to recalcitrate fusion. The technique of assemblage, popular in the 1950s (at the time of revival of Dadaism) has even enabled artists to assemble and

10. Cited from S.K. Langer's *Problems of Art*, London: Routledge and Kegan Paul, 1957, pp. 100-01. Italics added.

fix together such diverse materials as paper, wood, metal sacks or even crushed motor cars to create works that function as a three-dimensional whole. And in the region of Hindustānī classical music, masters have occasionally surprised us agreeably by incorporating notes which the grammar of the *rāga* being treated does not generally welcome (without expressly forbidding its use), of course, *after* working up a spell so intense and sweet that the little, *alien* detail was hardly experienced as an intruder.[11] Nor is our music lacking in diversity of materials, though of course all of them relate to sound. Words, formal graces like *soot, meeṇḍ, gamak* and meaningless bunches of letters (as in *tarānās*), and the beats of rhythm are obviously quite unlike each other. Nor can the *methods* of achieving coherence be determined for ever. Great artists can always devise new ones. Here, however, we may just speak of some simple ways in which a work of art is made to look coherent:

It may have an aesthetic focus, that is, a central or distinctive point, figure or region around which everything else appears organized, or to the meaning or beauty of which the other details may be said to conduce variously. Here, however, it is important to see that an aesthetic centre is pivotal in respect of effect, and is not necessarily in the very mid of an arrangement that is spatial or is thought of in terms of space. The *gandhār* of *Darbārī*, so crucial to the *rāga*, surely does not divide the scale into equal halves. It sways attention, and makes for melodic uniqueness by virtue of its own intrinsic quality. Generally, however, in Hindustānī music it is the *'vādī-saṁvādī' relation* that is really (or in principle) the focus of the *rāga*, though the *rhythm* of our music may be said to owe its cyclic or organized quality mainly to the single first beat (or *sama*). What is more,

11. The references here is to the deft use of *vivādī svaras*.

the impact of the *sama* itself may be lit up by what we have spoken as *āmad*, that is, a clear, well directed and winsome access to the *sama* of the basic *gat* or *sthāyī*. Quite a few paintings appear organized around one figure. A simple way to achieve this end is to suitably slant the looks of other figures. Here, indeed, to mark what is central in a work we speak not so much of *a* figure as of a dominant *line* of look. Coherence in art is also achieved by balancing the different segments of the work. This is done to ensure that no part of it may be merely missed. Positively, the purpose of balancing may either be to temper the unrelieved singleness of a big part of content, or to lend shape or tension to the work as a wholeness. Two simple kinds of balance are: *symmetrical* and *asymmetrical*. The first is provided by details that appear similar halves of one single object, like the wings of a flying bird. Asymmetrical balancing, on the other hand, works through contrast or opposites. Instances here are figures (or limbs)[12] put diagonally, or a white-black contrast at uneven levels. What is balanced may also be the *depth* of pictorial space. Thus, quite a few Cezanne landscapes employ not only such lines as take attention to the picture's background, but quite potent other lines which draw the eye again to the front so that, along with awareness of depth, we also duly heed what is closer to us.

Sameness of parts is another simple artifice by which a work may be made to look unified. In poetry this end is often attained by end-rhymes, or words that alliterate. The two may also work together, as in the following:

> घन घमंड गरजत अति घोरा।
> प्रिया हीन मन डरपत मोरा।।

In this extract from *Rāmāyaṇa* one cannot miss the ग, घ alliteration in the first line. But it is not so easy to see that the rhythmic brevity of अति, manifest in reading with due feeling

12. Say, in dance.

for the "short" (or *hrasva*) *mātrā* of ति, is balanced by being contrasted with the definite impact of घो in the next word. In developing such awareness, I may add, attention to the rhythms of our music can be of great help, for here the mnemonic syllables (or *bols*) provide a rich variety not only of tangential and emphatic *sounds*, but of flitting and steadfast pace. Grouping of similar segments is also freely seen in our rhythmic system, the most obvious of this device being the patterns that we call *tiyās*.

Finally, the singleness of a work of art may well be due in part to a clear and unremitting feature of the artist's style. Thus, the works of Botticelli owe their uniqueness (in a measure) to a liberal use of graceful lines; Van Gogh's, to vibrant, even frenzied brushwork; and El Greco's, to the evenly elongated, often bony look of figures.

Regional Qualities

As distinguished from the purely "local" character of a detail — say, the flitting or steadfast quality of a note, or a line's own fineness — a *regional* quality is one which arises out of some *relation* between parts or details. Such a quality may be purely summative — the result of simple addition, or emergent; that is, a quite new outcome of aesthetic ordering. The large extent of a mural is merely additive, because extension is a feature of its parts as well. So is the case of a music recital. Here, it is clear, the regional quality — say, the sheer size or temporal length — is clearly more than, but is not necessarily different in quality from the extent of its parts. Another instance of an additive (regional) quality is provided by the *variegated* look of the filling of *taans* in a *khayāl* recital, for this look is simply the result of a sequence of different *taans*.[13] On the other

13. This look of variety is indeed natural here, for in a *khayāl* recital *no taan* is repeated.

hand, the overall *compactness* of a musical pattern, and the rhythmic *ebullience* of a poetic line may be called emergent qualities; for, single notes or words cannot be credited with the qualities in question. It is only by registering the fullness of its verbal content and its divergence (so to say) from the technically requisite length that we are able to see the majesty of a line, and its appearance of overflowing. Take, again, the case of painting or drama. In a landscape drawing no shape is in itself near or away from the onlooker; the suggestion of distance here is due (in part) to the *relation* of superposition between figures. Nor can the *climatic* quality of a particular part of a play — such as that of the storm scenes in *King Lear* — at all be felt if we witness or read these scenes alone, and do not also follow what precedes the part in question, and (so to say) precipitates the big dramatic moment.

III

After this brief exposition of Beardsley's view we may now see if such a conception of the aesthetic viewpoint is quite tenable. In addition to formal unity of the whole work, Beardsley of course speaks of *regional* qualities too. But, what about such qualities as are different from both coherence and completeness, but can yet relate to the *whole* work, say, vibrancy and expressiveness? A Van Gogh painting may look vibrant through and through; and *bhajana*s of Kumar Gandharva, all along expressive of devotional fervour. Would our viewpoint here be aesthetic if we ignored vibrancy in the former case, and expressiveness in the latter? Obviously not. But the answer (on Beardsley's behalf) could readily be that, though their value is in many cases clear, such qualities do *not* relate to *all* art works, and so may well be ignored in our understanding of *the* aesthetic point of view. A *vilambit sthāyī* is rarely, if ever, said to be vibrant. Nor is a solo exposition of rhythm ever admired as being expressive.[14] *Coherence* and *completeness* cover a far more extensive region of art.

However, some of us may find it difficult to accept the phrasing of the following in Beardsley's account:

> To adopt the aesthetic point of view with regard to an object is to take an interest in whatever aesthetic value the object may possess or the value that is obtainable *by means of* the object.[15]

Here, exception can be taken to the words in italics. It may be contended that when our experience of a beautiful work *as art* is completed (for the time being) it would be truer (to actual experience) to speak of the joy that we have found *in* the work than to say that we have felt gratified *by means of* it. But the point of the protest is dissipated as we turn to the following words with which Beardsley forthwith supplements the extract cited:

> The aesthetic value of an object is the value *it* possesses in virtue of its capacity to provide aesthetic gratification.
>
> Gratification is aesthetic when it is obtained primarily from attention to the formal unity and/or the regional qualities of a complex whole, and when its magnitude is a function of the degree of formal unity and/or the intensity of regional quality.[16]

Here, Beardsley clearly speaks of the object's (or complex whole's) own gratifying character.

However, objections may also be built around the "capacity" nature of our definition. We have held (with Beardsley) that to adopt the aesthetic point of view is to care for the satisfaction

---

14. For a fuller treatment of this point see the third essay in this book.
15. Beardsley, "The Aesthetic Point of View", p. 43. My italics.
16. Ibid., pp. 43-46.

that an object provides or *can* provide by virtue of its formal unity and (/or) regional qualities. But is it not possible to conceive a work of art so great or artistically subtle that nobody may be able to see its greatness? Shall we deny it aesthetic value merely because *we* do not presently have the *capacity* to appreciate it?

Here, as we turn to meet the objection, we must open with a distinction. That a band of select (present) people lacks the power to admire a great work is one thing; that the work itself can or cannot satisfy us, is quite another. Our concern is here with the latter; and if this emphasis on the *work* be duly kept in mind, the protest can with ease be met as follows:

We may consider the matter either abstractly *or* in relation to fact. To *think* (or conceive) of a work as a masterpiece is at once to imply that it *can* give delight to at least some men of highly refined sensibility. What, otherwise, is the meaning of a masterpiece? It is self-inconsistent to think that a work is a masterpiece though it is not going to satisfy anyone. And if a critic, in his actual commerce with a work, speaks of it as an "unrecognized masterpiece," the meaning is not (merely) that it has satisfied nobody, but simply that, though it has gone generally unnoticed so far, *he* has been able to see its charm, and can be of some help to others too in gaining access to it. To sum up: *as a mere word,* a "masterpiece" at once means a work which can satisfy (some of) us deeply; and as a work that is *in fact contemplated,* it is one which has given deep delight to at least some men, maybe pretty long after its being put up for public notice.

Lastly, one may wonder, can we grant aesthetic value to an object merely because it *somehow comes to have* formal unity and striking regional qualities? Does a heap of street sweepings acquire aesthetic value when it appears to have such features to a man who is drugged?

Here, I think, we have to turn anew to a detail of the logic of our talk about the aesthetic point of view. Whereas the single word "view" just means notice, by senses *or* thought, *a point of view* is a specific way of considering a thing which is (and can be) more or less *consciously adopted*. The fact that a random heap of sweepings *appears* vivid and lovely to a man under the influence of say, L.S.D., does not mean that he *knowingly adopts* the aesthetic viewpoint in looking at it. The object's "appearing" here does not issue in response to the conscious adoption of a viewpoint. It is simply an instance of a thing's coming to gain some fictitious qualities; and is no real threat to the view being put forth. When the landscape *looks* washed and lit up in sun after a quick heavy shower, nobody says that the "look" is a sequel to our having adopted the aesthetic point of view.

What *I* find questionable in the extracts (from Beardsley) cited is their seeming failure to provide for the truth that at least in some cases a work's formal wholeness is in part made (not merely seized) by the *rasika*'s active sympathy; and that it is not always found in the works as a readymade fact.

IV

A more serious difficulty, however, appears when we reflect that what can be looked at aesthetically is not only art, but also Nature. Where the object is, let us say, a towering, but grey and straggling mountain range, we just do not care if it is formally unified or whether it appears self-complete. The source of delight here is just the mountain's hugeness, its look of limitlessness. Nor can we here be said to care, in the main, for any regional quality. Instances of the kind we have chosen may not offer to sense any beauty of detail. And yet our concern would here be aesthetic if what holds, impresses and (so) satisfies us is the mere look of the object.

Kant's view is here better. In his *Critique of Judgement* he argues that whatever be the object of attention, a spectacle of nature or a work of art, when we find it aesthetically satisfying we are not worried about its possible usefulness; and that we only contemplate what is given to the eye.[17] In other words, the aesthetic viewpoint cares only for that gratification which is quite non-utilitarian.

At this point, however, a question must be faced. Is it at all proper to say that one can look *at* (raw) *nature* from the aesthetic *point of view?* Or does common speech permit us only to say that our *attitude* to it can be aesthetic? In my view, I rejoin, it *can,* at times, be fair to speak about nature too from the aesthetic *point of view.* A viewpoint is a specific position from which one looks at anything, literally or merely in idea. It may be a (1) spot or angle from which we direct *our eyes* at something, or (2) a specific criterion — say, of goodness, utility or beauty — in the light of which alone we choose at present to *think of* the object. Now, even in its second sense we can have a "viewpoint" for nature:

Imagine an instance. Suppose a builder and I are both looking at a lush green and undulating plot of ground on which some flats are to be built. Suppose, further, that when he expresses his considered judgment that it would not cost much to level it into a *useful* playground, I advise him to let it remain as it is, *for the sake of* the sheer visual joy it now gives us. *My* angle (or viewpoint) in this case would be clearly aesthetic.

Our *attitude* to nature is aesthetic when in viewing it we do not raise any question of utility, reality or meaning, and just *remain lost in* the beauty of what meets the eye. But our *viewpoint* is aesthetic when we consciously *ascribe value to* the scenery *because of* its very look of delight. An attitude (we have seen) is a matter of how one is generally disposed towards an object; a viewpoint is a specific criterion in the light of which we

17. This, of course, is not the whole of Kant's view here; but it will get due supplement as the article proceeds.

consciously judge something. Both, I repeat, can be easily aesthetic in respect of physical nature; *but the viewpoint, in such cases, may not be one of formal unity.*

What is more, the point I am seeking to make is warranted by a specific genre of the art of music.

Consider, for instance, the case of some really good *ālapa*[18] as it is done by our *dhruvapad*[19] singers of the orthodox kind.[20] Is our ultimate response here determined *mainly* by any specific regional qualities of the singing? No, it is not. A particular melodic phrase may well seem effulgent or soothing. But ultimately we judge the *ālāpa* primarily as a whole; and, taken as the growing form of a single *rāga,* it appears (*as we follow it*) the build-up of a melodic atmosphere, a serene and intense diffusion, and certainly *not a completed composition.* When, after the recital, we use words to admire it we do not generally say that the *ālāpa* was coherent or well-structured. We prefer to say that it was sweet all along, and soothing, tranquil, deep, besides being a wondrous exhibition of the aesthetic potential of the chosen *rāga*.

I here feel tempted to put forth another cognate idea. Our *ālāpa,* at its best, is often said to be *great* music. But how is this greatness estimated? Surely not in the way in which we praise a *vilambit khayāl.*[21] In the case of such *khayāls*, our awareness of

18. Taken generally, *ālāpa* in music is the proper unfoldment of a *rāga* in (wordless) *akāra*. As done by our *dhruvapad* singers, *ālāpa* is singing without words *and* also without (beat-) measured rhythm.

19. *Dhruvapad* is the *song* which generally follows *ālāpa* as done by the traditional classical vocalists of north India. The word also means the general style or *form* of such songs as are distinguished from, say, the *khayāl* style of classical Indian singing.

20. In specifying the kind of *ālāpa* I here wish to exclude the way it is done by *khayāl* singers of the *Agrā* school.

21. *Vilambit* means adagio or slow and reposeful. *Khayāl*, I repeat, is a distinct form of classical north Indian music, much more popular today than its other form, *dhruvapad*.

greatness is in part calculative. We go by the slowness of the cycle; and the adagio here is the *measured stretch of a number of beats*. But in *ālāpa*, as we know, there is no counted rhythm. How, then, do we manage to call *ālāpa* great? The answer may be had by turning once again to Kant. In his view, we experience the "absolutely great" when we are aware of something which seems greater than everything else, but the greatness of which is *not* known by resorting to measure. He calls such awareness *aesthetic*. Now, all this fits *ālāpa* to perfection. It is a fact that good *ālāpa* which is consummate makes us feel *uplifted above everything*; and that, what is more, the feeling is not a sequel to the use of any calculative device. Such experience is no mere awareness of a *form* which (I repeat) implies limitation, according to Kant.

Happily, he says something more, and of obvious value about the concept of "form." This should become clear as we turn to consider some recent thinking on the subject:

S.K. Langer and L.A. Reid, though they both pay due attention to the objective meanings and analysis of "form," agree in concluding that the form of a work of art is not quite communicable discursively, and that it is truly known only in the direct contemplation of the work itself.[22] This means that every work of art has its own individual form. Now, this is a thesis to which few would object. But for aesthetic *theory* we need concepts too. We must have some idea as to what the form of art signifies in general.

Now, what *general* remarks can be made about "form?" Langer uses two words to distinguish the general character of form in art: *expressiveness*[23] and *articulation*. But neither word, I

22. Thus, see Reid's *Meaning in the Arts*, London: George Allen and Unwin, 1969, pp. 32-33, and Langer's *Problems of Art*, p. 68.

23. "The work of art is an expressive form created for our perception through sense or imagination, and what it expresses is human feeling." Langer, *Problems of Art*, p. 15.

fear, applies to *every* art. Expressiveness is surely *not* a feature of our art of rhythm. Yet, as it appears in its solo expositions, our rhythm *is* an independent art with its own unique material, artistic devices and criteria of evaluation.[24] *Articulation*, of course, should always be there in rhythm. In speaking of this feature, we may note, Langer emphasizes the requirement that a work of art should be a perfect balance of the individuality of its parts and its overall cohesiveness; or that neither the parts should be so individual as to ruffle, tug at, and detract from the whole-form, not the unity so coercive that it may seem simply to swamp the parts into utter indistinctness. And in the region of our rhythm we indeed always insist on both the clarity and proper organization of the syllables (or *bols*) as played. Yet, I must add, there *are* works and some good features of art which do not appear articulate; and I turn now to develop this particular point.

But, first, an obvious question. What exactly do we mean by form as articulate? Langer explains the concept as follows, by pointing to music:

> Music, like language, is an *articulate form*. Its parts not only fuse together to yield a greater entity, but in so doing they *maintain some degree of separate existence*. . . . The greater entity we call a composition is *not merely produced by mixture* like a new colour made by mixing paints, but is articulated, i.e. *its internal structure is given to our perception*.[25]

Two ideas are here implicit. First, an articulate form is *not* the unity of mere mixture. When "a new colour (is) made by (merely) *mixing* paints," the latter, the different paints, can no

24. As for the propriety of the (Indian) view that rhythm may well be regarded as an independent art too, even from the viewpoint of aesthetic theory, see the fourth essay of my book, *Avenues to Beauty* (Sangeet Natak Akademi and D.K. Printworld, 2009).

25. S.K. Langer, *Feeling and Form*, Routledge and Kegan Paul, 3rd Impression, 1963, p. 31. Italics added.

longer be distinguished. In the articulate form of art, on the other hand — as in a musical composition — the *parts* do not wholly cease to look individual. Secondly, what is again not possible in the case of a mere mixture, in the articulate form of art "the internal *structure is* given to our perception."

Now, what exactly does it mean to say that an artistic form is articulate because its internal structure *is given* to our perception? "Is given" can have two different meanings: is actually given, *or* given in principle; that is, directly manifest or capable of being realized. Now, take the first meaning. Is the structure or organization of details actually manifest in the case of every work of art? Certainly not. Consider, for instance, the masterpieces of Turner, the famous English painter of seascapes and landscapes. Think of his well-known work, *Snowstorm.* Turner himself feared that its details would not be manifest to the onlookers. That indeed is why he had to exhibit the work with a long, descriptive rubric.[26] And yet the work *is* a masterpiece, "one of the finest representations," as Ruskin said, "of the sea in motion, and of clouds and light."[27]

If it be said that the details are after all *distinguishable* or that we *can* distinguish them with more or less effort, is such discrimination, I would ask, not at all possible even in the case of a *mixture? I* may not be able to do it, but perhaps a gourmet may well find it possible to distinguish the many spices consumed in the making of a dish. What can be, and what cannot be made out in a given complex is undecidable *ab extra.* But one thing is clear, and I mention it assuredly. In north Indian music *meeṇḍs* or glides, if suitably employed, are found to vivify rather than to weaken the form of music; that the notes which a *meeṇḍ* covers cannot be said to have, *because they*

26. This rubric was: "Snowstorm — steamboat off a harbour's mouth making signals in shallow water, and going by the lead."

27. Giuseppe Gatt, *Turner,* A Dolphin Art Book, Thames and Hudson 1968, p. 37.

are not seen as having, any "degree of separate existence." Such existence is here neither present nor desired. In fact, what distinguishes a *meeṇḍ* as a formal device is the quite opposite fact that the notes it traverses seem only *to flow into one another*. Notice may here be taken also of a remark that Langer herself makes elsewhere:

> In artistic production, the composer's materials must be *completely swallowed* up in the illusion they create.[28]

And to speak quite generally, where *harmony* dominates the music I wonder if the notes of music (as heard) can be credited with *any separate* existence. So I conclude: the form of *all* art cannot be said to be expressive *or* articulate.

Let me now turn to Reid. He speaks of artistic form as *embodiment*. Now, I am quite aware of the special meaning that is given to the word. Reid amplifies it as "creative aesthetic embodiment," and regards the inseparability of "peceptua" from aesthetic meaning as the key emphasis in his thesis of *embodiment*. Yet my protest is here ready and definite. A very clear instance of perceptua-meaning inseparability is provided by the harmony of (verbal) sounds and sense or meaning in poetry. But, we may note, where the words' very sounds chime with what they signify, the meaning is revealed with such directness and so unmistakably that expressiveness rather than mere shaping or embodiment becomes the final, felt quality to be lauded.[29] What, then, is the alternative left? How can we speak of "form" in such a way that *every* art may be covered?

---

28. S.K. Langer, *Problems of Art*, p. 39. Italics added.

29. Often, and not merely freakishly, as (one could say) in the case of painting. I have here in mind the art of Michelangelo Pistaletto. His "photographic figures (are) fastened to mirror backgrounds in which the spectator sees himself reflected, thus completing the composition. . . . " Edward Lucie Smith, *Movements in Art since 1945*, London: Thames and Hudson, 1969, p. 132.

Let us see if Kant's views on the matter can be of help here.

In the case of arts like painting and scultpure, he maintians, form is a matter of spatial relationships between *co-existences*. The "form" of music and dance, on the other hand, lies in relations among *successives*. However, two (of the) arts which our word *sangeet* signifies are not "formed" identically. For whereas musical form is a relatedness of successive auditory *sensations in time*, in the case of dance it is successive *figures in space* that blend to give us "form." In the case of every art, however, form (or relationship between sensations) is perceived "intellectually." Nowhere, says Kant, is form provided to sensation alone.

Now, the view that "form" is not a *direct feature* of what is given to sense may seem questionable to those who look at it as merely a matter of shape. But in the context of art it is difficult to challenge the suggestion, implicit in the view of Kant, that apprehension of form is not a matter of mere sensing. For, to consider an instance, we can hardly hazard the opinion that *any one who just* lends his *ear to* the presented sequence of *svara*s is able at once to see the form of the music composition that they go to make. The right response, here, is an *intellectual* awareness of *interrelations* of tonal phrases (and rhythmic beats) and not the mere listening, howsoever attentive, of a mere sequence of individual sounds.[30]

Yet, I cannot roundly ascribe to Kant the view that apprehension of interrelations and overall organization *distinguishe*s our seizure of form *in art*, for he holds that, as objects of sheer sense, even colour and tones are *successions* of sensations, hence "formed"; and that what can be beautiful is

30. Kant himself says that music is not an art of merely agreeable sensations, but a *fine* art of beautiful auditory sensations (*Critique of Judgement*, 190/Academy Edition, p. 325); and that here *composition* constitutes the proper object of the pure jedgement of taste (Ibid., 68/Academy Edition, p. 225).

not merely an ample, intricate symphony, but an individual note. Now, this is bound to look odd to us, for no one speaks of *organization* in respect of the beauty (or beautiful form) of a single tone. In short, the difficulty here is that by regarding form as a manifold or as a matter of mere co-existence or successiveness (not of *inter*-relation or organization) Kant is not only enabled to speak of the beauty of single tones and colours along with that of (complex) works of art, but is somewhat weakened in respect of his suggestion that apprehension of form is, in a way, necessarily *intellectual*. However, in his general emphasis on form, as distinguished from the way he interprets it, Kant would seem acceptable to many. He insists that "perceptua," such as bright colours in painting, "only make (the) form more clearly . . . intuitable, as they excite and sustain the attention directed to the object itself";[31] that, in respect of the arts, the fundamental prerequisite for taste is "not what gratifies in sensation merely but what pleases by its form";[32] and that all such embellishments as do not "enter into the composition of the beautiful form" are merely finery which takes us away from the work's genuine beauty.[33]

This clearly foresees the value we set on form in art today; and we may also note, in passing, that Kant lays stress not only on the universal forms of experience — that is, space-time and categories — but on the empirical form of objects.[34] For our present purpose, however, it is the following ideas of his that are really of value:

First, "form" is beautiful when we contemplate art (or

---

31. Kant, *The Critique of Judgement*, tr. J.C. Meredith, Oxford: Clarendon Press, 1969 Reprint, 68/Academy Edition, p. 225.
32. Ibid., 67/Academy Edition, p. 225.
33. Ibid., 68/Academy Edition, p. 226.
34. Kant's remarks on "empirical form" have not received due attention. See T.E. Uehling's *The Notion of Form in Kant's Critique of Aesthetic Judgement*, The Hague: Mounton, 1971, p. 79.

nature) with disinterested delight. Secondly, the object of delight is here the mere presentation. In other words, the object is liked for its own sake. It is not regarded as a mere instance of some kind. Nor is it admired because it conforms to any plan or concept. Finally, when we find a painting beautiful, the *immediate* ground of our judgement is not any objective criterion, but subjective feeling. This feeling, however, is no mere delight of sense. It is rather one of restful contemplation which is no inert sensation, but the reflex of an active, yet harmonious working of our cognitive powers. Kant insists that aesthetic delight issues from the accordant functioning of understanding and imagination. Beautiful form is essentially a matter of the object's *being apprehended in a particular way.*

Of these three emphases it is the last that is distinctively Kantian; and I think it necessary to clarify it, by commenting on a passage from *The Critique of Judgement.*[35]

Beauty, we have seen, is essentially a matter of form. The faculty which perceives beauty is taste. It estimates an object by judging that the imagination conforms to law freely. But what does this *free conformity of imagination to law* really mean? It means, to begin with, that the activity of imagination here is not merely reproductive. For, reproductive imagination is not free, but subject to the laws of association. In a judgement of taste, on the other hand, imagination is free in the sense that it is productive and exerts an activity of its own. It is here seen to originate "arbitrary forms of possible intuitions." Yet, where (in the region of nature or the arts) what is apprehended is a definite object of sense — quite unlike a poem, the form of which cannot be said to be essentially perceptual — the activity of imagination is "to that extent" not free; for it does not quite

35. The reference here is to the passage which opens the "general remarks of the First Section of the Analytic" on p. 86 (Academy Edition p. 240), and covers almost the whole of the next page of the *Critique of Judgement.*

desert, but has in general to conform to the object. This restraint, however (in the case of beautiful form) is not so rigid as to deny all freedom to imagination. The object is such a readymade arrangement of the manifold as would be projected freely by imagination itself, were it allowed to do so, in *general* conformity with the law of understanding. To illustrate, a painting showing some figures *and Christ* may present the latter as visibly and prominently, yet not spatially central;[36] and this, further, could be the way in which imagination may itself like to organize the figures as an intelligible unity. As an object of attention, such a work would certainly control *apprehension* by *imagination*, but it would do so without seeming to constrain[37] the latter.

Here, we must remember, Kant is speaking of the freedom of *imagination*, not of the will. In respect of *the will*, it seems proper to say that its determination by (its) law does not detract from its freedom. In fact, according to Kant, freedom of will is nothing but autonomy — "that is, the property which will has of being a law to itself." But the freedom *of imagination* lies in its originating "arbitrary forms of possible intuitions."[38] So, it would be a contradiction to say that imagination is both free and of *itself* (directly) conforms to the law of understanding; we must rather say it *has to* do so.

But this having to conform to law cannot mean "being compelled to follow a course laid down by *a definite* law"; for

---

36. I may here refer to works like: "Adoration in the Forest" by Filippo Lippi (included in C. Bazin's *A Concise History of Art*, London: Thames and Hudson, Second Impression, Part I, 1964, p. facing 240); and "Resurrection" by El Greco (Ibid., Part II, p. facing 308.)

37. In all matters of taste, Kant holds, regularity in the shape of constraint is to be avoided as far as possible. Kant, *The Critique of Judgement*, 88/Academy Edition, p. 242.

38. Ibid., 86/Academy Edition p. 240. Italics added.

in *that* kind of conformity, the form of the product is determined by concepts. To illustrate, a figure may be adjudged and acclaimed as conforming admirably to the definite concept of circularity. Here the delight would relate to the formal perfection of the figure, not to its beauty. So when we speak of the *free* conformity of imagination to understanding in a judgement of taste, we can mean only that imagination has here (roughly) to conform not to a determinate concept of the understanding, but to the (general) law of understanding, which is judgement. In other words, though the object *is* here judged, it is not judged definitely according to a specific concept. This is what Kant means by "conformity (in general) to law without *a* law" or "finality apart from *an* end" or "a subjective harmonizing of the imagination and the understanding *without an objective end.*"[39] And this is exactly what makes imagination "free." It is free in schematizing without a concept.[40]

To turn to our earlier reference to painting, we may now say that when the work is found beautiful, it is only because of the *feeling* which results from the accord of imagination with the general discursive manner of understanding — or, with an indeterminate idea of centrality — not with the precise concept of a mathematical centre. The play of the two powers is here "free" because it is not at all constrained by any stiff or mathematical regularity, "the contemplation of which affords us no lasting entertainment."[41] This is what Kant means by the general accordance of the *faculty* of imagination with the *faculty* of understanding. For him, "beauty" means "a free and indeterminately final entertainment of the mental powers."[42]

---

39. All these phrases are Kant's own (Kant, *The Critique of Judgement*, p. 86/Academy Edition) p. 241. But the italics are mine.
40. Ibid., p. 143/Academy Edition, p. 287.
41. Ibid., p. 88/Academy Edition, p. 242.
42. Ibid.

When it is *pure,* says Kant, a judgement of taste "combines delight or aversion immediately with *the bare contemplation* of the object irrespective of its use or of any end."[43] "The subjective formal condition" of *every* judgement is the harmonious accordance of the two powers of representation,[44] but the *aesthetic* judgement is "free" in the sense that it is determined neither by any concept nor by the criterion of utility. I may add that where the unity of a manifold is just apprehended by referring it to a *definite* concept, it is only grasped, not explored; *and that such form is clearly abstractable.* Kant, on the other hand, speaks (we have seen) of "free and *indeterminately final entertainment* of the mental powers." This means that, in his view, the unity in question is *experienced by indwelling,* and as a mutual quickening of imagination and understanding. A form that is thus experienced is clearly not abstractable; and, what is more, this emphasis is of help to us in avoiding the mistake of regarding aesthetic experience as a mere *inert* "absorption in the fullness of artistic meaning."[45] Kant's emphasis on the self-complete or autonomous *and active* character of aesthetic experience is indeed unmistakable. He says:

> We dwell on the contemplation of the beautiful because this contemplation strengthens and reproduces itself.[46]

We must also here mark another significant detail of Kant's thinking. The accord of imagination and understanding of which he speaks does not mean *coordinate* activity of the two powers. Kant in fact says openly that whereas in a cognitive judgement — such as: "This is a perfect circle" — imagination is at the service of understanding, in a judgement of taste,

43. Kant, *The Critique of Judgement,* p. 88/Academy Edition, p. 242. My italics.

44. Ibid., p. 143/Academy Edition, p. 287.

45. Reid, *Meaning in the Arts,* p. 88. Reid, I may add, speaks of our actual experience of art as (merely) "a time to be silent." Ibid., p. 89.

46. Kant, *The Critique of Judgment,* p. 64/Academy Edition, p. 222.

"understanding is at the service of imagination."[47]

In other words, Kant explains *beautiful* form in terms of subjective feeling,[48] not by referring to objective properties. For him, the beauty of art or nature means that the *form of the object* delights the contemplator because, in apprehending it, his understanding does not dominate, but subserves the working of his imagination. In other words, the unity of the given manifold is here judged not as determined by any definite concept, but *in accordance with* whatever varying syntheses imagination may like to put on the given,[49] consistently, of course, with the overall unity of the object itself.

The "accord," we may further note, is merely formal. For, understanding is the faculty of the *forms* or rules of thought, and *that* in imagination which corresponds with understanding is therefore nothing material or specific, but temporal and spatial relationships. The question as to what precise concept is an analogue of a synthesis of imagination is left open by Kant. But the fact that an analogue *is* found is indicated by the resultant feeling of pleasure.[50]

The "analogue" is found, I must add, in our dealing with the *object*. The two cognitive powers are not to be regarded as

---

47. Kant, *The Critique of Judgement*, p. 64/Academy Edition, p. 222.

48. "The judgement of taste must found [itself] upon a mere sensation of the mutually quickening activity of the imagination in its *freedom*, and of the understanding with its *conformity to law*." Ibid., p. 143/ Academy Edition, p. 287.

49. This specific suggestion would seem warranted by Kant's own view that what distinguishes a judgement of taste is "a principle of subsumption not of intuitions under concepts, but of the *faculty* of intuitions . . . i.e. of imagination, under the faculty of concepts" (Ibid.) provided we remember that imagination makes for the intuition *and* the arrangement of the manifold of intuition" (Ibid.).

50. J.E. Uehling, Jr., *The Notion of Form in Kant's Critique of Judgment*, pp. 60-61.

working only in relation to each other. Where "form" seems *beautiful* the object appears "pre-adapted to our power of judgement," though not to any plan or concept. In our experience of the *sublime*, on the other hand, the object may seem "to contravene the end of our power of judgement, to be ill adapted to our faculty of presentation, and to be, as it were, an outrage on imagination."[51] To sum up, the apprehension of beautiful form means, first, that the object seems adapted to our powers; secondly, that these powers work in harmony with each other; and thirdly, that the delight here does not rest on any thought of utility, reality or accordance with a plan or concept. This is what Kant means by his emphasis on disinterestedness and by the "definition" of the beautiful which he derives from the "third moment:"

> Beauty is the form of finality in an object, so far as perceived in it *apart from the representation of an end.*

Such a way of speaking, it is true, gives nothing detailed about form in the various arts. But that, I rejoin, is not the business of general aesthetics. The alternative to Kant's way is to characterize form less abstractly, by turning to *objects* of art; and to speak of it, say, as "expressive" or "embodied." But the inadequacy of such efforts has already been brought out.

Finally, we may ascertain the bearing of Kant's thought on the question as to how to relate the beautiful to religion and morality. How exactly is the question problematic? We cannot, of course, doubt the possible togetherness of the good and the beautiful. As we listen to good music, a finely rendered note may seem not merely sweet, but uplifting; and the mixedness may not at all strike the listener as odd. Nor would anyone murmur if a concept from the good life were woven into an accent of poetic beauty. The fusion, on the other hand, may

---

51. Kant, *The Critique of Judgment*, p. 91/Academy Edition p. 245.

only delight us. This is, for instance, surely the way we react to Kiekegaard's image of the rainbow as "a portal of grace across the heavens."[52]

One feels like protesting only when art is subordinated to, and is used as a mere vehicle of some ulterior purpose, moral or religious. Here, we may rightly object, there is a weakening of aesthetic values, an encroachment on the autonomy of art. And Kant would here readily support us. He in fact opposes all determination from the outside, all objective finality. If a work of art appears to be made according to some formula, moral or merely technical, he would set little value on it. On the other hand, Kant's position is far removed from the view that beauty has nothing to do with the good life. But, to see how the two are (in his view) related, one has to do a little creative thinking around some of his own key utterances.

His well-known phrase: "purposiveness without a purpose" is here of help. It makes for the idea that art can be purposive in the sense of *being incidentally adapted to* a basic feature of the good life *without seeming to pursue any purpose*, moral or otherwise. Thus, it may well be — in Kant's view, it really is — that when I take delight in the beauty of art or nature, my implicit approval is not determined primarily by any consideration of sensuous charm or utility; and that such relative freedom from the easy lure of sense is at once a necessary sign of being (somewhat) moral.[53] This indeed is the

52. Perry D. LeFevre, *The Prayers of Kierkegaard*, Chicago and London: The University of Chicago Press, 1963, p. 27.

53. And also, Kant would like to add, an active step towards the good life. Thus, see: "Taste makes . . . *the transition from the charm of sense to habitual moral interest* possible without too violent a leap, for . . . it teaches us to find, even in sensuous objects, a free delight apart from any charm of sense." Kant, *The Critique of Judgement*, p. 225/ Academy Edition, p. 354. Italics added. This perhaps explains why Kant regards "beauty as the symbol of morality."

meaning of Kant's own remark that the beautiful and the sublime are alike

> final in reference to the moral feeling; [and that whereas] the beautiful prepares us to love something, even nature, *apart from any interest*, the Sublime to esteem something highly even in opposition to our [sensible] interest.[54]

Kant's thought here may not be identical with, but — if taken along with his emphases that our experience of beauty is not one of objective finality, and that, in both art and nature, form is the real thing — it seems fairly akin to the modern view that, if a (literary) work is morally interesting, in adopting the aesthetic point of view with regard to it we only mean to see if the moral theme is nicely interwoven with the plot, and does not seem to have been forced into it.[55]

---

54. Kant, *The Critique of Judgement*, p. 119/Academy Edition, p. 267.
55. F.J. Coleman, *Contemporary Studies in Aesthetics*, p. 10.

6

Our Rhythm and Croce[1]

It appears to me that some seeming obscurities of Croce's aesthetic theory are lightened if we view it in relation to Hindustānī rhythm, and this essay is but an attempt to argue for this impression.

But why do I choose rhythm rather than the better known arts of, say, music, poetry and painting? Is rhythm an independent art at all? The answer to the first of these questions will emerge only towards the end of the argument, that is, when we have seen how *rhythm* is specially illustrative of Croce's ideas. As to the independent status of this art, I may here make some very brief remarks because the matter has been already discussed, at fair length, in my earlier book, *Avenues to Beauty*.

Rhythm as an Art

a. There is, to begin with, the clear evidence of *fact*. In some of our prestigious music festivals even today, *solo* expositions of rhythm are sometimes presented as important items in a whole session of music; and if the

---

1. This essay is a slightly modified form of my article "Aesthetic Theory of Croce and the Rhythm of North Indian Music" first published in the Italian journal *II Veltro* (3-4 - Maggio-Agosto, 1976) and of the paper presented, under a similar heading, to the Dante Society of Delhi at the University of Delhi on 15.2.1975.

drummer is a really good one — I have here in mind the late Ustād Habeebuddin Khān of Meerut[2] — such rhythmic recitals can captivate both lay and knowledgeable listeners.

b. One can also appeal to aesthetic *theory* to prove that — insofar as it has its own unique material, creative devices and criteria of evalution — rhythm may well be regarded as an autonomous art too, and not merely as an art of *accompaniment*.[3]

c. Further, our rhythm (or *tāla*) quite meets the contemporary requirement that art should be significant because of its own inner organization, rather than through a convincing representation of external reality. It is indeed easy to see how this adequacy of rhythm is traceable to its various features. There is, first, the fact that our *tāla* admits of ever newer inner shapings. The basic form of rhythm is *a specific* number of beats as forming a *regular* succession, like moments marked *evenly* in time. But in Hindustānī rhythm, within the chosen extent of flow — and remaining *on the whole* true to its tempo — some little slowdowns and spurts can also be brought in adroitly.[4] Nor is there any limit to the number and location of improvized accents, in addition to the set ones of a cycle, within the speed

---

2. Regarded by many as a model of technique, fluency and appeal among the drummers of north India. *Tablā* is the two-piece drum popular today in the fold of north Indian music.

3. See, in this context, my article "Aesthetics of Hindustānī Music", in *Sangeet Natak* (Official Journal of Sangeet Natak Akademi, New Delhi), no. 28, April–June, 1973, pp. 14-15.

4. That is, according to a design; or intentionally *and* with an eye to some effect of beauty.

and measure of the flow in question, it being largely dependent on the creative skill of the drummer as to which particular moment of the flow can be accented to make for added beauty. The syllables (or *bols*)[5] that make the filling of the flow even *between* the beats are also quite various, in respect of both number and character.

Secondly, and this is noteworthy, insofar as the *syllables* here are all without ordinary meaning or quite non-representational — and (positively) sounds of changing step, character and embedment — attention is not only invited to rhythm, but is entirely prevented from straying towards thinking of things and happenings in reality. Aestheticians sometimes speak of art as a *presentational* symbol;[6] and in so doing they seek to provide for the truth that, though a work of art does say something, its "meaning" is quite fused with what we find presented in it. Now, of the truth of *this* particular idea, our rhythm is perhaps the best available instance. The "meaning" is here *indivisible* from — and not only embodied in — what directly meets the ear; and the mind follows only the varying sound and movement of rhythm.

Now I may outline some key ideas of Croce's aesthetics before turning to see how our rhythm is of help in understanding them. What first claims attention is here his singular view of intuition and expression.

Croce: Intuition, Expression

By *intuition* Croce means the spiritual (or inner) *activity* of

---

5. A *bol* is a mnemonic syllable, a letter or a tuft of letters, alike meaningless. It is a means to identify the various sounds that the drums produce when they are struck (or pressed) variously at different places. These *bols* are therefore the material of our rhythm.

6. The reference here is to the view of Susanne K. Langer.

having a *vivid* image *or* perception. According to him, it is intuition when I see this paper clearly; and when I vividly *imagine* myself as writing in another room, that too is intuition.[7] This may be taken to imply, as Croce indeed believes, that "the distinction between reality and non-reality is . . . secondary to the true nature of intuition."[8] But what I here want to emphasize is his view that (a) intuition is an *activity*, and that the spirit intuits "only in making, forming, expressing."[9] Elsewhere, however, Croce also says that:

> (b) To intuit is to express; and nothing else (nothing more but nothing less) than to express.[10]

Here, there is a seeming discrepancy. In the second utterance (b) Croce says, quite categorically, that intuition is nothing but expression. But in the first (a) he seems clearly to hold that intuition is not merely expression, but also making, forming; or that expression is just a part, however necessary, of intuition. *This* is more clearly held in the following:

> Be it pictorial, or verbal, or musical, or in whatever form it appears, to no intuition can *expression* in one of its forms be wanting; it is, in fact, an *inseparable part of intuition.*[11]

How are we to reconcile the two sides? Perhaps the only way to do this is to regard "expression" itself as *including* forming, making, etc. In the light of this suggestion, the first utterance — that the spirit intuits "only in making, forming, expressing" — may be regarded as *a gradual ascent to the full meaning of intuition*, so that expression (as understood by Croce) may be

7. B. Croce, *Aesthetic — As Science of Expression and General Linguistic*, London: Vision Press, 1962, rpt., p. 3.
8. Ibid.
9. Ibid., p. 8.
10. Ibid., p. 11.
11. Ibid., p. 8. Emphases added.

said to be truly a making too. This is, in fact, borne out by his own following words:

> Intuition . . . is distinguished as *form* from what is felt and suffered, from the flux . . . of sensation, or from psychic matter; and *this* form, *this taking possession, is expression*.[12]

So "expression" is really a form *at work*: or it is at once a forming. For the sake of understanding we may indeed distinguish *intuition* from disorganized sensations by saying that it is a form; but as manifest in experience — or as it is found — intuition is this form as actively organizing ("taking possession" of) the psychic material. This *activity* is expression. It includes, or is itself a "forming." "Expression" which Croce regards as being inseparable from intuition is not any expression, but *formed* expression. Intuition, correspondingly, is not the mere having of suggestions or sensations, but their active organizing.

Further, and this partly follows from the remarks just made, though the fact of intuition is (in Croce's view) never separate from expression, a distinction between the two may be made *from the viewpoint of their individual relation to knowledge and experience in general*. Thus, whereas intuition — as that "knowledge of . . . individual things" which is provided by imagination — is opposed to the knowledge of *relations* between things provided by the intellect,[13] "expression" is (by Croce) distinguished from impressions on the one hand, and from expression in the sense of the external activity of making art, on the other. The latter dual distinction *is* present, if not quite manifest, in the following basic thesis of Croce:

> Art is the expression of impressions, not expression of expression.[14]

---

12. B. Croce, *Aesthetic — As Science of Expression and General Linguistic*, p. 11.
13. Ibid., p. 1
14. Ibid, p. 13.

The way "expression" is here related to "impressions" enables us to make another distinction between intuition and expression. Quite generally, expression may be regarded as the (necessary) objectification of intuition:

> That which does not objectify itself in expression is not intuition.[15]
>
> (Here, however, Croce would like us to remember that what he calls "expression" is no external activity, but only the holding up of some content, as it were, before the mind.)

And where he speaks of art and the aesthetic, "intuition is used to emphasize the *individuality*, and "expression," the *manifestness* of an experience. This is borne out by the following:

> What *intuition* reveals in a work of art is . . . character, *individual physiognomy*.[16]
>
> When we have . . . conceived *definitely and vividly* a figure or a statue . . . *expression* is born and complete. . . .[17]

But, I repeat, the difference is only one of emphasis. It is not to be regarded as warranting a separation of intuition from expression. Croce indeed is careful to add that expression *too* has the unity (or continuity) of a process:

> A corollary of the conception of expression as activity is the indivisibility of the work of art. Every expression is a single expression.[18]

Finally, the fact that Croce keeps it *so close to intuition* may be taken to suggest that "expression" is an inner activity. This is indeed (we have seen) a view which he professes.[19] And from

---

15. B. Croce, *Aesthetic — As Science of Expression and General Linguistic*, p. 8.
16. Ibid., p. 20. Emphases added.
17. Ibid., p. 50. Emphases added.
18. Ibid., p. 20.
19. Ibid., pp. 50-1.

the other side, the coupling of "intuition" with "expression" means that, though it cannot be seen from the outside, *intuition* is, so to speak, always the setting up of something before the mind.

Our Rhythm and Croce

But if, as Croce indeed maintains, intuition is formed expression, where exactly do we find that intuition, that having of a vivid *image* which is at once and *clearly* a "forming" or "making?" The answer, I fear, is not quite provided by some of Croce's own favoured instances:

> . . . The perceptions of the room in which I am writing, of the ink-bottle and paper that are before me, of the pen I am using . . . ; — these are all intuitions.[20]

A. But, one may at once ask, what, if any, is the element of forming or making here? To answer this question, I suggest, we have rather to look at those arts where the very first step is obviously a kind of making; and here, I may add, the case of rhythm is markedly relevant, because the moment one begins contemplating rhythm, a speed is *actively* set for all subsequent work. Here, indeed, the very first intuition (or clear awareness) or a beat *as a mātrā*[21] is at once a forming or making of *laya*.[22] But this must be clarified:

To put it roughly, the manner of rhythm is similar to counting steadily at a chosen speed; and, as we know, *our* rhythm is cyclic. But, and this is precisely what is here noteworthy, the temporal character of the very first beat — that is, the time which one takes, more or less, in speaking (*or* playing) it — directly determines the pace at which the *entire*

20. B. Croce, *Aesthetic — As Science of Expression and General Linguistic*, p. 3.
21. The word *mātrā* literally means "measure."
22. Quite generally, *laya* may be taken to mean the *flow* of musical time which the beats serve to measure and articulate.

cycle is to be played.[23] Thus, if one begins counting *sharply*, the inviolable norm of steadiness demands that the same *quickness* be kept throughout. If, on the other hand, the opening is slow and deliberate, what follows immediately, nay, the full cycle too must move and seem leisurely, in response to the same basic requirement.

In other words, the moment I begin the right kind of rhythmic counting, I choose the pace to be followed throughout. The clear awareness or utterance of a beat, *as the beginning of rhythm*, is thus at once regulative of the process to follow. The "intuition" here is clearly a forming.

B. We may dwell a little longer on the fact that an essential aspect of the whole rhythm — that is, its moving at a set pace — is determined by the length or brevity of the very first beat. This is in fact necessary because it bears out a key aesthetical idea. Insofar as determination of the character of the whole by that of the parts is a clear meaning of the concept of organic unity, what we have just said of rhythm also lends point to Croce's following utterance:

> (The activity of artistic expression) is a fusion of impressions in *an organic whole.*[24]

I may add here that the "individual physiognomy"[25] of which Croce speaks is, as a rule, quite manifest in our rhythm. What it here means, however, is not merely the cyclic self-completeness referred to earlier, but the ordered character of the inner accents of rhythm.

C. In Hindustānī rhythm, indeed, the formed character of an

---

23. What follows is very well known to every classical musician.
24. Croce, *Aesthetic*, p. 20.
25. Ibid., p. 5. The Hindustānī word here, in the region of rhythm, is *shakl* which literally means a face with its individual features.

articulate whole is the main ground of appeal.[26] And insofar as this character is obviously an inseparable part of what is directly presented to us, if we at all speak of rhythm as "symbol" the word cannot be taken as signifying something to which "meaning" is *merely conjoined*:

> The symbol has sometimes been given to us as the essence of art.. . . But if the symbol be conceived as separable — if the symbol be on one side, and on the other, the thing symbolized, we fall . . . into the intellectualist error.[27]

D. Finally, our rhythm is, in my view, of greater help than any other art in seeing how (in some cases) the following words of Croce could seem quite warranted:

> The aesthetic fact is altogether completed in the expressive elaboration of impressions. When we have achieved the word within us, conceived definitely and vividly a figure or a statue or found a musical motive, expression is born and complete. If after this we should open our mouths — *will to* open them to speak . . . this is all an addition . . . a *practical* fact, or fact of [the] *will* . . . The work of art (the aesthetic work) is always *internal*.[28]

Croce's meaning here is that artistic expression, or the real making of a work of art is a purely internal happening; that the moment I have been able to form a tune and to hear it sung in the mind, the music *as a work of art* is quite complete; and that if I then sing it out to others I certainly *share* it with them, but do not add anything to the music itself. The work of art is completed *within* the mind.

---

26. I say, "main," not "the only" ground, because the heard sweetness of playing also counts.

27. Croce, *Aesthetic*, p. 34.

28. Ibid., pp. 50-51.

In support of this rather unusual view, Croce appeals to the evidence provided by some very eminent artistes. Thus, the great Michelangelo tells us:

> One paints, not with the hands, but with the brain.[29]

Again, there is the case of Leonardo who once stood just gazing at *The Last Supper* for days together — without touching it with the brush — and then made the following remarks on this attitude of intense, but tranquil attention:

> The minds of men of lofty genius are most active in invention when they are doing the least external work.[30]

Now, it is difficult to accept the view that the making of a work of art is, in general, a *purely* internal affair; and most of the artists and aestheticians today would here disagree with Croce. Thus, Reid cites with approval Barbar Hepworth's explicit mention of how, in her own abstract drawing, the process of creation is vitally determined by the *material* (therefore, visible and *external*) character of lines and curves.[31] Our own *ālāpa* singing too is a challenge to Croce. Here, what happens is this. The notes which open the music are naturally heard by the singer, and they may seem to be tender or firm. Now, this specific character of notes as heard may *itself* seem to call for a particular phrase or turn of voice. So the making of music is here not merely subjective. We cannot deny that some thinking too *is* here done. Distinguishing two adjacent notes or linking two distant ones by means of a shapely pattern is as

---

29. B. Croce, *Aesthetic — As Science of Expression and General Linguistic*, p. 10.
30. Ibid.
31. L.A. Reid, *Meaning in the Arts*, London: George Allen and Unwin, 1969, p. 108.

clear a demand on the mind[32] as the act of relating two concepts. But *here* the thinking is done essentially on the basis of what is sung *and heard*. The making of Hindustānī music, which is often embellished with *improvizations in response to open* (or quiet, yet registered) *reactions of the audience*, is clearly, though of course not wholly, an overt process.

Our *rhythm*, however, may be said to support Croce's view — to a very large extent, if not entirely. My point here is that rhythm can be composed *and enjoyed* very largely within the mind: for in both these aspects the essence of rhythm is a steady movement *of the mind* across a chosen extent of beats. In the act of composing rhythm the mind just goes on pecking the flow, held and followed quite ideally; and the absence of real hearing does not vitally affect the form and inner accents of what is composed, exactly as one can do mental counting with ease. In respect of enjoying rhythm too, though the heard quality of playing may well affect the fullness of delight, what makes the response really intelligent is, in essence, one's ability to follow *with the mind* the measure and meander of rhythm. If we add to all this the non-representational quality of its syllables, rhythm would at once seem to be much more capable of being independent of *outer* activity, meaning and values than any other art.

---

32. Cf. John Dewey, *Art as Experience*, New York: Capricorn Books, 1958. (Seventh Impression), p. 46.

7

The Spiritual and Hindustānī Music

Perhaps the most glibly talked about topic relating to our music is its relation to spirituality. But one cannot fail to be struck by the fact that our best known musician of the day, Bharat Ratna Pandit Ravi Shankar, is convinced that "the highest form . . . of music is spirituality."[1] To the question if he had ever experienced a divine touch while creating music, his answer to (at least) one interviewer has been categorical:

> Oh, many times. It just happens. The atmosphere, my own mental condition, some good vibrations — all play a role. I have had this experience playing for a single person also . . . [namely,] Paramāchārya Kāmakoti Śaṅkarāchārya. Sometimes I also have this feeling while playing in Albert Hall, London . . . [Even generally,] if you listen to a finely tuned *tānpūrā* in isolation and with a quiet mind . . . [or] with absolute concentration to a church organ or Bach or a truly good musician performing any *rāga*, you shall have a fantastic sense of peace.[2]

Nor are our Carnatic musicians slow to voice such a view. See, for instance, the following remarks by the violin *vidwān*,

---

1. From Saurabh Bhattacharya's conversation with the Sitar maestro, reported in the June 1999 issue of *Life Positive*, pp. 34-35.

2. Ibid.

Narayana Iyer, who has given us virtuosios of the calibre of T.N. Krishnan, his son, and N. Rajam, his daughter:

> Our music has a divine origin and it will assert itself out of the present turmoil. Spoken languages . . . are prone to create . . . divisions. But not *sangeet which is the language of the soul*. It cannot die, you see![3]

It would, however, be wrong to suppose that it is only in India that music has been related to the life of the spirit. Beethoven does the same, if (or rather necessarily) in his own way:

> It takes spiritual [*geistigen*] rhythm to grasp music in its essence. . . . All genuine [musical] invention is moral progress. To submit to its inscrutable laws . . . to overcome and control one's own mind, so that it shall set forth the revelation: that is the isolating principle of art. . . . Every true creation of art is independent, mightier than the artist himself. . . . Music gives the mind a relation to the [total] harmony. . . . [4]

It is not easy to make sense of the extract just cited. But, on the other hand, insofar as it issues from the mind of one of the greatest composers of the world, we *have* to struggle to see what it could possibly mean. Anyone who looks at a maestro's utterances critically is indeed often faced with a challenge. My own humble attempt may roughly run as under:

The essence of music can be seized only by means of *spiritual* rhythm. Such rhythm (or regulation) is no mere disposition of beats, but it rather an intense focusing of mind on the effort to invent or produce new music. The focusing is at once a curb on the mind's natural tendency to flit from one thought or image to another; and may therefore be said to be a step in self-control or moral progress. Yet *the effort to create*, however intense

---

3. From Mohan Nadkarni's interview with the *vidwān* as it appeared in the *Economics Times*, Delhi, on 27 March 1983.

4. Cited by Susanne K. Langer in her book, *Feeling and Form*, Routledge and Kegan Paul, 3rd Impression, 1963, p. 131.

and focused it be, cannot quite predetermine the ways to necessary fruition; and though it is surely required, it has to keep itself reverently open to the emergence of something which may outstrip prefiguration vitally. This is why the creation of a new musical work, or of the "total harmony," strikes the composer as a kind of *revelation*, and makes him bow to the exhaustless mystery of music-making. This is how the creation of art may be said to be "mightier than the artist himself"; and this is how music is felt as putting the mind in a relation of happy subservience to the "total harmony" *of the work*.

In the Indian tradition, however, music has been related to man's spiritual *destiny*. In his well-known work, *Saṅgīta Ratnākar*, Śāraṅgadeva goes to the extent of saying that even by merely looking at or touching the *veeṇā* one attains emancipation of the spirit and redemption from heinous sins.[5] According to one legend, if out of the two wives of the sage Yājñavalkya, Gārgī and Maitreyī, only the former needed her husband's assistance in attaining *mokṣa*, it was essentially because Maitreyī (we are told) could achieve the same supreme objective quite on her own, *in virtue of her expertise in playing the veeṇā*.[6] Another similar story relates to the Buddha. There was a *veeṇā* in his chamber, we are told, the strings of which would emit such an ethereal sound on being stirred by a breeze that it "aroused in him that great dispassion which led to his renunciation of earthly pleasures."[7]

Finally, to turn to contemporary musical practice, Ustad R. Fahimuddin Dagar, who is the eldest living member of the famed Dāgar Gharānā, is fond of singing a *dhruvapad* in *rāga*

5. S.C. Anantapadmanabhan, *The Veeṇā — Its Technique, Theory and Practice*, Delhi: Gana Vidya Bharati, 1954, p. 5.

6. Ibid., p. 8.

7. Ibid.

Bihāg, the opening line of which runs thus: *sur tattva gyān tab pāve jab jīvan mukti ko rūp sādhe.*[8]

Now, views (and compositions) such as the ones referred to above surely fascinate me; and they are very likely to impress the traditional Indian mind because of its ingrained interest in spiritual matters. But, on the other hand, I cannot ignore the evidence of the present either. Today, indeed, the fact is that a considerable amount of our music — of Hindustānī music, I mean — is pretty good without having anything to do with *mukti* or *nirvāṇa*. And as for the references I have made to traditional views and beliefs, the way they relate music to life's nobler values or its surpassing end is surely not quite clear. To the critical eye it may even suggest some immediate questions such as the following:

What exactly is meant by *spirituality*? Is it an invasive orientation of one's whole being and attitudes or just an occasional, though very satisfying experience? If it is the latter, is it to be *identified* with the feeling of a *peace* that "passeth understanding"? Could it not occasionally take the form of an intense yearning for the divine? And if it is the former — that is, a pervasive colouring of one's whole being — and if the act of music-making always calls for *tādātmya* or intense (if ideal) oneness with the act in question, may not the *lifelong* practice of this art of melody and rhythm be expected to make for the visible spiritualization of one's conduct and attitudes in daily life? But how many of our top musicians can fairly claim to have *become* spiritual, as against the mere having of a passing experience of peace, through the practice of music? Do their lives and personalities appear to be blessed with what the Bible speaks of as "fruits" or "riches of the spirit" and the *Gītā* as

8. As sung by Ustad Fahimuddin Dagar, this composition was one of the many *dhruvapads* recorded by me at the Central Production Centre (CPC) of Doordarshan (New Delhi, 19, 20, and 24 July 1999) on behalf of the Indira Gandhi National Centre for the Arts.

daivī sampadā? Is the craving for ever higher fees and honorific "awards" a mark of spiritual growth?

Questions such as these cannot be answered straight away. I must first carefully determine what exactly *the concept of sprituality could mean in relation to music*, and how this meaning is to direct our thinking from now on. The word music, of course, does not present any semantic problem. We all know what it means. We may not find it easy to *define* music. But, in a general way, it is known to us all as the art of melody and rhythm. It may also be generally agreed that what we are here concerned with (in principle) is not music as merely notated *or* recorded, but live music — that is, music in the process of being made, and also as being heard, at least by the musician himself (or herself), say, during the course of *riyāz* (private/personal practice) at home. In my view, it would be a clear error to reflect on the subject without keeping the *rasika* too in mind. After all, music which claims to *be spiritual* must in fact *appear* so to knowledgeable listeners. The full truth indeed is that *the precise spiritual significance that a work of art may be said to reveal depends also and importantly on what kind of a person the individual contemplator is and not only on what the work itself may be said to contain*. On this subtle point, however, I will focus a little later; and presently I may deal with a more obvious question.

What do we mean by the word *spiritual*? Quite a few things, one may say. Some of these meanings are clearly religious, others quite secular. The *non*-secular meanings of the word in question are:

> belonging, referring, or relating to the spirit or soul rather than to the body or to physical things;
>
> belonging, referring, relating to religion; or sacred, holy, divine.

The *secular* meanings are:

belonging to or arising from the mind or intellect; or highly refined in thought or feeling.

Now, the secular meanings are easy to deal with. Our music may indeed be said to be *spiritual* in the sense that it is importantly a matter of the artist's independent thinking, recall, integration and imagining during the actual course of performance, and surely not of just following some pre-fixed notational plan. *Thinking* is there because the *rāga* being sung has to be saved against intrusions of the idioms of "neighbouring" *rāgas;* and also because the distribution of time over the *vialmbit* and *drut* compositions has to be done (generally) in felt accordance with audience-response. *Recall* is present because the *sthāyī* has to be repeated (as an anchor), say, after every two or three *taans*. *Integration* may be seen in the way different phases of the singing — say, *sthāyī-antarā, baṛhat, taans* (and again *sthāyī*) — are proportioned to one another. And *imagining* obviously helps the vocalist in determining what is to come after, or is rather demanded by, the present detail of creation. During the act of singing or playing (I repeat) one has to take great care to ensure that the treatment of the present *rāga* is not at all disturbed by glimpses of those *rāgas* which employ the same *svaras*, if in a different way. Thus, while singing *rāga Bhūpālī,* one has to guard against the influx of (alien) idioms of *Deskār* and *Shuddha Kalyāṇ*. What is more, when after a lucid and elaborate treatment of the opening melody-mode, the musician has to switch over to a quite different *rāga*, maybe in response to a request from a respectable *rasika* in the audience, the transition is surely a strain on the vocalist's intellectual powers.

Let me turn now to the other meaning of the word *spiritual* — the spiritual as relating to matters of the spirit, the religious, holy or divine. How *exactly* does our music appear to be spiritual (in this sense) *where it really does*? Here, I have to make four points by way of an answer:

a. First, the text of the composition — I mean the words which it builds on — must speak of matters relating to the spirit. Thus, the *bandish* (or the composition) may be an invocation to some god or goddess; or it may glorify the attributes of the Lord, or sing of the value of reciting His Name. It may even be a prayer of the musician himself for a fuller insight into the mysteries of music. There is a *dhruvapad* composition, passed on to me by my mentor in music, the late Ustad Rahimuddin Khan Dagar, a part of the text of which runs thus:

तू ही है सुमिरन जोग मोरे दाता
किरपो करो मोपे
दीजे स्वर ज्ञान . . .[9]

b. But, however rich and significant be the verbal content of a composition, the music will not actually appear spiritual to a *rasika*, unless it is sung *sweetly* and in a *tranquil, yearning or ecstatic* manner. But I must explain why I pick these three particular adjectives, besides the adverb *sweetly*. Melodic charm is, of course, the basic requirement. A good many *dhruvapad* singers commit the mistake of believing that if they only pack the *sthāyī-antarā* twosome with high-sounding words of ethico-religious significance — or with the names of gods and goddesses — their singing will impress the listeners as spiritual, and so respectable, even if sweetness is sacrificed for the sake of emphatic utterance. This is, I may add, one of the main reasons because of which the *dhruvapad* form has gradually lost its pristine appeal. The loss is also due, of course, to the average *dhruvapad*-singer's penchant for wayward and hectic *layakārī*, which often only shows how the singer can (somehow) arrive

9. This composition too was included in the recording referred to in Note 8.

at the *sama* after (randomly) improvized variations in rhythm, not how beautifully the pace of *singing* can regulate itself.

To turn now to the three (italicized) aesthetic predicates I have listed in the preceding para, the word *tranquil* is important because tranquillity or serenity and humility have been commonly regarded as the essential marks of a man who is truly spiritual. In his *Epistle to the Galatians*, St. Paul includes *peace* in his list of the *fruits* or *riches* of the spirit. And the *Gītā*, in its 16th chapter, speaks of *patience* and *humility* as important marks of *daivī sampadā* or *spiritual* plenitude. It is, of course, very difficult to fix the precise *laya* required for a look of serenity in singing. But it is possible to make two general remarks in this context. On the one hand, *laya* cannot be too slow here; indeed, I have not heard any *bhajans* in *jhoomrā/tilawāḍā tāla*s. On the other hand, in our classical vocal music where a manifest structure or form is of pre-eminent value, the semblance of a spiritual look cannot co-exist with a pace so quick *and so assertively used* that the singing may appear hectic. The *laya* chosen should rather appear unhurried all along, without seeming wobbly or anaemic, of course, at any stage.

c. Further, and this is a point which is relevent to *live* music alone, the manner of singing has to be such that the vocalist may become *and appear* truly lost in contemplating the glory or divinity of the deity or of the Name to which the composition relates. This is necessary because where the singer wears a look of *tādātmya* — or appears quite absorbed in the act of (sweet) singing — the *rasika*s also tend to get imbued with the lofty import of the song. Such transmission of a mood is indeed easy where the listening is marked by what has been called an attitude of "wise passiveness."

d. But, we may note, the attunement of the singer himself (with the ongoing music) depends upon quite a few different factors: first, the individual quality of his own personality and *set* attitudes, chief of them being his religious orientation; second, his *present* ability to focus on the singing; and third, the *structural cohesion* of the composition itself. How exactly this particular quality counts here can be easily explained. If the fabric of the rhythm, the structure of the *sthāyī-antarā twosome*, and the verbal content of the composition all seem to share a common character, the entire *bandish* will appear gathered, and easy to handle, so to say; and the singer will be able to focus his attention quite without effort.

Here, as illustration, I may refer to a *dhruvapadāṅgī* composition[10] which is set in *rāga Gurjarī Toḍī* and in a rhythm-cycle of 11 beats, the syllabic structure of which (probably improvized) runs as follows:

धा	धिन्ता	कत्ता	कत्तागदिगिन	कत्तागदिगिन	कत्तागदिगिन
1	2 3	4 5	6 7	8 9	10 11

The identical bunches of *bols* that follow the first five beats are clearly *three*; and the text of the song too (as given below) projects the concept of three, in the way of a *triple* recitation of His Name, or by referring to the *three main deities, and three basic functions of God* — namely, creation, preservation, and dissolution; as also to the *three kinds of suffering* (see ताप त्रिविध)

10. This *dhruvapad* was presented by me, first on December 1, 1998 during the course of my Bhatkhande Memorial Lecture (on Hindustānī music) at the University of Delhi; and, again, as a part of my talk on "Spiritual dimensions of Indian Music" at India Habitat Centre on June 3, 1999, while participating in a seminar organized by *Svaralaya,* an association devoted to the promotion of Indian music. In the first case, the composition was sung jointly by me and Pooja Srivastava; and, in the second case, by Pooja and her elder sister, Smita.

and *the three guṇa*s distinguished freely in traditional Indian philosophy. Here is the full text of this composition.

स्थायी: सुमरौं तेरो नाम, तेरो नाम, तेरो नाम
अन्तरा: तू ही ब्रह्मा, तू ही विष्णु, तू ही है महेश
तेरो ही गुन गावें, गुन गावें, गुन गावें सब
अन्तरा: जनमदाता, पालक तू, संहारक तू ही
ताप त्रिविध गुनातीत पारब्रह्म तू है
तेरो ही गुन . . . सब

It is noteworthy that, after the 5th beat, the three rapid occurrences of कत in the rhythm-cycle go well with the three repetitions of ते in the *sthāyī*. Incidentally, it should here be clear that tranquillity of pace is by no means indispensable for a spiritual look in music. The devotional practice known as *japa* uses repetition at a fairly quick pace; and where the text of the song permits it, even a fervent and yearning — and so impatient — manner can make for the look in question. It may even be necessary in some cases. Thus, if the vocalist has chosen to sing that well-known *bhajan* of saint-poet Sūrdās which opens as follows — say, in *rāga Sohnī* and *madhya laya tritāla* — a yearning way of singing (at the *taar svara*s, in particular) would be both apt and requisite:

हमारे प्रभु अवगुन चित न धरो[11]

The whole composition is a beautiful blend of soulful — and so impassioned, not serene — prayers of praise and petition, and some devout argument; and hence, though the pace of singing cannot be hectic here too, the overall manner of singing has to be animated (though not frenzied) rather than tranquil. Be it noted that an impassioned utterance is not necessarily a loud one. Even where it wells up from the very depths of one's

11. I have here in mind the way this *bhajan* used to be sung by the late Ustad Rahimuddin Khan Dagar, or as it is sometimes sung today by Ustad Iqbal Ahmed Khan, the present doyen of the Delhi Gharānā.

being, a woebegone sigh may just kiss the ear delicately; and, in the instance we have taken — of a *bhajan* sung in *rāga Sohnī* — where it occurs in singing words like "न धरो" or "पार करो" — the *rishabh* in *taar saptak* may easily appear as an emerging luminous line of longing for pardon or release, and may be perceived by the *rasika* as imbued with intense feeling.

The question as to how pace relates to a song's spiritual look is, however, a tricky one. Much would depend, here, on the text of the song and on the vocalist's ability for modulated utterance as demanded by verbal meaning. But a fairly safe remark can well be made here. Aesthetic pace (or *laya*) is surely as vital a determinant of the semblance I am talking about as the *mumber* of beats in the rhythm-cycle chosen. I must, however, explain the point. *Ektāla* comprises twelve beats and *sūl-tāla* only ten: yet the pace at which a *'drut ektāla khayāl* is generally sung does not seem to admit of a spiritual look, whereas *dhruvapad*s in *sūl* are not so commonly handicapped. At this point, however, I cannot claim to be perfectly sure; for I have heard some *sūl-tāla dhruvapad*s sung so hectically by some members of the illustrious Dagar family that, quite apart from *layakārī*, even the basic composition would appear helter-skelter rather than the patient and careful laying of a melodic base. In such cases it is impossible for the music to appear spiritual. On the other hand, in the Dhrupad Samaroha of 1998 I was gratified to listen to a duly serene presentation of a *shankarā dhruvapad* in *sūla-tāla* by a pupil of Ustad Fariduddin Dagar; and the singer in this case was not a member of the Dagar family.[12] I could also here refer to a *rāga Bhairava dhruvapad* in the same *tāla* presented by me as far back as the year 1970, at the Sangeet Natak Akademi's seminar on "Science and Music." The *sthāyī* of this composition is a duly reposeful singing of the following words:

---

12. The vocalist in this case was Dr A.K. Sanyal of Banaras Hindu University.

प्रथम नाम लेत, शिव, शिव, शिव[13]

But, is the semblance of spirituality in music inseparable from appropriateness of the meaning of its *verbal* content? If yes, what shall we say of *ālāpa* of the *dhruvapad*-singer? It is clearly quite without any filling of (meaningful) words. Is it therefore to be taken as intrinsically incapable of appearing spiritual? Finally, where music does in fact look spiritual, what is that which it demands and draws upon *in those to whom it appears spiritual*?

Before, however, I begin to address these questions, let me quickly distinguish the different feelings or states of being which are commonly thought to characterize experiences that are generally called *spiritual*. The feeling of tranquillity is perhaps the best known of these. It is, in this context, instructive to note that whereas poets who are fond of contemplating nature claim to experience, at times, a "peace that passeth understanding," *mantra*s in our sacred texts freely link the sacred syllable, *auṁ*, with *shānti* or peace.

This peace is, of course, not kept confined to our inner being; in some Vedic prayers even the vegetable kingdom is devoutly petitioned to be kept free from disturbance in its natural processes of growth. But, on the inner side, the experience is not *quite* the same in the two cases — that is, mainly inner *or* environmental. I admit that, as in the case of a sensitive poet, habitual communion with nature may well instil in our inner being a calm that is too deep to be ruffled by thoughts of plurality and divisiveness, and may even quicken in us the elevating sense of a profound underrunning unity. This is indeed the message of poetic utterances such as the following:

13. This *dhruvapad* was presented by me on 28 March 1970 in the morning session of the Akademi seminar already referred to. For the full text and notational analysis of this composition, see Dr Anjali Mittal's *The Concept of Form in Hindustānī Music*, D.K. Printworld, 2000.

> . . . And I have felt
> A presence that disturbs me with the joy
> Of elevated thoughts, a sense sublime
> Of something far more deeply interfused
> A motion and a spirit, that impels
> All thinking things, all objects of thought,
> And rolls through all things . . .[14]

But such inner *peaceableness*, desirable though it admittedly is, issues only from what has been called "a wise *passiveness*," that is, from the attitude of just being there in the lap of nature, moving about in its ample stretches, and keeping alive to its soothing sights and sounds, say, of moonlit waves and rippling brooks. It is not the fruit of any active regulation of our innate psychic propensities, and so it differs widely from the *equimindedness* of which the *Gītā* speaks in its account of the man of steadfast wisdom. Yet the two forms of tranquillity are not quite dissimilar either. They alike seem to rise above that facile sense of plurality which often clouds for us the underrunning unity of things and persons. Where it is heartfelt, the prayer (of which Gandhi was fond) that *one and all* may be granted *sanmati* or the right sense of discrimination is surely an index of authentic spirituality. Nor is the poet merely using words when he records his intuition of a "sense sublime/Of something far more deeply interfused. . . ."

Turning now to our music, I may venture to express an opinion which may seem to be merely subjective, but which I find it difficult to shake off. It seems to me that in the opening stages of *ālāpa* on the *veeṇā* — that is, so long as the music is (at least) as much a flow as abidance at individual notes — when a competent musician builds upon *svaras* in the *mandra saptak*, the *rāga*'s unitary form appears *to wriggle out*, so to say, from

14. Wordsworth, "Lines Composed a Few Miles Above Tintern Abbey", lines 95-104.

the discreteness of the notes that are commonly taken to make it, and to help us identify it; and that, what is more, the manifest depth and power of playing (at notes in the *mandra*, I repeat) evoke an *awesomeness* that is commonly regarded as a mark of the sublime, and may even make the music appear "like a god yearning in pain."[15] If this awesomeness is also a feature of intense religious experience — as it is perhaps said to be in Otto's well-known work, *The Idea of the Holy* — the kind of instrumental music I have just referred to may also be said to be somewhat spiritual. By way of illustrating the point, I may here cite the following from one of my "critical" pieces written long ago, on Ustad Dabeer Khan's *bilāskhāni ālāpa* on the *veeṇā* in his (A.I.R.) National Programme of May 1956:

> [I was struck by] a consistently immaculate rendering of *re* as emanating *from within* the basic *sa* . . . deeply bestirred, sweet and souful . . . Here, at once, one feels impelled to compare . . . *veeṇā-ālāpa* with the quivering sensuousness of touch seen [at times] in *sitār*-playing, as in the hands of. . . . Wilayat [Khan] or Halim [Jaffar]. The secret of the difference seems to be this. A note which turns and twists before it has [duly] steadied itself seems [a little] flippant. . . . The vibrant *trail* of a steadily rendered [*veeṇā*] *svara*, on the other hand, produces, specially when the tone is . . . [emphatic] . . . an irresistible impression of deep inward feeling [and] power.

In vocal *ālāpa*, on the other hand, a semblance of spirituality can be evoked by an unremitting austerity of manner coupled with, say, the following qualities: quintessential sweetness — that is, a melodic charm which is *very easy* on the ear, but does not weaken anywhere; tranquillity of pace; and such a manifest inwardness of manner that the *svara*s appear to well up on their own, without any effort on the part of the vocalist. I cannot decide which of the qualities I have listed is most important

15. Keats, "Eve of St. Agnes", 56th line.

for evocation of the semblance of spirituality in music; but I do find it possible to offer some argument in support of the one which opens the list, namely, *austerity of manner*. I believe that, quite as truly in music as in a person's way of daily living, abstention from mere ornament is one of the surest marks of spirituality. As I speak thus, I have in mind an unforgettable treatment of *Gurjarī Toḍī* by Ustad Rahimuddin Khan Dagar in the Radio Sangeet Sammelan of 1956. The music critic of the *Times of India* came out with a very apt comment on this recital:

> The finest recital of the day came from Rahimuddin Khan Dagar whose treatment of *toḍī* was *an embodiment of repose and tranquillity*.

Here, I think it necessary to add that, along with the general manner of musical utterance, the *specific* visual or emotive hue with which *individual* notes may be sometimes tinged can also play a vital role in evoking a spiritual look in vocal music. The *Sohnī rishabh* in *taar*, to a specific way of singing which I have already referred (p. 143) can easily wear a faraway look. But how exactly this look strikes a particular *rasika* would depend largely on his own individual make-up. If the interests which dominate his life are only mundane, what the note in question makes him visualize may be merely physical distance. But if they are religious or spiritual, the same note may suggest to him not mere remoteness, but qualities like *transcendence, detachment, and renunciation*.

Here, at once, some comment on three distinct points seems demanded by the context: first, the relation of an aesthetic appearance of singing to strength or gentleness of utterance; second, the need for using aesthetic, and not merely grammatical terms in our talk about music; and, third, the part played by the *rasika* in determining the overall, emergent look of the music he is listening to. In respect of the first point, I may make only one simple remark — just one, because the other determinants of the look of a *svara* as sung, such as the precise quality of voice and measure of involvement with the making of music, are peculiar to every singer, and so defy a thorough estimation. I may only say that the look of transcendence (or detachment) is by no means inseparable from gentleness of utterence, though so far, it may seem, I have taken this relation to be necessary. In some *bhajans* presented by Kumar Gandharva, the *komal re,* appearing quite early in the singing of *sthāyī* itself, would be quite full-throated; but it would yet seem (to me) as suggestive of detachment, though not quite without assistance from the meaning of the text of the song. On the other hand, in *ālāpa* which is done without the aid of words, the same note may be sung as just a slender, luminous line (in *taar*), as Rahimuddin Khan used to do, and yet be quite evocative of a look of transcendence on its own, though (obviously) not without being quietly perceived as being a little higher than *shadj.* I hasten to add, however, that though the two cases of the use of *rishabh* I have just adverted to may both be said to look "detached" (or to suggest renunciation), the semblance as it appears to a watchful *rasika* is *not exactly* the same in the two cases, though (I repeat) both are *generally alike* in suggesting what they do. The point is that the state of renunciation (or *vairāgya*) itself admits of a distinction. If the state in question arises automatically from a moderately watchful journey through the course of life — which may itself make one aware of the (ultimate) fickleness of the common sources of worldly joys, as also of human relations — the feeling of moving away from attachment to the world and its contents is likely to be tinged with a little sadness at what one has for long been fond of, but is now about to turn away from. For such a slightly nostalgic (so to say) and not quite settled state of renunciation, a sylphlike singing of *komal re* would do, as an apt melodic image. But where the state in question is a firmly established one, by virtue of being the fruit of some hard and purificatory lifelong disciplines; and is, in addition, aglow with a feel of the higher reality against which the joys of the world easily pale into vapidity,[16] a rich and vibrant *rishabh* would be needed as a melodic index.

As I recall my own actual experience of the two aesthetic shades of *komal re* which I have just distinguished, I feel impelled to dwell upon a thought which has just dawned upon my mind, during the very course of writing these words. The thought issues from a careful phenomenological analysis of an experience (which I now recollect) of listening to a bit of *ālāpa* in *rāga Śrī*. The note *pa* is clearly more distant from the *mandra ni* than the adjacent *rishabh* — adjacent to *sa*, I mean. Yet, whereas the *ni-re* twosome, in case the second note is elongated a bit after a fleeting touch of *ni*, may well evoke the suggestion of "moving away from or rising above" — both everyday ways of referring to what I have called the semblance of transcendence or detachment — the *quick* shift from *re* to *pa* is not so suggestive, though the melodic distance traversed is here obviously greater than in the ascent to *re* from *ni*. This is a clear instance of how the aesthetic semblance of 'moving away from' can be quite different from the actual shift of music from one *svara* to a higher one.

A cognate point to be noted here is that the language that we commonly use in identifying and remembering the notes that go to make a *rāga* is not quite adequate to show how the same notes actually appear in a *bandish* or in a passage of *ālāpa*; and I can only wonder why the indequacy has not been noticed by our musicologists so far. A parallel should make the point clear. To distinguish colours as red, blue or green is to take them merely as they are before being mixed on the palette,

---

16. Here, I am thinking of the following profound couplet of saint poet Kabīr:

    हम घर जारा आपना, लिया मुराड़ा हाथ
    अब घर जांरू तासुका, जो चले हमारे साथ

and also much before they come to appear as determinants of the overall look of a picture where they may appear and be said to be *warm* or *cool, recessive,* or *vibrant*. None of these qualities is or can be *actually* there in the picture; yet the trained contemplator would insist that they really seem to be there in the work. Similarly, though in respect of the bulk of our music as practised today, it may be difficult to accept the following remark of Tagore —

> Indian music concerns itself more with human experience as interpreted by religion, than with experience in an everyday sense. . . . Our music . . . takes us to . . . [the] lonely region of renunciation. . . .[17]

it should not seem improper to use aesthetic (or even ethico-religious) terms in respect of individual *svaras* as they appear in the living course of music. To illustrate, one may well characterize the *pañcham* of *rāga Śrī* as *kamalvat* if the singer's voice rises from *re* to *pa* with the slenderness of the stem of a flower and then opens and gathers itself at *pa* in one undivided instant of audio-visual charm! And if the *komal rishabh* of *Bhairava* is, in *avaroha,* visualized as offering *arghya* (sanctified water) at the *shadj,* what would be the harm in calling it *rishabh* of the *arghi* variety? Similarly, if in a *Sohnī* recital the *rishabh* in *taar* appears to look detached and satisfying in itself, why should we hesitate to call it *sanyastha*? My own considered view is that if, during the course of singing, the vocalist contemplates the appearance of *rāga-svaras* used *in terms of such ethico-religious terms,* his attunement with the ongoing music will deepen a little more happily than it commonly does; and, what is more, he will be saved from letting the recital lapse into a merely technical exercise in keeping to the grammar of *rāga* and *tāla*.

---

17. Such a view is obviously not true to *rāgas* which are *chañchal* (or lively) in temper, and to compositions the text of which aims at evoking *śṛṅgāra rasa*.

But it is obvious that the way of looking which I am pleading for can be adopted only by those who prefer to look at music as an art, rather than as only a matter of dealing with melody and rhythm in predetermined ways. I admit that there are works of art, as some of the creations of Mondrian, which only tease perception and may not be said to convey anything; and that, what is more, proper attention to every work of art surely sharpens our percipience. But most works of art have a meaning — or rather *import*, because the meaning is here inseparable from what meets the ear or the eye, or from the word-bound images that a literary work, say, a poem, may directly evoke — which is surely not confined to the work as it appears to the untutored eye or intellect, and has to be filled in, importantly, by the *rasika*'s individual ability to perceive and integrate, as also to visualize on the basis of, what is directly presented to sense or to literal understanding.

I may buttress the point I am seeking to make by citing an instance which I have found irresistible. I acclaim it because of two reasons. First, it convinces me of the sanity of the traditional Indian emphasis on the role of the *rasika* in art contemplation. Second, it makes me realize that what has been spoken of as *tādāmya* by our ancient theorists of art is not the mere coincidence of two inert points, but an imaginative growing one with the essence of the other; and that, insofar as imagining and getting at the core of what a work of art signifies are both processes — and alike never-ending, because they are both determined (if in part) by the *rasika*'s own growth in respect of both experience and capacities — we can never circumscribe the meaning of a (great) work of art. But let us now turn to the work, a *picture*, that I have in mind.

The Return of the Prodigal Son is one of the best known paintings of Rembrandt. Many have reacted to it in their own individual ways. But if a particular *rasika* — say, Henri J.M. Nouwen, a Dutch Roman Catholic priest who has authored a remarkable book on the Biblical parable[18] — sees in the painter's depiction of the powerful Gospel story three distinct states in Man-God relationship (such as the errant soul's turning anew to God, restoration of sonship, and the Holy Father's compassion) by means of a deeply personal and resonant meditation, the interpretation cannot be dismissed as a mere imposition on the work, because the intense reaction proceeds all along on very close attention to the minutest perceivable details of the masterpiece, that is, not only its larger-than-life size, and "abundant reds, browns, and yellow,"[19] but even the subtle tenderness of the way in which the Father is seen to embrace the son in the picture.[20] But if all this can happen in contemplating a picture, what is the warrant for believing that the meaning of music is *confined* to its sensuous elements? Why should the *rasika* be denied freedom to react to art not only on the basis of its grammatical norms, but also in accordance with his own intellectual and moral equipment as a person? In practice, however, the *rasika* does not have to ask for this freedom; he has it already, and he exercises it.

To conclude, the look of spirituality in music depends not only on what is objectively there in the play of melody and rhythm, but on how the given appears to, and directs the uniquely trained (and burgeoning) sensibility, imagination, and value-sense of a *rasika*.

---

18. *The Return of the Prodigal Son — A Story of Homecoming*, St. Paul's Bandra, Mumbai, 1998. This fascinating book was very kindly presented to me by Father J.K. John, (S.J.) Professor of Religious Studies at Vidya Jyoti, Delhi.
19. Ibid., p. 13.
20. Ibid., p. 10.

8

To Kathak Anew[1]

THE Kathak Kendra (New Delhi) Festival of 2003 (October 28-31) and the quite as ambitious workshop organized by Birju Maharaj's Kalāshrama in the same year (November 24-30) both gave me a chance to participate as a speaker, and the present article is based on what I said on these two occasions. Participants at the Kendra festival spoke on "Challenges that face the solo Kathak dancer today." At the Kalāshrama workshop, on the other hand, a wide variety of topics were discussed; and I was kindly allowed to speak on a subject which suited one of my major interests, namely, *Kathak and art theory in general.* My book, *Swinging Syllables: Aesthetics of Kathak Dance* was brought out by Sangeet Natak Akademi about eighteen years back. So I am now able to say a good deal which does not figure in that book.

The two topics referred to above are not quite disparate. I believe that the most important challenge which faces a solo Kathak dancer today is the general failure to realize the true value of Kathak as an art form; and the resulting tendency to cling to the age-old view that in the region of *sangeet*, vocal music is pre-eminent, *vādya* comes next, and dance is the lowest in rank. Now this is a view which I challenge straight away. If by vocal music we mean the singing of religious souls like Swāmī Haridās and Saint Tyāgarāja, the main purpose of which

1. This article is a slightly modified form of the way it appeared, under the same heading, in *Sangeet Natak*, vol. XXXIX, no. 1, 2005.

was growing closeness to God, it may well be said to be superior to *any* human activity in general, and not to the art of dance alone. But the kind of classical singing that is heard today aims directly at performing well and eliciting listeners' applause, and ultimately at the monetary gain which results from growing popularity. How such singing can be ranked higher than Kathak dance is not clear to me. On the other hand, I can give at least two cogent reasons against such ranking.

First, just as it is not possible to say that dance calls for a greater measure of *sādhnā* than vocal or instrumental music, so it will be equally difficult to hazard the view that good dancing is in any way easier than *gāyan* or *vādan* of comparable excellence. The *khayāl*-singer's attainment of the *sama* of a *sthāyī* is not more difficult than a Kathak dancer's bringing *his whole bodily frame* immaculately to the *sama*-point where a *toḍā/tukḍā* completes itself. What is more, dance is definitely an art of the whole personality. Thought and imagination are both vitally involved in presenting thematic numbers, and very clearly in *bhāva-pradarshan* (popularly called भाव बताना in a seated posture), where the meaning of some words of a song has to be expressed visibly and appropriately in terms of varying but *winsome* gestures and bodily turns. As for the body, it is all along involved in Kathak as *aṅg*, that is, not as what the body itself is, but as carefully adapted to the aesthetic demands of dance-syllables and semantic content of the various thematic numbers.

Second, besides some similarities, an important difference has to be noted between the constituent *svaras* of a *khayāl-aṅg taan* and the *bols* of a Kathak *toḍā/tukḍā*. Just as every *dānā* (or discreteness of the individual *svaras*) of a *taan* has to be clear (though not obstructive), besides being true to its location in the scale — and hence sweet — so every *bol* in a Kathak pattern has to look articulate and rightly related to the *laya*-flow. But, whereas there is, as a rule, hardly any great difference in the *way of singing* the constituent *svaras* of a *taan*, in Kathak, on the other hand, many of the *bol*s of the *selfsame* pattern have to be danced quite differently. Thus, in the pattern which opens thus: ताओ थुंगा तकिट थुंगा (*tāo thuṅgā takita thuṅgā*), the very opening *bol*s have to be danced varyingly, because it is a basic and well-known requirement of Kathak dance that the sound of footwork (पदचाप) *and* bodily figuration (अंग) have to accord maximally with how every individual (uttered) *bol* strikes the ear. The simplest difference in Kathak *bol*s is the one that obtains between *khule* (open) and *bund* (closed) syllables; but even this cannot be ignored in the way they are danced. Thus, where the chosen syllabic tuft is, say, धात्रक धिकिट the second segment calls for a figural adaptation which is quite different from the one required by the first segment. No *such* (acrobatic!) effort is generally involved in singing a single *taan*.

The need to focus on the details of a Kathak composition not only in dancing them, but also in thinking about them, should now be clear. However, there are at least two other ways in which one has to look at Kathak for a proper understanding of its nature and value an an art-form: the viewpoint of language and the viewpoint of art theory. The former viewpoint again admits of a distinction. The Kathak repertoire itself has its *own* language, I mean the names of the intra-forms (or numbers) it comprises, such as *thāta*, *āmad*, and *tatkār*, etc. Nor can we ignore the word "Kathak" itself, for the very definition of this dance-form has been freely derived from the meaning of this word. And then there is the language which our traditional *guru*s generally use in talking *about* this art-form, and which at times appears quite obscure, but cannot be neglected if the truly creative work involved in this dance-form is to be properly realized.

Take the word *Kathak,* to begin with. Going by its very meaning, a Kathak dancer is defined as one who tells a story or recounts an incident, actual or merely visualized. The definition, कथन करे सो कथक कहावै (*kathan kare so Kathak kahāvai*), has for long been freely bandied about. It obviously implies (the view) that story-telling or narration is the only (or main) thing that a Kathak recital does. But such a view obviously misses out the truth that the entire *nṛtta* (or pure dance) part of Kathak is quite without story-telling (because of being devoid of language) and appeals to us essentially by virtue of its rhythmic form and clarity of execution. So, I conclude, the suggested definition is inadequate. However, this need not worry us unduly. In other fields of thinking too, incomplete definitions abound. For instance, one definition speaks of *rāga* as that which fascinates people at large (*rañjako janachittānām*). But it is obvious that speaking of *rāga* in this way simply fails to mark it off from, say, the *tamāshā* of a wayside juggler who may well be able to draw and entertain a large crowd effectively. Therefore, to seize the full nature of *rāga* we have to supplement the definition we have cited with other definitions which take due notice of the inner details and emphases of a *rāga*. Indeed, whatever be the aesthetic principle, concept, or art-form that we choose to reflect on, its relation to the details of artistic *practice* has always to be kept in mind. Otherwise, our thinking will be merely vacuous, however self-consistent and detailed it may itself appear.

Another important word relating to the Kathak repertoire is *tatkār* or pure footwork. What the word as such may be taken to mean is "giving *ākāra* or shape to the *tattva* or the essential feature of *sangeet* (which is *laya*)." Rhythm or *tāla* (which is beat-measured) is just not there in a recital of *ālāpa* of the *dhruvapad* genre; and, it is obvious, no singing contributes to the charm of instrumental music and the pure dance numbers of a Kathak recital. *Laya* or temporal flow, regulated with an eye to the needs of art-making or aesthetic appeal, is the only element which pervades the whole of our *sangeet* through and through.

What is, however, far more important is attention to the language that our traditional Kathak *gurus* use in talking about the art they are committed to, specially where this language appears unclear. To illustrate this particular point I take pleasure in recalling some instances from my own experiences at Kathak Kendra. I may put them briefly, and all in the present tense, because I recall them so clearly that I virtually see them (in my mind) happening anew:

(a) A student (Durga Arya) is dancing to *dhamār tāla*. I admire her dance. Birju Maharaj, sitting by my side, concurs and says: "हां, हमारी तरफ देख नहीं रही है, पर नाच रही है हमारे लिये". Now, I choose to interpret and amplify this remark as follows:

The attention of the danseuse is not at us (the audience), but is all taken up by what she is dealing with, that is, the rhythmic patterns as they are being danced. This intense focusing on the inner accents and overall designs of the patterns — and also on varyingly accordant *aṅg* — makes it all quite pellucid to us, assuming, of course, that we are genuine *rasika*s. *Tadātmya* or contemplative oneness with the art-object (here, art-mak*ing*) is quite as essential for the artist at work as for those who are looking at it. For the artist, it makes for effective presentation, and a concomitant feeling of subdued delight which is reflected, effortlessly, in the dancer's face, producing (not *contriving*) what is called *mukhvilās*. Important though it surely is, this winsome facial bearing is in truth but a by-product of correct and sincere dancing, and not something to be aimed at wilfully.

But what does the dancer's focusing on the work being done really mean? It means an unremitting watch not only on the *laya* chosen and the overall design of the pattern being danced, but on the *dharam* (as they say, in traditional Kathak parlance) of individual *bols*, that is, on how exactly they sound, and on *their own intrinsic laya*. Here, in passing, a distinction may be noted. Setting some *bols in a particular laya-frame* is one thing; caring for the *laya that is intrinsic to bols* is quite another.

Consider, for instance, a rhythmic pattern which opens thus: घिननन नागे तिट क्ड़धेत धातिट घेघे तिट घेघे नातिट। (*ghinanana nāge tiṭa kḍedhet dhātiṭa gheghe tiṭa gheghe nātiṭa*): Here, it is obvious, घिननन (the very first *bol*) cannot be recited (or danced) at *too fast* a pace, because otherwise the successive individuality of the three न-s will just be compressed into mere indistinctness. On the other hand, the utterance (or dancing) of क्ड़ cannot be *decelerated*, if we are to avoid the *bol*'s unwarranted distension into कड़. Only if these details of individual *bol*s are duly heeded can the total pattern (as danced) appear duly articulate. Otherwise, as our *guru*s would protest, the syllables' *dharam* (or individual character) would be merely ignored, warranting admonishment like the following: "तुम नाच नहीं रहे हो, नाच रगड़ रहे हो, चबा रहे हो" — words which Birju Maharaj freely uses in the class when his pupils begin to dance but cursorily.

(b) At times, however, it is far more difficult to interpret the Kathak *guru*'s cryptic language. At a particular seminar, where the topic of discussion is *āmad*, the maestro surprises me by declaring that *āmad* is the "item" with which the dancing really begins. On my interjecting with the question, "What, then, about *thāṭa* which is the traditional opening of a Kathak recital and which, as a rule, precedes *āmad?*," Birju Maharaj turns a little uneasily in his chair, but yet manages to repeat his remark just referred to.

I leave the seminar wondering why the maestro was insisting on what is obviously questionable. What could his words really mean? I begin ransacking my mind, and suddenly recollect that in a particular music conference (Delhi, Ramlila Maidan, 1954) a lady had remarked "अब गाना शुरु हुआ है," when Ustad Bade Ghulam Ali began singing in his resplendent *ākāra*, even though some recitals (including a vocal one) *had already preceded* his appearance on the stage. The recall makes me see a distinction at once. A literal beginning at a point in time is one thing; we mark it with devices like a watch. The sudden emergence of what is aesthetically noteworthy is something quite different; what registers it is no external aid but our percipience and sensitiveness to sensuous charm and artistic design. And now I come to see in a flash (so to say) what could possibly be meant (justifiably) by Birju Maharaj's (seemingly) cryptic remark. It is simply this: if, as only seems fair to hold, eye-catching *rhythmic movement and accordant configuration of the body* (or *aṅg*) be regarded as the essence of a Kathak recital, it may well be said to begin with *āmad*, because it is here that the two (distinguished) essentials almost force themselves upon our notice. By means of an *āmad*, so to say, a Kathak recital heralds its own advent unmistakably.

(c) As a part of her test, a candidate at the ongoing examinations (in Kathak Kendra) prepares to give a brief demonstration of actual dancing. The *sāraṅgī*-player begins playing the *lehrā*; but the moment it completes a cycle, Guru Kundal Lal (sitting on my left) exclaims: "अहा! सक्सैना साहब! क्या ज़मीन क़ायम होती है!" Now, how are we to interpret the two words, ज़मीन and क़ायम? The ज़मीन which is literally (or actually) क़ायम (or stable, moveless) is the ground that we freely walk on. Even in such everyday talk: वो अपनी बात पे क़ायम है, the word क़ायम means literal fixity or utter absence of moving away from one's chosen position or view. In a *lehrā*, on the other hand, an up-and-down *movement* (or *āroha-avaroha*) is clearly there. Yet it *appears* to be क़ायम or steadfast because of two reasons: first, because the time-interval between every two *mātrā*s is kept identical; and second, because the completion of an *āvṛtti* lends to the rhythmic flow a look of self-completeness, or of staying in its own orbit, *and so not straying*, so to say, from where it is — and therefore of appearing क़ायम.

Here, if in passing, I may dwell on the value of a distinction which is vital for both the making and contemplation of art, — I mean the one which marks off the *virtual* from the *actual*. The virtual is a mere semblance; it surely *seems* to be, but is not actually there in a work of art. So long as one keeps contemplating the work, the seeming *is* an appearance; yet, it is not literally there. Take, for example, the distance that we may easily (seem to) see in a landscape painting comprising, say, a dense undergrowth of tiny shrubs in the *foreground*; a few tall, stately trees *behind* them; then, a little more *remote* from the eye, a range of craggy hills; and, *beyond* them, some clouds overhanging the hills hazily. Here, if they are taken together, the words in italics all stand for our (illusory) perception of *growing recessiveness*, so that the clouds in the picture appear furthest from the eye. But actual distance (or the third dimension) cannot actually be there in a painting; its canvas does not in fact *extend* backwards. In other words, the growing remoteness of objects that we "see" in the work in question is but a seeming, just appearance, though (I repeat) it *really* seems to be there to the contemplating eye.

Now, Kathak dancing too is by no means devoid of such virtual elements. Thus, if the dance floor is traversed by a Kathak diagonally and daintily *in a rapid succession of very short steps*, the distance covered will appear to be much greater than it really is. And if a Kathak dances a well-designed pattern in such a way that the footfalls relating to some *bols* that immediately precede the *sama* are gradually heightened in intensity, *the pattern itself* would appear heading for the *sama*, though in point of fact it is really *the dancer* who is doing so. In good Kathak dancing, I may add, the *sama* is (in principle) not the mere terminus, but also the destiny, so to say, of the pattern being danced.

I may turn now to the word ज़मीन. For a Kathak dancer, the *lehrā* is indeed the anchor of the total dance. If for his *riyāz* at home, the *tablā* and *sāraṅgī* accompanists somehow fail to turn up, the drummer's absence will be borne with relative ease, but the *lehrā* will generally have to be repeated by the dancer as implicit speech, that is, within his (or her) own mind.

However, for the Kathak dancer and others who are wedded to this art-form, the *lehrā* is no mere anchor, but a stimulus too. It indeed is a verifiable fact that the moment they listen to a *lehrā* played sweetly and steadily, they cannot help feeling bestirred to think of what the playing normally demands, that is, actual Kathak dance.

I may now reflect, in brief, on Kathak dance from the viewpoint of art theory taken generally. My procedure will be simple. I will just take, one by one, the theories of art that have figured in the history of Western aesthetics and show how almost all of them are relevant to Kathak dance, though no one of them is quite able to seize the whole range of this form of dance. The earliest of these is the imitation theory. It was quite popular in ancient Greece. As is widely known, even the *philosopher* Aristotle subscribed to it in his theory of drama and even music. As for the *artists* of ancient Greece, a fascinating story of the rivalry between two eminent painters may be cited here as a perfect instance of imitation in art. One of them, Zeuxis, painted a few bunches of grapes in such a realistic manner that birds began to peck at them. Thereupon, Parrhasius made a painting with such meticulous imitativeness that when Zeuxis came to look at it he had to ask the curtain (painted) on the picture to be taken off so that he could see the picture itself, though what looked like a curtain was but a mere semblance. Today, however, though *imitation of the perfect kind* we have just referred to surely calls for a great deal of skill, the theory which makes *it* the essential purpose of art is no longer in vogue, and is even looked down upon. In the region of Kathak dance, luckily, *literal* imitation of the details of any act or happening, actual or mythological, has never been the practice. In my fifty years of active interest in Kathak, I have seen but one attempt at utterly truthful mimesis, that is, when (during the course of presenting *panghat-kī-gat*), a well-built male dancer tried to make the act of pulling a *heavy* (water-laden) bucket from the well look convincing *by actually straining his facial muscles* vigorously. The result was an outrage on *mukhvilās* (pleasing facial bearing) which is a cardinal requirement of Kathak.

However, the more important point here is that literal imitation makes the onlooker *see* everything; *leaves nothing for him to imagine*; hence recalcirates *tādātmya* or *contemplative* oneness with the essence of the aesthetic object; and so makes it impossible for *rasa* to emerge.

Of all the other theories of art as well we have very good examples in the region of Kathak. *Representation* of outer situations and happenings, both everyday and mythological; and *expression of navarasas*, specially of *karuṇa* and the various shades of *śṛṅgāra* — all this abounds in thematic numbers like *gats* and *chālas* (*gaits*) of different kinds, *nāyikābheda*, and *navarasamālika*, though (so far as I know) the subject of *navadhā-bhakti* (or nine types of devotion) is yet to be used as a theme for our Kathak numbers. As for the expression theory of art, it has not only been the most popular of all theories in Western aesthetics, but has always been given a pre-eminent place in Kathak dancing too. It is noteworthy in this context that here a whole intra-form (or number) is called *bhāva-batānā,* that is, varying expression of different emotions that can arise in a particular situation (which is also represented) *and* in a seated posture which utterly skips what is commonly regarded as पैर का काम (or footwork). Above all, the theory which is dominant in some areas of Western art and aesthetics today, namely, the view that art is essentially a matter of formal organization of the material it builds on, and that it must shun all relatedness to things, happenings, and emotions of actual life, is admirably illustrated in our purely rhythmic numbers like *toḍā, tukṛā* and *tatkār*. The last of these, *tatkār,* may also be taken as an excellent illustration of the plausible view which looks on beauty as essentially a matter of unity in variety. For here, in this traditionally final item of a Kathak recital, just one rhythm-cycle, usually *tritāla*, is chosen for beauteous treatment, and the content of the number is nothing but a trelliswork of adroit variations that cut and cross the basic rhythm in different ways.

Kathak is indeed quite open to aesthetic analysis in the way of the dominant slant in contemporary theory of art.

9

Altaf Hussain Khan[1]

CHANDNI MAHAL is a well-known block of houses in "Suinwālān," near the Jama Masjid of Delhi. The area is a queer medley of all sorts of people — pedlars and *pānwālās*, blacksmiths and tobacconists. Yet, here, in its narrow streets, live more musicians of note than perhaps in any other single region of the city. In terms of both fact and legend the area has plenty to interest a lover of classical music. One finds here, for instance, a street named after the legendary Tanras Khan; and Ustad Chand Khan's *Mosiqui Manzil*. *Chandni Mahal* is hallowed by the memories of such great masters of the past as the vocalist Tanras Khan; the *sāraṅgī* wizard, Bundu Khan; and Natthu Khan, who, as the story goes, could make the *tablā* "talk." To lovers of classical music this Mahal is even visually reminiscent of the maestros named, say, by virtue of its very state of decay.

It was here that I first met Ustad Altaf Hussain Khan, in June 1963, to be precise. Though more than ninety-five years of age, the Ustad appeared to be in fairly good health. The wrinkles and the stoop seemed merely physical; for when the talk turned to the excellences of our traditional styles of singing, he argued his points with perceptible zeal and vigour. I wondered how, with such a burden of years, he could be consistently ebullient in both approval and criticism. His sons, who had gathered around us during the course of the

---

1. This is a modified reprint of my article, "Altaf Hussain Khan" as it appeared in *Sangeet Natak*, no. 2, April 1966, pp. 92-104.

conversation, told me that the Ustad was still fond of some daily exercise. The news of his death, only a few months later, therefore surprised me.

Behind his undimmed spirits there is a long story of many-sided endeavour, coupled with a healthy, conscious sense of achievement. He won the Akademi Award in 1960 and deservedly. Some of the older musicians today assure me that in his younger days Altaf Khan had impressed them unforgettably with a number of effective performances in the company of our most distinguished musicians of the past. What is more, the Ustad could justly claim to have initiated quite a few pupils into the subtleties of classical Hindustānī music. Many of his pupils today are princes from various states. His eldest son, Wahid Hussain Khan, learnt from him for quite a few years and is presently a vocalist of no mean merit. What is more, one of our better known musicians, Azmat Hussain Khan, was trained by Altaf Hussain Khan for full twelve years.

However, it was for sheer musical scholarship of the orthodox variety that Altaf Khan was revered all over the country. Paying a compliment to the remarkable humility of the man, he would gently recall how such a connoisseur as the late Ustad Vilayat Hussain Khan would often consult him on matters of musical technique and grammar; and that, for his insight into *aprachalit rāgas*, as also for his mastery over some very ancient compositions of diverse designs, he did not have many peers in his day. The following, he added, were prominent in the list of his favourite *rāgas*: *Tirwan, Lalitabasant, Suhā, Bhankār, Nat, Gaurā, Śrī, Jayat, Lacchasākh, Hem, Khem* and *Shahānā*. As for his repertoire of compositions, he referred happily to varieties of *Gaurī, Bihāg, Naṭ, Bilāwal* and *Malhār*. His aged eyes twinkled as he recalled that in his younger days his expositions of such *rāgas* as *Basant-bahār, Śrīgour* and *Gourā* had often moved the audience to tears.

His sons, who assisted him in recalling some of his past recitals, assured me that he was also thoroughly conversant with such rare innovations of Amīr Khusro in the world of music as *quol, qualbānā, naksh, gul,* and *havā*. The maestro himself provided the added information that the aesthetic riches he had inherited from his own ancestors included some such compositions as provide hints of great value for better *riyāz* of diverse elements and genres of vocal music. As an instance, he referred to a *tirvat-prabandh* composed by his father, Zahoor Khan "Ramdas." In this composition meaningful words are blended with mnemonic syllables drawn from the realm of rhythm, and its purpose too is therefore dual. On the one hand, it heightens the contrast between meaning and sheer sonant effect, making us alive to the immediate and varying appeal of the mere manner of utterance; and, on the other hand, it familiarizes the learner with some intricacies of rhythm.

The ideal that a vocalist should have a firm hold over all the different elements of singing, has indeed been the professed objective of Altaf Khan's *gharānā*. Consider, for instance, the way in which patterns of note-names appear embodied in some of his father's characteristic compositions. They have, of course, the usual twofold *rāga-tāla* setting, but what makes them distinctive is the effect of sparkle, leisureliness or rapid upgathering evoked by articulation of *sargam*s against the seamless stretches of sheer *akāra*. *Sargam*s, according to Altaf Khan, serve as an intermediary between *ālāpa*[2] and textual singing. As we know, *ālāpa* of the orthodox *dhruvapad* variety avoids language (and *tāla*) totally. Textual singing, on the other hand, cannot do without at least a whole line of meaningful words. The ideal here occasionally is to heighten, at places, the effect of music by reinforcing the meaning of words with a

2. In the present context, because the reference is to the *dhruvapad* genre of our vocal music, *ālāpa* is to be taken as signifying singing without the aid of *both* language and rhythm (as *tāla*).

duly corresponding manner of singing. *Sargams* stand for a stage between these two extremes. We have here a far greater measure of diversity and syllabic successiveness than in the leisurely continuities of pure *ālāpa*. And yet the variety at the level of *sargams*[3] is utterly unlike differences of verbal import and expressiveness.

Altaf Khan's own style of singing was not only appealing but instructive to authentic *rasikas*. They would admire him for his correct rendering of *vilambit sthāyī* in such *tālas* as *tilawāḍā* (16 beats) and *jhoomrā* (14 beats). A reference may here be made to a *toḍī khayāl* composed by his father, in *jhoomrā tāla*, which he would sing in the truly orthodox manner and yet with pleasing effect:

तब योंही, प्राण पिया बिन, घरी घरी आवत मो मन में,
'रामदास' तुम जब ते रहत हो, विरहा घूम परी तन में।

The piece has been recorded and has the following likable features: The *sthāyī* is sung exactly as it should be — in a firm, even-tempered manner, radiating repose. Care is taken to keep out *drut* embellishments altogether and the unity between different parts of *sthāyī* is maintained by resorting to what is popularly called *kanbharnā* — that is, by interspersing them with thin musical, flowing lines rather than with tonal turns and twists.

Why is a *vilambit sthāyī* to be sung thus? And, in the piece referred to above, why does the *sama* occur at प्रा, the first letter of the third word, and nowhere else? Altaf Khan's answer here was illuminating. "If you are asked to walk slowly and with dignity, it is patently wrong to resort to occasional jumping or running. Similarly, if a *sthāyī* is expected to bloom when it reaches the *sama*, the latter — the focal beat — must carry a sparkling letter like प्रा."

3. *Sargam* stands for disposition of notes as named, say, as *sa, re, ga, ma.*

Now the theorist can certainly develop the point here hinted into full-blown ideas, rationally more defensible. He may say that it is self-inconsistent to lay claim to *vilambit* singing and yet to incorporate flirtatious embellishments; and that not merely being, but *appearing* as the focal point requires the *sama* to be placed at a letter which looks distinctive by virtue of its very sound. However, the truth here involved can be realized only in the light of actual singing. Altaf Khan would openly insist that the detailed reflections of a musicologist have got to be grounded in details of actual aesthetic practice. Or else, the veteran warned, the quintessential truths of music may be not merely ignored, but dismissed as nonsense. He would refer, at his point, to the following *marwā* composition of his father, Zahoor Khan "Ramdas":

वादी अनुवादी विवादी समवादी
उदात अनुदात स्वरित प्लुत
तान मान और उपज कठिन होत है
आरोही को अवरोही कर
तीव्र में कोमल प्रकाश
'रामदास' तब गुनियन में गिनती पावे

Here, the fourth and the fifth lines seem to recommend what is plainly contradictory. But, when requested to account for the (seeming) inconsistency, Altaf Khan came out with his critical best. "*Aroha* and *avaroha*,"[4] he contended, "do not really stand for the physical acts of moving up and down the scale. They stand rather for the rise and ebb of thought or feeling. You *can* sing, if you so desire, what is grammatically *teevra* with the pathos of a fading tone. And unless the musician can do so, what does he *create*, instead of merely going by the rules of grammar?

4. That is, ascent and descent along the scale.

Like many others of his kind, Altaf Hussain Khan would bemoan that "educated" musicologists had on the whole been indifferent to this truth — the truth that what appears far-fetched or absurd in mere theory may, in practice, be the very essence of beauty. So far as I remember, this was the only point at which he tended to grow a little bitter. Otherwise, his talk in general was objective and controlled. Even in recounting his *yādgār gāne* (or memorable performances), he never grew hyperbolic. Referring to the most popular classical vocalists of today, he once said to me meaningfully, "*Khayāl*[5] is different. The difference between *khayāl* and *ṭhumrī* consists not only in what patterns you use, nor even (merely) in how precisely the voice moves in rendering a particular pattern but primarily in the *temper* which permeates your singing. Differences in manner of execution then follow automatically." Much that is happening in the world of classical music today was, without doubt, disagreeable to him; but Altaf Khan was never spiteful in expressing his disapproval. It seems to me that a quiet but abiding sense of deep, inward fullness — of knowing intimately what in music is of lasting worth — prevented him from getting embittered over the relative neglect of the *gharānā*s by the educated musicologist of today. He would lament, but nobly — in a tone of restraint and quiet self-confidence. "It does not matter," he would say, "when they wake up to what is worth presenting and listening to, they will turn to us, the torch-bearers of tradition." It is good that his two young sons share this self-assurance; for, it steadies them today when they are not much in demand. They know what rigours their father had to bear, and how well he withstood them. They are, therefore, neither impatient to succeed nor willing to barter tradition for music of an easier appeal.

5. *Khayāl* is the popular style of our classical vocal music today.

Personal Life

Married in 1890, at the age of twenty-two, Altaf Khan was blessed with three children — two sons and a daughter. Their simple way of life was entirely free from that pervasive abandon which has come to be regarded as being characteristic of musicians. The Ustad himself was a deeply religious man. Even when sick, he would maintain religious abstinences, such as fasting during the period of *ramzān*. He was proud of the fact that he had once been a pilgrim to Holy Mecca — "and on my own money," he would quickly add. Religion, indeed, was one of his permanent interests. Up to a few months before his death, his one main concern was to get a mosque built in Champanagar — a city in district Purnea where he lived for the last twenty years of his life with the Raja of Banaili, and which, as his sons now tell me, had for long been the nursery of authentic musical culture.

Considering that, as a musician, he had (in general) to keep the company of his kind, Altaf Khan's austere living was indeed exceptional. His sons cite it as an index of the general tenor of his life that, as a rule, he would avoid even such simple indulgences as the use of oil and pickles. This should not, however, be allowed to suggest that he ever ignored the legitimate needs of the body. In fact, right from the age of 17, he never missed his regular physical exercise till before the advent of real old age, and he would often recall with legitimate pride how, as a young man intent on working his way up, he never failed to do his daily 100 *dands*[6] or to consume one *seer* of almonds and half a *seer* of milk before or after *riyāz*,[7] in addition to a substantial quantity of *ghee* along with his two regular meals. This bodily discipline produced its desired effect. Altaf

6. *Dand* is the best known form of our traditional physical exercises.

7. *Riyāz* is the traditional Hindustānī word for the regular practice of music or dance.

Khan's *akāra* grew broad and rich. Notes very high in the upper register could now be sung with the greatest of ease and without any distortion of voice. What is more, he developed the capacity to practise and perform for long hours without the least sign of fatigue.

The severe and methodical quality of his early training is a clear clue to what he finally grew up into — a veteran respected for his insight into the subtleties of our traditional *khayāl*-singing; a musician with an impressive record of performances against some of our greatest vocalists of the past; a simple individual with a perceptible measure of self-control and quiet dignity, revealing, in daily talk, a continual firmness of manner which seemed surprising to those who knew that the greater part of his life was spent under the wing of *rājā*s and princes who generally expect utter subservience from their subjects.

Gharānā: Its Style and Tālim

As is generally admitted, Altaf Hussain Khan has been, in our day, the best known representative of the Khurja school of *khayāl*-singing. The style of this school is naturally not without its characterstic features. Some of these are: emphasis on openness of *akāra* during the execution of *taans*;[8] avoidance of abrupt changes in their structural design; and a relatively infrequent employment of *boltaans*.[9] What is perhaps more distinctive of this school is that the *tarānā*[10] is here sung, in

8. A *taan* is a pattern of *svaras* (or notes). It is longer in range than a mere phrase.

9. A *boltaan* is a melodic pattern which comprises not only *svaras* but some words of the song as well.

10. A *tarānā* is a composition which builds mostly on mere letters or their collocations, all alike meaningless *to the generality of listeners*, that is, barring maestros like Ustad Amir Khan who believed that the mnemonic syllables of rhythm have some mystical significance. Anway, every *tarānā* is necessarily set in a specific *rāga-tāla* frame.

part, after the manner of *khayāls*. In others words, to speak negatively, the closing stage of a recital here is not marked by that hectic, repetitive articulation of *dir, dir,* which is a conspicuous feature of quite a few *tarānās* as they are commonly sung; and, positively, not only are the *taans* executed at subtly regulated speeds, but the access to the *sama* is made to arise from varying and unsuspected accents in the rhythmic cycle.

However, the man who brought the *gharānā* into limelight did not belong originally to Khurja. Altaf Khan's grandfather spent the major part of his life in Dankaur, another small town in Uttar Pradesh in the district of Bulandshahr, before he moved to Khurja. Here, Altaf Khan was born in 1868. His music lessons began at the tender age of five under the watchful eye of his father Zahoor Khan, whose name appears as "Ramdas" in many compositions remarkable for their structural excellence. The training was vigorous and traditional in manner. For even the slightest slackness in daily practice, physical punishment was meted out promptly. Altaf Khan would recall with amusement how, on a chilly winter night, his hands and feet were once tied firmly together and he was hung up on a pole at the top of the house — bundled out because of a mere lapse in practice. The severity, however, was useful. By the age of 13, the growing boy had acquired mastery over at least thirty compositions in three different genres: *dhruvapad,*[11] *khayāl* and *horī* — after undergoing a thorough training in the patterns of *sargams* which form the basis of our practical equipment for classical vocal music. But, at this very age, in 1881, he lost his father. This was a heavy blow to the boy, still quite young and by no means ready to meet the challenges of life. However, his training did not suffer. He began learning from his uncles, Ghulam Haider Khan and Munshi Ghafoor Khan, both of whom were not only accomplished musicians, but well versed in

11. *Dhruvapad* is the oldest extant form of our classical vocal music.

Persian and Sanskrit. They initiated him into the subtleties of *suradhyāya*[12] and *surbyorā*;[13] and though during all these years he put in only two hours of daily practice, the proficiency acquired was both intensive and many-sided. The emphasis, throughout, was on method and musicality rather than on mere speed. It was, therefore, understandable that even at the ripe age of ninety-five Altaf Khan could sing with remarkable robustness.

Career

On attaining the age of 17 Altaf Hussain Khan proceeded to Mathurā and stayed there with Seth Laxmi Chand for a few months. Those were the days of the well-known brothers, Chukkha-Ganeshi Lal, the former known for his skill as a harmonium player, and the latter as an exponent of the *dhruvapad* genre of singing. Mathurā, in those days, was ringing with the stately sonorities of *dhruvapad* and *pakhāwaj*.[14] Altaf Khan did not fail to imbibe some of their high seriousness. Then, in 1886, he moved on to Mursānā, an adjoining State, and spent two years with Rājā Ghanshyam Singh. Luckily, the Rājā's nephew, Bhoop Singh, was fond of music. So, taking full advantage of the congenial conditions, Altaf Khan put in intensive daily practice, from midnight to 4 o'clock in the morning. Another stay of about 4 years with Raja Sadashiva Rao Peshwa of Chitrakoot State was similarly helpful, and the young rising musician could feel his powers growing every day. This was followed by a series of employments in various States, such as Giddhaur and Panchkoot in Bengal, Bhāvnagar,

12. As the maestro explained these terms to me, *svaradhyāya* is correct *identification* and singing of individual notes; and *svarabyorā* is their *disposition* in different ways during the course of actual singing.

13. Ibid.

14. As distinguished from the *tablā*, *pakhāwaj* is a one-piece drum which provides rhythmic accompaniment to *dhruvapad-dhamār* singing.

Kaṭhiāwāṛ, Dujānā, Gabhānā and Nepal. His longest stay was, however, at Purnea, with Rājā P.C. Lal. This association lasted for about 20 years. Even during the closing years of his life he remained mostly with the Rājā of Banaili.

Beginning at the age of 17, Altaf Hussain Khan took part in most of the important music conferences of the country. Some of these participations were in his view memorable. One of them came about more than a century back — at Laxmi Bhavan, in Bombay. Among those who performed on the occasion were such distinguished musicians as Bhaskar Rao Bua Bakhle and Waze Bua. Vilayat Hussain Khan and his elder brother were also present. Altaf Hussain Khan was asked to sing after Bhaskar Rao. He sang a rare variety of *Gaurī* for about four hours. It was followed by an exposition of *Basant* and *Lalitābasant*. The recital was acclaimed both for its technical accuracy and emotive content, and created quite a stir in the city.

About the same year he gave another remarkable performance in Calcutta at the residence of Duli Chand Babu, a well-known patron of music. Participants here included Nanhey Khan of Rampur; Dhunni Khan; Chhotey Khan, elder brother of Ghaseet Khan; and the famous harmonium player, Bhayya Ganpat Rao. The concert opened with exquisite recitals by such consummate artistes as Alladia Khan and Maujjuddin. Altaf Khan sang on the following day. The distinguished audience sat spellbound for more than three hours, admiring every subtle turn of musical phrase and the singer's adroitness in rendering difficult *rāga*s.

Had he ever sung better? Altaf Khan thought he had — in 1902, though he was not very sure of the year. It was in the garden of a well-known patron of music and musicians, Shri Ashu Mallik, about 14 miles from Calcutta. Here too the participants were musicians of the highest order, chief of them being Malikā Gohar Jan; Alladia Meherban, pupil of the well-known Fateh Ali Khan; and Fayyaz Khan, then working his way to the top, slowly but unmistakably. The young "Fayyaz," as Altaf Khan put it, sang for more than ninety minutes, interspersing, as was his wont, movements of remarkable profundity with light, tickling curls of readier appeal, because of which device even the sweetest songstresses of those days regarded him as a formidable rival. The impact on the audience was so overwhelming that no one was prepared to "attune his *tānpūrā*," as they say, when Fayyaz Khan had finished.

But Altaf Khan came forward, to do *jugalbandī* with Fayyaz Khan. The two began singing together — the same *rāga*, matching phrase for phrase, either as a parallel or as a foil, and drawing repeated applause from all those present. For full four hours they sang uninterrupted. Both were young, and neither was prepared to be humbled in the eyes of the audience, spiced with not a little feminine glamour. And so the music went on — without respite, till at last Gohar Jan's elderly mother put her hands firmly on the *tānpūrā*s, signalling the end, and exclaiming, with her eyes fixed on the ladies: "What! do you want to kill my sons?"

Beside his overall ability as a singer, the remarkable range of Altaf Khan's voice (in his younger days) was of great help in swaying vast audiences. It was precisely this, he believed, which enabled him to hold a very big gathering in rapt attention for well over ninety minutes on the occasion of the marriage of the son of Raja Chandra Shamshere Jung of Nepal which was attended by more than a thousand musicians. At the same time he would insist that he had never betrayed tradition by sacrificing methodical singing for the sake of easy appeal.

Did he never sing ineffectively? Altaf Khan would readily admit he had, on quite a few occasions. Thus, in one music concert at Calcutta — in the "thirties" — in which Bade Ghulam

Ali Khan also took part, the first half of his recital was distinctly colourless; but it brightened up perceptibly when, accompanied by the inimitable Habibuddin Khan on the *tablā*, he switched over to *lalitābasant*.

There was at least one more such incident which Altaf Khan could vividly recall. Once, after eight months of intensive practice, he set out for the state of Giddhaur — brimming with confidence. But, as ill luck would have it, he developed fever in the train. His condition worsened and when he found himself at the royal court, all set for a session of competitive music, he could hardly stand erect. It was impossible for him to withdraw, for he was the main artiste of the evening. So when his turn came, he had to sing. But so unwell was he that even the *sthāyī* could not be completed. He put down the *tānpūrā* and stopped unceremoniously.

It was surely an odd thing to happen. The entire gathering, including the Rājā, was disappointed. Determined to make good at his next appearance, Altaf Khan rested for one full day. And when on the third day he was again invited to sing, he responded magnificently. He sang for six hours — and with remarkable effect. The Rājā was delighted. The Ustad was given a befitting present in the court. What is more, the prince became his pupil.

Altaf Khan's Preferences

Being a veteran, Altaf Khan had naturally heard all the master musicians of the day, right from the age at which he stepped out of his home to win laurels for himself. To turn first to the *khyāliyā*s, he would cherish the memories of Bahadur Khan of Delhi; Natthan Khan Agrewale, father of Wilayat Hussain Khan; Zahoor Khan "Begumwala" of Delhi; Fateh Ali of Patiala; and Quadratullah Khan of Sikandrabad, in Uttar Pradesh.

Did he ever have the privilege of listening to the music of

Rahmat Khan who, as is widely known, used to tour the country along with the circus of Sri Vishnupanth Pagnis? Altaf Khan regretted he had not, though when he was only 8 years of age, he did accompany his father to meet the maestro when the latter visited Khurja — with the circus. He also remembers one particular incident which illustrates how hard it was to please the great Rahmat Khan. It occurred at Bombay. In a well attended musical gathering, Fayyaz Khan provided the opening recital. He was followed by Altaf Khan. They had both hoped to win at least a nod of approval from the great Rahmat Khan. But he sat absolutely unmoved. However, when Alladia Khan began, Rahmat Khan opened his eyes and wondered meaningfully: "Has singing begun?"

If asked to name the more important of the *ālāpiyā*s and *dhruvapad*-singers he had heard, Altaf Khan would refer to Murad Khan of Delhi; Maula Bux and Nawab Khan of Tilwandī Gharānā; the famous brothers, Allabande-Zakiruddin Khan; and Karamat Khan of Jaipur. The last of these, Altaf Khan would add, was remarkable for his thin yet exceedingly musical voice.

Recalling the great *tablā*-players of his day, Altaf Khan would refer, in particular, to the following: Natthu Khan and Muzaffar Khan of Delhi, Abid Hussain Khan of Lucknow, Beeru Misr and Gopi of Banaras and Maulvi Ram of Mymensing. His favourite *sitāriyā*s were some of the best known names of the day: Ameer Khan of Gwalior — a true representative of the *seniyā* school — and Imdad Khan, grandfather of Vilayat Khan, the well-known *sitāriyā* of modern India whose recent demise (2004) has been widely and deservedly mourned.

This list does not include Babu Khan of Gwalior, of whom Altaf Khan preferred to make a special mention. Babu Khan, we are told, used to tend cattle; and though his *sitār* would rarely have all the strings or frets, he could always produce out of it the loveliest of music. As for the *beenkārs*,[15] Altaf Khan was confident that the best of them, over the last one hundred years or so, had been Murad Khan, pupil of Bande Ali Khan; and of all the *sarod* players that he knew, he had a special word of praise for Ghulam Ali Khan, grandfather of Ustad Hafiz Ali Khan and a pupil of Tanras Khan.

Did he gain anything by listening to these masters? Altaf Khan would answer affirmatively and refer with perceptible thankfulness to two vocalists in particular — Bahadur Khan of Delhi and Alladia Khan. Again, he felt proud of the fact that Tanras Khan's sister was married to his mother's father. This is indeed an important detail of Altaf Khan's musical heritage. He would, however, hasten to add that, formally and directly, he had learnt only from his father and uncles.

Sensitiveness to Folk Music

Classical music had thus been Altaf Khan's main interest. Yet he was duly sensitive to the charms of folk music too. This is borne out by some actual incidents in his life. One of these occurred at Khurja. He was proceeding in a tonga towards the railway station for going to Purnea, when the following simple song gently closed in upon him:

तू मत कर काया का गुमान, तनक तेरी ज़िन्दगानी
इस काया पर दूब जमेगी, खेती करेगा किसान
तनक तेरी ज़िन्दगानी

The singer was a grass-cutter. He sang as he worked in utter oblivion of the world around him. Altaf Khan was overwhelmed by the soulful quality of the song and by the vital significance of its theme. He lost all inclination to proceed, paid off the *tongāwāllā*, and went on listening enraptured till it grew dark, whereupon he quietly trudged back home. Altaf Khan was then

15. A *beenkār* is one who plays at a *veeṇā*.

only forty years old, but even when as an old man of ninety-five, he recalled that song he grew tearful. The lapse of time had in no way bedimmed the impact of the folk song. The maestro candidly cofessed that with all his musical training (or perhaps because of it) he had never been able to sing so effectively as that simple man had done.

Altaf Khan had another such experience at Qualan-Dargarhai, a suburb of Khurja, about a mile from the railway station. It occurred at midnight. Sweet rural strains suddenly awakened him. He looked around. The music seemed to come from a neighbouring house. Some women were singing to the accompaniment of the spinning stone-mill. And they sang so sweetly, of basic human trials and sentiments, that Altaf Khan lay listening nightlong — and with brimful eyes.

There is, he would clarify, nothing mysterious about the ready appeal of folk music. The theme here is what it should really be — the common affective drives and joys of human life; the *akāra* is simple and unaffected; and, above all, the entire singing is such a direct outpouring of the heart that a spell is created because of sheer soulfulness.

But if this is what makes music irresistible, how can *a training in classical technique* be said to be indispensable? Does it not estrange us from the deeper sources of appeal? To questions such as these Altaf Khan would not venture to give any answer. But he made no secret of it that many a time he had himself been transported by the simplest of music. Music must have appeal, above everything else; technique is secondary. This was Altaf Khan's considered opinion. Even in the realm of classical music, he would add, the emphasis should be on sweetness of *svara* and beauty of design, rather than on mere intricacy and speed. To a musician seeking to grow as a performer he had the following orthodox advice to give: regular *riyāz* under the eye of an Ustad; good, nourishing diet; and above all, simple, temperate habits. What is more, the aspirant to fame must be wary of his friends; for they often tend to admire uncritically and may therefore mislead one.

In music, as in life, Altaf Khan was a traditionalist. As far back as he could think — and he would revel in recalling the more important names in the past ten generations of his family — he saw an unbroken succession of eminent musicians and composers. This awareness of his rich heritage kept him, on the one hand, continually self-critical; and, on the other hand, studiedly averse to glib experimentation.

Characteristically enough, Altaf Khan kept thinking of music till almost the last breath of his life. Paralysis struck him on March 8, 1964 and he passed away on the 15th at about 3.30 p.m. In the hospital, however, a strange thing happened. After four days of fruitless treatment, the Ustad rallied strongly. Being unable to articulate words, he resorted to pure *akāra*;[16] and, in a pathetic struggling manner, he succeeded in indicating to his son, Wahid, the form of a rare *rāga* which the young man had for years been eager to learn.

It was the last flicker of a will that had glowed intensely and for long.

---

16. *Akāra* is sheer musical voice, that is, without any words and note-names.

10

Ustad Amir Khan:[1]
The Man and His Art

THIS essay is no mere homage.[2] It is a serious, if modest attempt to determine what exactly we lost in the death of Ustad Amir Khan about thirty-five years back.

My first thought is that the Ustad was an artist of singular courage. It is today common to criticise our listeners. They are not eligible, we sometimes protest, to receive truly good music. Now this may be justified partly. But I wonder if it is proper to blame the listeners alone. What they learn to like is vitally determined by what is offered to them; and the latter is, in the main, *musicians'* own choice. They do not only present their music to listeners but also determine the taste of those who listen.

Consider, in this context, the practice of our very best instrumentalists. Their general practice is to regale audiences

---

1. With some substantial changes, this essay reproduces my article, "Ustad Amir Khan: The Man and His Art" which appeared in the 31st issue of *Sangeet Natak* (Jan–March, 1974, pp. 5-12).

2. Though, in the view of many lovers of serious music even today, Amir Khan does deserve some kind of *abiding* homage. Decidedly the most significant homage to the maestro is the book, *Ustad Amir Khan*, authored by his devoted pupil, Tej Pal Singh (the elder of the well-known Singh Bandhu twosome) and Tej Pal's own leading pupil, Dr Prerna Arora; and published by Kanishka Publishers, New Delhi, 2005.

not only with the quality of their own playing, but also — and importantly — by resorting to bouts of rhythmic exchanges with the drummer, specially in *drut* playing where structure and *svara* both tend to weaken at the expense of sheer speed; and where listeners who applaud are only vaguely excited, instead of being appreciative discriminatingly. Some vocalists too resort to things and devices that are not really integral to good classical music. Superfine *kurtās* and beauteous rings bejewelling fingers — things such as these are often used to impress lay listeners. A common artifice is recourse to some *ati drut taans* that often seem to stampede. The *akāra*, here, often becomes ungainly; sweetness, clarity and design — all tend to suffer; and what is utilized to impress and excite us is sheer speed with some vocal acrobatics. *Vilambit* singing, indeed, is often given much less attention than it deserves. Then, there are those who try to impress audiences more by crowding the composition presented with words of serious ethico-religious import, than with the help of purely musical values, such as tonal sweetness and the various formal graces. This is perhaps truer of *dhruvapad* singers than of *khayāl*-singers generally.

Amir Khan was different; and, in this difference, solitary. I must mention in this context his absolute indifference to reactions of the audience. During the course of singing, his music would be the only object of his attention, and he would sing all along as directed by his own view of what classical *khayāl gāyakī* truly is. Generally, *our* response, or the lack of it, had just no effect on him — at least not visibly. As a rule, his music would impress us mainly with its remarkable blend of poise and serenity. Yet, because of his effortless manner, he *never seemed to make a conscious endeavour to please the audience.* This I regard as the hallmark of a very great artist, that is, absolute commitment to the basic values of classical music, which can be (to genuine *rasikas*) a welcome relief from that abject pining for growing popularity to which quite a few of our Hindustānī musicians are today clearly subject.

Amir Khan would indeed face audiences with a kingly self-confidence, and with absolute faith in unmitigated classicism. He never expected *the drummer* to add to the charm of his singing. All that he needed was a reposeful *ṭhekā* as steadfast accompaniment, first, to provide ample space for his imagination to unfurl itself; and, second, to serve as a ground for his intricate criss-cross of *taans*, highlighting thereby both the *ṭhekā*'s peaceableness and the nimbleness and variety of the patterns. And though he often sang *sthāyī*s with a devotional text, the meaning of words (which he, as a rule, uttered pretty clearly) never seemed to dominate the melodic and structural aspects of his *gāyakī*, or the winsome mellowness of his *akāra*.[3]

It is true that the Ustad would take special care to sing a *tarānā-antarā* in open *akāra*; and that — as in the case of his *lalit tarānā* employing the words, *dar ā jane mun* — he would often try to invest even mnemonic syllables with a tissue of meaning.[4] Yet, I repeat, the distinctive effect of his singing never seemed to issue *mainly* from the meaning of the words used. The *way* of rendering would always be paramount. To illustrate, and this is something which might have struck the more knowledgeable, the effect of the Persian couplet of Hafiz — in Amir Khan's well-known *suhā tarāna* — was certainly

3. From here onwards, I am generally (and quite heavily) indebted to two sources: first, the late Pandit Amar Nath for supplying not only information about Ustad Amir Khan's life, but insights into his art as well; and secondly, to Tej Pal Singh's book referred to in note 2. This book, in particular, has enabled me not only to enrich the essay, but to remove some errors in it as it first appeared in *Sangeet Natak*.

4. Prof. Manfred Junius of the Venice Institute of Comparative Music once assured me that, in the opinion of the Ustad, *tarānā* syllables had a mystical significance.

heightened, if not actually outweighed, by the nimble *taan* following the couplet, emanating from the offbeat and proceeding in a subdued voice, *because of which the pattern would seem quicker than it really was.*

As for *ṭhumrīs*, it is not that Amir Khan could not manage them. He would often sing them to his pupils at home; and with immaculate effect. His pupil, the late Pandit Amar Nath — who was thoroughly imbued with the *temper* of the Ustad — would often fondly recall the delightful ease of the master while singing the *Bhairavī* composition: *chailvā ne māri katār*. Yet, as we know, no one speaks of Amir Khan's *ṭhumrīs*. The reason simply is that he was convinced of the charms of the truly classical *khayāl* form itself and so never sang *ṭhumrīs* at public concerts.

We all know the *rāgas* that the Ustad would generally prefer to sing. The more important of these are: *Bhairava, Pūrbī, Naṭgourī, Ābhogī, Mālkaus, Lalit, Darbārī* and *Marwā*. Most of us remember his expositions of the last three. But I personally think Amir Khan had the remarkable ability to invest *whichever rāga* he chose to sing with a tissue of high seriousness. And I may here be allowed to repeat, with some changes, what I wrote about his *Darbārī* on 3 April 1957, as a part of the Seminar recitals organized by Sangeet Natak Akademi; for, it seems to seize the very essence of his *gāyakī*:

> The secret (of Amir Khan's singing) lies *not* so much in the slowness of the rhythm-circle to which he sings — be it *jhoomrā* or *tilawāṛā* — as in the *contrast* which he freely brings about between a meteoric *taan* and the resposeful articualtion of a *vilambit sthāyī*. The flitting figures tend to deepen the [look of the] ground, and so a tissue of thought appears to encompass the whole singing. Not any great ebullience of feeling — such as one associates with the music of Omkarnath or Kumar Gandharva — but a certain contemplativeness, depth and serenity — these are the qualities which

> distinguished the art of Amir Khan. *An Amir khan svara*[5] *(or tonal phrase) is at once a tuning of the singer's own being, and the source of a calm that spreads; Ghulam Ali's, glows — with a pulpy luminosity; and that of Kumar Gandharva is often a* [*manifest*] *upsurge of feeling.*

Such sketchy remarks, however, are no *explanation* of what makes Amir Khan's music appear so impressively overlaid with a tissue of high seriousness, and I therefore think it necessary to add the following by way of elucidation:

First, as he sets out to sing, Amir Khan's very presence on the stage is markedly collected, not only because of his sitting posture (or his *baiṭhak*), but because of his half-open, downward eyes which rarely looked at the audience. And I venture to suggest that as the singing began he would use the first line of the composition (or the *sthāyī*) as much to compose himself as to provide the usual opening to the recital. Here, I also feel impelled to make an intriguing addition. On one occasion he complained of noise even when the venue was a perfectly quiet room; and when the host, a devoted pupil of his, wondered at the oddity, the maestro was quick to explain that the "noise" he had referred to was his own inner tumult.[6] Be that as it may, it is unquestionable that Amir Khan *looked* perfectly focussed as he opened his singing.

Secondly, the rhythms that he would generally choose — that is, *tilawāṛā* (16 beats) or *jhoomrā* (14 beats) — were obviously wider in range than *ektāla* (12 beats). What is more, because

5. Here, the *gandhār*, of which I wrote:

   > Some consummate renderings of the cardinal *gandhār* . . . one of them being so steady, yet fine that, though moveless in fact, it *suggested* oscillation, bringing out the *svara*'s real charm which nestles in a look of tentativeness, even like a fading tint.

6. Tej Pal Singh and Prerna Arora, *Ustad Amir Khan*, p. 91.

leisurely pace is an intrinsic demand of these bigger rhythms, they would provide the maestro ample room to focus on the task ahead.

Thirdly, the reposeful pace of rhythm and the tranquil presence of the artist on the stage also conjoined to quietly induce serious listeners to get set to pay close and patient attention to what the stage had to offer to their ears and imagination. What is more, the unusually long pauses between the words of the *sthāyī* as sung would make genuine *rasika*s look for what musical utterance was going to relieve the immediate moment of silence. Such looking-for, we may note, is neither difficult nor unpleasant. And it is surely no bewilderment; for, first, as *rasika*s we are (in principle) able to follow the rhythm and also feel assured that, whatever it may be, the next musical step is not going to present anything that falls beyond the *rāga*'s determinate melodic plan; and, secondly, the perfect quiet in the hall makes the duly tuned *tānpūrā* fill the pauses agreeably. The net result is that, not only because of our sustained attention and expectancy, but because of the musical filling provided by the *tānpūrā*, the pauses, though admittedly actual, are not felt by us as literal breaks, but rather as integral to the run of music. Nor is this uncommon as a happening. Even our daily conversation does not look disrupted by the inevitable moments of quiet that punctuate it; and, to turn anew to Amir Khan's music, our patient attention, the quiet majesty of the rhythmic pace, mellowness of musical utterance, the utter absence of frolicsome touches in the melodic run, and the artist's own visibly serenity — all would make his music look a veritable picture of dignity.

Of the many other excellences of Amir Khan's singing, the following seem noteworthy:

Unhurried evocation of the *sthāyī*'s full form; reverential and so leisurely access to the core of the *rāga* being rendered

— technically called *baṛhat;* due repetition of *sthāyī* after every few *taans*, so as to make it appear as their *aesthetic ground,* and not only as *the first line* of singing; and due attention to the *mandra* where, as in the *madya* region, a rich mellow voice, with its (cultivated?) husky umbra,[7] would directly evoke a semblance of both depth and serenity.

These effects of Amir Khan's music have been irresistible to many of us. Yet it is not easy to appease the wonder as to why he had such a penchant for unusually slow *sthāyī*-singing. It would not do to say, as has actually been suggested by some, that his purpose here is to saturate himself with the character of the *rāga* to be sung; for if (as is well known) he could begin a different *rāga* almost at once after the first composition, why should he need so much time in getting set to begin the first *rāga*? My own view is that Amir Khan wanted to incorporate in *khayāl*-singing the serenity of the opening stages of *ālāpa* of the *dhruvapad* manner; and yet differently, that is, within the ultimate confines of *tāla*. This I regard as an innovation which is an index of his creative prowess.

Yet I do not wish to suggest that Amir Khan's music never left anything to be desired or that it clicked unfailingly. Overdone *vilambit*, which occasionally tended to make for some insipidness; and a little loss of tonal colour and fulness of *akāra* in some *atidrut* patterns — these are perhaps the only flaws that one could at times complain of, in respect of his recitals. But I must also add here that those who please quickly — and even the lay listeners — often *try* to do so, by employing devices which are not quite laudable; and that in the process they cannot but lower the quality of the music that they offer.

Amir Khan never stooped to do this, even at the risk of incurring public indifference. In one of his "interviews" he not

7. This partly explains why Amir Khan's *drut taans* emanting from the *mandra* would often seem to upgather themselves like a cloud.

only admitted that in the Mirzapur Conference, which was his very first chance to sing on a big occasion — and in which such great names took part as Ustads Faiyaz Khan, Pandit Omkarnath Thakur and Smt. Kesar Bai (all vocalists) and instrumentalists like Ustads Inayat Khan (*sitār*) and Abdul Azeez Khan (*veeṇā*) — he could sing only for about 15 or 20 minutes because of hooting by the public. But (he added) when, with a view to mending matters, the Organizing Secretary of the Conference requested him to switch over to *ṭhumrī*-singing, he preferred to just quit the conference, *without being shaken at all in his own view of good khayāl*-singing.[8]

Amir Khan was indeed a man of very strong convictions. What is more, he had some admirable personal qualities which made him the singular artist that he was — very steadfast in commitment to the art of his choice; and very simple and human in some respects, yet well above the average in virtue of his exalted sense of fairness and decorum. I say so on the basis of some actual happenings. While participating in the five-day East-West Encounter at Azad Bhavan in 1964, Amir Khan had to stay at Asoka hotel with the other participants; but instead of exulting in the regality of the place, where he had to conform to its formal living style throughout the day, he would prefer to spend a relaxed evening (in a *luṅgī*) at the homely residence of his dear pupil, Tej Pal Singh.[9]

As for his attitude towards other musicians, it was always fair, duly cognisant of their merit, and utterly free from jealousy. Thus, when he had to sing at the Swami Haridas Sammelan of 1968 (Bombay, April 23) he began by openly declaring that, because of the sad news of the demise of his dear friend, Ustad Bade Ghulam Ali Khan, he was not really in a mood to perform, but just had to do so, to avoid upsetting the organizers'

8. Tej Pal Singh and Prerna Arora, *Ustad Amir Khan*, pp. 72-73.

9. Ibid., p. 86.

schedule, adding (in the end) that he may please be pardoned for the shortcomings of his recital on this occasion.[10] Further, it was at Amir Khan's express insistence that D.V. Paluskar was chosen (by Naushad Sahib) to provide Baiju Bāorā's voice in the film named after Tansen's vanquisher. What is more, when (after seeing the film) some of the Ustad's close pupils asked as to why he had condescended to appear "defeated" in the film by a younger artist, Amir Khan's forthright answer was: "A 'defeat' in a film is no real index of actual inferiority; and, after all, he (D.V.) is the son of (no less a person than) the lion-hearted Vishnudigambarji."[11] Even in his relations with *shāgirds*, Amir Khan was always very fair and sympathetic, ever careful to avoid straining them financially, and never averse to teach the choicest compositions in his repertoire to those who were keen and deserving. Thus, at his *gandā-bandhan* ceremony, Tej Pal Singh was explicitly advised by the maestro to offer *nazar* only to Ustad Chand Khan and an elderly lady, and not also to "my distant relatives."[12] What, however, seems to be most directly related to the quality of his music is the maestro's own personal equanimity in life. In spite of many inhibiting factors — such as the loss of his mother when he was just a child, a more or less unsettled married life, and rejection by the audience at his very first appearance on a big stage — he stuck gamely to the task of bending public taste towards his uncommon *gāyakī*. As a result, the recognition of his merit was so rich and manifold that it could well be the envy of the best of our musicians. The following is a quick listing of the more important ways in which he won accolades:

India's sole representative at the East-West Music Encounter in 1964; the only classical vocalist to perform at the Red Fort

10. *Ustad Amir Khan*, p. 88.
11. Ibid., p. 128.
12. Ibid., pp. 108-09.

> on the occasion of the Silver Jubilee of our Independence; automatic exemption from A.I.R.'s audition test, along with placement in the top grade; the very first artist to be invited to sing in the Sunday Morning Sabha of A.I.R.; also the chosen vocalist to inaugurate the A.I.R. auditorium on 15.8.1962; repeatedly invited to sing in Radio Sangeet Sammelans, and included in those select musicians who were billed to give a two-hour performance;[13] and one of those *very* few musicians whose recorded music is drawing increasing attention in the music market even today.

In addition to all this, there is hardly any important music conference of the country where Amir Khan did not perform creditably. I personally recall a particular *lalit* rendering of his at the Constitution Club, New Delhi, many years back, and well before sunrise. After the first few minutes of *vilambit* treatment — relieved and deepened by a sprinkling of *drut taans* — the music seemed strangely *disembodied* from *rāga-tāla* distinctions, and appeared as just an intense musical atmosphere that looked ethereal; and this without much help from the meaning of the words about the distinct articulation of which the *Ustad* was fairly particular. *His music, at its best, was rarely a dazzle. It would rather be an influence* that just stole into us and kept us wrapped up, so to say, *till long after the end of the recital.*

Such uncommon excellence, however, cannot accrue suddenly; and so it is necessary to look at the maestro's early years, and influences. Born at Kalanaur in 1912, Amir Khan spent his early childhood and the greater part of his adult life at Indore. Here, thanks to his father Shah Mir Khan, his impressionable years were spent under the influence of the music of two very great masters: Rajab Ali Khan, the vocalist; and Murad Khan, the *veeṇā* expert. Shah Mir Khan himself was

---

13. *Ustad Amir Khan*, p. 121.

a *sāraṅgī* player, and so quite conversant with the subtleties of vocal music. The two musicians from whom the growing boy *himself* tried to benefit, however, were Abdul Wahid Khan, and Amanat, brother of the well-known Aman Ali Khan.

A look at these early influences gives us a clue to understand quite a few features of Amir Khan's own music. Rajab Ali Khan would revel in *drut* singing. Abdul Wahid Khan, on the other hand, was a master of the *vilambit* idiom generally and of assiduous singing of *sthāyī* and *baṛhat* at a leisurely pace. The genius of Amir Khan lay in synthesizing the two rival emphases. His *taans* would be subtly designed, like Rajab Ali's: and his slow singing had the poise of Abdul Wahid Khan at his best. Aman Ali's influence was also here manifest — mainly in the compositional excellence of Amir Khan's *sthāyī*s. Ever eager to learn from the knowledgeable, the Ustad even "took" an Aman Ali Khan *bandish* in *rāga Shahānā* from Prof. Shiv Kumar Shukla of Baroda University.

The one thing that Amir Khan liked to emphasize about his early training was that, for the first 25 years of his life, he devoted considerable time to *sargam* singing. To the question why *this* aspect of singing should be deemed so important, Amir Khan's set answer would be that, besides helping identification of notes — and so facilitating watchful improvization and fidelity to the *rāga*'s set character — *sargam*s lend variety to singing by virtue of their *audile* diversity. Now, this is not only interesting but true. *Pa* keeps the *akāra open; ni* shows the voice as clearly *subdued;* and *ma,* if steadily sung, has about it a clear measure of *nasal resonance* — which the *ālāpiya*s may speak of as a touch of *anuraṇātmaka* utterance — though not as manifestly as it can appear in a steadfast singing of *ni*. Such variform effects do much to relieve the monotony of singing all along in open *akāra*.

With regard to *taans*, Amir Khan's considered opinion was

that, whatever be their individual *design* — which is obviously essential, because a *taan* is no mere collocation, but an orderly disposition of notes — their actual singing should always involve a measure of *gamak* and *lahak*. The first of these formal graces gives to *taans* a measure of depth, which is so necessary for classical singing; and the second — that is, *lahak* — tempers the *gamak*, preventing (on the one hand) the *akāra* in *taans* from appearing *affectedly* deep; and (on the other hand) their *dānā* — or discreteness of constituent notes — from jutting out from, and so inhibiting the run of the *taan*. Such *taans*, the maestro believed, can certainly be made fairly fluent in *laya*, yet without any harm to sweetness and clarity of *svaras*.

Allied to what we have just said (and following the maestro), two more points may be made here. First, the right kind of depth accrues to *akāra* only when it has mellowed through proper *riyāz* for a number of years, specially in respect of *svaras* in the *mandra;* and not from any immediate wilful effort in the course of singing. Secondly, formal devices, like *mīṇḍ, gamak* and *lahak* have a major role to play in the proper management of *rāgas* which are *narrow* — that is, those which employ, say, four notes, and have built-in gaps between their constituent *svaras*. These gaps cannot be bridged properly by voices that have not been trained to use the devices just referred to, because they (the devices) alone enable a singer to let his voice *soar and sweep with perfect control*. This is precisely why — Amir Khan would add, with a twinkle in his eyes — music *schools* which revel in quick coaching are forced to advise their pupils to follow the easier method of creating *taans* in *rāgas* like *Guṇkali, Hindol* and *Meghrañjanī* by employing *two successive emphases of the same individual note*. This device is surely an affective short-cut; but, *I* protest, it also precludes the requisite semblance of inner roominess which can be a distinctively pleasing feature of these *rāgas*, precisely because of the limited number of *svaras* that they build on.

Amir Khan's own voice, I may add, could soar to, and sweep across far-off *svaras* with grace and felicity. This has in fact been a feature of his *drut taans*. It variegates their nimbleness with a touch of flightiness (उड़ान), so that the run of music does not look merely single or seamless on the inside, but also on wings, so to say. All this, however, is the harvest of a lifetime. Amir Khan, incidentally, was thoroughly opposed to the idea of short-cuts to success in music; and if he could sing compositions in a *rāga* like *Megharañjanī*, such as the *tritāla* one which opens as follows:

Ek oṁkāra niraṅkāra

for hours together, and with unflagging effect,[14] it was mainly because of his superbly trained voice and *svara*-sense born of mastery of solfa-singing.

Yet, as an artist, the Ustad was by no means *confined to* mere practical comptence, but could also argue for his view of good singing. Thus, to the question why he prefered *such* slowness in *vilambit*, his answer would readily run as follows: in a slowly moving *ṭhekā* the *sama* does not recur very soon, and so the mind gets plenty of time to attune itself with the mood of the *rāga*, well before having to conform to the eventual constraint of rhythm.[15]

Of his other views on music the following may be picked for special mention:

---

14. As, I am assured, he often did for his pupils, privately. I got this assurance from the late Pandit Amar Nath, in my interview with him on 12-3-1974. Incidentally, Amar Nath himself sang the composition here referred to with remarkable ease and effect, on 26-2-1974, at Rabindra Bhavan, New Delhi, on the occasion of the memorial meeting organised by Sangeet Natak Akademi.

15. I find this unsatisfactory. In principle, rhythm should not merely contain or encompass, but *permeate* a good *bandish*. On the other hand, I cannot deny the remarkably reposeful effect of Amir Khan's singing.

So far as possible, the *sama* should be marked with an *akāra-bol*, so that the *sthāyī* may appear to flower, so to say, at the focus of rhythm. The *antarā* would seem not merely to follow, but belong to (its) *sthāyī* if the two have similar endings — similar in respect of flow. *Lagāo*, or the manner of applying voice to *svaras*, is at least as important as sheer physical sweetness. An abrupt and full blown application of voice to *svaras* is never welcome to ears. Singing is superior to instrumental music in two clear respects: expression is here more direct, and the voice is able to embrace far-off *svaras* more gracefully than stringed instruments generally can. Proper treatment of *taar* notes *is* desirable,[16] but mastery over the *mandra* is more important for effects of seriousness. An assiduous practice of *merkhand* is, of course, indispensable for every learner of classical music; but the teacher's personal attention, and the persuasive example of his own way of singing are even more important. However, what is of maximum help in progressing as a vocalist is the pupil's own intelligence and industry. Musicologists and the present-day *schools* are not of much help, so far as *classical singing of the highest quality* is concerned Their only clear superiority over the Ustads lies in their knowledge of English.

All this makes sense, but there is one view which has been attributed to Amir Khan, and which I find difficult to accept. The view, as put forth in a recent publication, runs thus:

> Look! a good voice has to model itself after the shape of a pyramid; that is, it should be broad at the base (or lower notes); and become increasingly slender and pointed as it traverses the higher notes.[17]

---

16. Amir Khan would emphasize *this* competence while praising Ustad Bade Ghulam Ali.

17. *Ustad Amir Khan*, p. 48.

If this view is accepted we will have to withdraw the very wide acclaim that has so far been given to the legendary Rahmat Khan whose *taan*s were admired precisely because they appeared to bloom and sparkle at the *taar svara*s, like an *anār* used in a display of fireworks; and to Ustad Faiyaz Khan whose singing of *taar* notes in *Jogiyā*, as energized with the formal devices known as *lāga-dānt*, used to thunder, so to say, with poignant, powerful• feeling.

Amir Khan, however, never sought to impose his views or even his *gāyakī* on anyone. This is why his pupils do not all seem to conform to his *gāyakī* meticulously. The music of the late Pandit Amar Nath, though he was himself a composer of no mean merit, was of course a pretty good image of the master; at its best; it would be generally deep, spacious and at times moving too. I say so on the basis of listening to his music more than once, and at my own residence. But the well-known Singh Bandhu,[18] who have won the Sangeet Natak Akademi Award (2004) for excellence in classical music, have a style of their own. All those, however, who have come under the spell of Amir Khan as pupils (and they number about twenty) are alive to the best in our classical music; and it is noteworthy that, led by Singh Bandhu (Tej Pal Singh and Surinder Singh), nine of them have been put in the "top grade" by A.I.R.[19]

The Ustad, indeed, has been able to instil — by the very example of his own art — a deep love of serious, contemplative music into the hearts of many young listeners all over the country. This itself, I believe, is ample warrant for the many honours he received, including the following: Fellowship of Sangeet Natak Akademi (Bihar); the central (New Delhi)

---

18. This is how we commonly designate the well known pair of Tej Pal Singh and Surinder Singh.

19. *Ustad Amir Khan*, p. 68.

Sangeet Natak Akademi Award for excellence in classical vocal music (1967); and Padma Bhushan in 1971.

I wonder if, in independent India, any other Hindustānī classical musician has been more unbending in his aesthetic taste, and more successful *without organised support* than this great *khayāliyā*, Ustad Amir Khan. His passing away heightens our duty to care for those who are wedded to his kind of music, so difficult and yet so open to greatness.

It is not enough to remember him. We must cherish the values that he did. Luckily, quite a few living vocalists *are* doing this assiduously today.[20]

20. This is probably truer of lovers of classical music in Bengal than in any other part of the country. Be that as it may, this is undeniable that Amir Khan's music continues to draw growing attention today.

11

Ustad Bade Ghulam Ali Khan

A Master of Melody[1]

A LITTLE abrupt though it may look, I begin straight away with some categorical, yet truthful remarks. In respect of sheer musical appeal Ghulam Ali could stand comparison with, if not positively outshine, the sweetest singers of the silver screen. His appearance at a music festival would invariably draw a packed house. The audience, impatient to listen to the music of this maestro who — because of his acknowledged pre-eminence — generally came to the stage last of all, would often grow visibly impatient to see that the earlier recitals ended quickly. To a south Indian audience he was just as welcome as to *rasika*s of Hindustānī music. The late G.N. Balasubramaniam once gave the following superlative compliment to Ghulam Ali: "There is no one like him. He sings a music which is impossible to imitate or reproduce."[2] I may add that quite a few classical singers, of no mean merit themselves, have fallen low in their own esteem after listening to the "great" Ghulam Ali. In one such moment of self-reproach an eminent vocalist once confessed to a friend

---

1. With but a few changes, this essay reproduces my article, "A Master of Melody — Ustad Bade Ghulam Ali Khan" included in the book, *Ustad Bade Ghulam Ali Khan — His Life and Music*, authored by Malti Gilani and Quaratulain Hyder, New Delhi: Harman Publishing House, 2003.

2. Prakash Wadhera's essay, "The Phenomenon that was Bade Ghulam Ali Khan", ibid., p. 281.

of mine that he felt like giving up singing and selling vegetables instead! How many present-day vocalists can give such a feeling of despair to other top class artistes sitting in the audience? I cannot think of any apart from Ghulam Ali.

However, it is not enough to say that Bade Ghulam Ali Khan was a vocalist *par excellence;* we must also account for his title to greatness. The right way to do it is to show how exactly the maestro's art met the basic criteria of excellence in music. I may list these norms, as I did during the course of my talk at the 1996 *Sabrang Utsav* of the Ghulam Ali Yadgar Sabha (Indian International Centre, 14-15 September) quite simply, as follows: first, unremitting euphonic appeal to impartial *rasika*s, that is, to those discriminating listeners who have heard the music of the major *gharānā*s, but are not tied down to any one of them; second, congruence with music's ultimate aim which, according to our traditional thinking, is *mukti* or spiritual liberation; and, third, due evocation of some magical or virtual effects.

Now, no one would object to the first criterion; but the second one may be passed over, for hardly any exponent of Hindustānī classical music today strives for spiritual upliftment through music. The third criterion needs some explanation; for, though it is important, it is not given due thought by our *rasika*s and musicologists.

Goethe once extolled the art of music for its magical power to create, out of its scant material of just seven notes, suggestions of infinite depth, height and power, and of almost every emotion known to man. This, I believe, will surely find favour with those of us who have heard the music of vocalists like Abdul Karim Khan, Omkarnath Thakur, Rahimuddin Khan Dagar, and Kumar Gandharva; and the *veeṇā* playing of instrumentalists like Abdul Azeez Khan and Dabeer Khan. The "suggestions" referred to are so irresistible during the course of actual listening that we may later feel somewhat averse to acquiesce in the down-to-earth reminder that, after all, they were all *mere semblances*. Yet they were, and have to be taken as such. The locus of *real* emotion is a human heart; and quite unlike their parallels in *actual* life, the depths and heights that we (seem to) see in music are not measurable.

But, one may ask, how exactly are these magical effects evoked? One key way to do it, I rejoin, is what Susanne Langer speaks of as *transformation* and which she explains as the:

> rendering of a desired appearance without any actual representation of it, by the production of an equivalent sense-impression rather than a literally similar one, in terms of the limited, legitimate material which cannot naively copy the desired property of the model.[3]

The actual application of the above device is easy to illustrate. A painter can convey a sense of motion by means of dynamic lines, "without picturing [any] attitude or events that connote it."[4] Actors on the stage often highlight the dramatic character of a situation by resorting to "well-timed silences instead of exciting statements."[5] Turning to music, if in an exposition of *rāga Sohnī* the *taar rishabh* is projected finely and sweetly, and if the immediately preceding *sa* has been sung as a mere instant of sweetness, the *rishabh* will appear to be looking *far away into the distance*, in spite of the fact that the two *svaras*, *sa* and *komal re* are in fact *very close* to each other. However, as I propose to bring out a little later, such virtual effects can also be evoked in music by the intrinsic quality of the singer's own voice *and* by the deftly regulated pace and direction of tonal passages. How Ghulam Ali did it will be brought out a little later. Let me first speak of some obvious excellences of his art.

---

3. Susanne K. Langer: *Problems of Art*, Routledge and Kegan Paul, p. 98.

4. Ibid., pp. 98-99.

5. Ibid.

Here, the very first thing to be said is that his art was a veritable paradigm of euphonious singing, essentially because of his meticulously trained voice. His *akāra* would strike us all as sweet, round, unconstrained, mellow and luminous all along, quite without any rough edges or crease on the inside. Even during the course of *ati drut taan*s, in which his music abounded, it never lost the aforesaid qualities. However, with regard to his weaving of patterns, I think it necessary to make the following additional points:

First, he generally preferred the easy-to-follow *ārohī-avarohī* patterns to those that run in involutions, though he could also reel off the most intricate *taan*s impeccably, if and when he so desired.

Second, his *taan*s were exemplary in the sense that, besides being utterly free from the slightest loss of tonal colour, they would always be perfectly true to the norm which enjoins: ना तान फंसे, ना दाना दबे। These words occur freely in the casual talk of our more traditional Ustads, and what they thereby mean makes admirable sense. The constituent *svara*s of a *taan* should be so adroitly regulated in their *singleness* that neither the run of the pattern may suffer the slighest check nor their दाना or discreteness any loss of clarity. Ghulam Ali's *taan*s indeed, which generally dazzled the listeners with their electric pace, would always resemble a rosary of close-grained, but perfectly discernible and shapely beads. I know of no better illustration of what aestheticians have spoken of as the *articulate* form of music.

Third, the maestro would often make a *taan* gain access to the *sama* with such a brief but *meteoric* phrase that one could *restfully* notice, though not without a gentle shock of wonder and delight, only the pattern's immaculate *advent* at the focal beat and *not the passage towards it.* This singular resort to a flashing pace enabled the maestro to achieve, if unwittingly, a wondrous though merely apparent transformation of the actual, successive order of notes into a more or less simultaneous presentation. The terminal passage would generally be so fast that one felt like seeing its beginning and end almost *at the same time*.

Of the other "virtual" or magical elements in Ghulam Ali's singing, I may mention only two, because these alone I can still recall quite clearly. His descent into the *mandra saptak* would evoke a suggestion of depth quite easily, because of the sheer majesty of his *akāra* in this region. Here he never resorted to an intentional deepening of voice as many others do. And as for the semblance of height, I remember to this day that, during the course of singing a devotional composition at the first National Festival of Music at Delhi, the maestro made his utterance of the word, *mahādeo*, ascend to the *taar* region with *such a fluent tonal run-up* that I felt virtually *upraised* to a temple's very pinnacle. Such a look of height (or depth) in music is clearly a mere semblance. What here works is no measuring device, but just our aesthetic sense. The essence of Bade Ghulam Ali's *gāyakī* may indeed be put thus: a truly amazing blend of fluency with unwavering tonal power, sweetness, softness, and a lit-up quality — or, as I have preferred to christen it in some of my write-ups, the *pulpy luminosity* — of *akāra*. In respect of these essentials of good music, *taken as one*, hardly any other vocalist of the country has been comparable to him.

Yet there are some who are likely to sniff at this attempt to put Ghulam Ali on a pedestal. Indeed, quite a few experts of musical theory and veteran listeners insist that he is really a master of the light classical variety, not of authentic *khayāl-gāyakī*. This may be taken to imply either that Ghulam Ali is better as a *ṭhumrī*-singer than as a *khayāliyā* or that his *khayāl*-singing does not really bring out the dignity or high seriousness — as distinguished from other attributes, such as imaginative richness and melodic appeal — of this particular genre of vocal music. The first implication, I believe, is reducible to the second.

To say that Ghulam Ali is better as a *ṭhumrī*-singer than as a *khayāliyā* is clearly to mean that his *khayāl*-singing does not approximate as closely to the ideal of this art-form as his *ṭhumrī*-singing does to the ideal *ṭhumrī*. So let us now reflect over the respective ideals of these two forms of our vocal music. It may be said that whereas *ṭhumrī* revels essentially in the erotic and the fanciful without, however, being confined to them, *khayāl* traverses the entire gamut of human emotions with a sustained imaginativeness which is not the same thing as little, isolated acts of fancy aiming merely at a varying, rather than at the deep and seamless evocation of a distinct melodic ambience. In the process of doing so, one may add, *khayāl* can even look contemplative and serene. In the context of such a view, the protest being considered would mean that Ghulam Ali's *khayāl*-singing does not have the requisite amount of expressional variety and depth or power of treatment. Now, admitting that he could sing the light classical varieties of vocal music such as *ṭhumrī*s, *ghazal*s, *pahāṛī*s and *bhajan*s remarkably well, let us now proceed to see how far his *khayāl*-singing can be fairly accused of being deficient in respect of the true classical idiom.

Here, I would like to open with a question at once. Can any one say, justifiably, that Ghulam Ali's *taan*s lack imaginative quality or creative spontaneity? My answer is negative and is based on my personal experience. I can also justify my stance with due reason. During his repeat performance at the Khadi Exhibition held at Delhi, which I had the privilege of organizing in April 1954, the maestro himself declared that his patterns were spontaneous outpourings of a feeling imagination and not a mere reproduction of something pre-planned. I think this is true. When I say so, I am not oblivious of the fact that Ghulam Ali had devoted long years of rigorous *riyāz* to the mastery of the patterns he appeared to execute so effortlessly at every concert. After all, spontaneity is not really a complete breakaway from the past. Not only in the case of music but in artistic creation taken generally, spontaneity only means that what has been assiduously cultivated in the past, but is not an object of conscious thought, right now — that is, till just before the actual moment of its present use — becomes readily available for the purpose of creating beauty. Here the element of freedom resides in the very facility with which some suggestion from the present may quicken the fruits of a long and arduous discipline into operative impulse. These suggestions can arise either from the outer environment, or from the artiste's own awareness of what is demanded as the next step, by the present moment in the run of music itself.

As I say so, I am happily reminded of what once happened at the residence of the late Ustad Chand Khan, the well-known vocalist of the Delhi Gharānā. The occasion was a feast given in honour of Ghulam Ali. When he had just finished a song and was tuning his *sur mandal* for another, a cat suddenly jumped into the centre of this gathering and then shuffled away. This movement caught the maestro's watchful eye; and, looking amused, he readily remarked, "this is how it went"; and so saying he at once produced an improptu *taan* which, in respect of the manner of its run, appeared an almost perfect parallel of the way the cat had rushed into and out of the gathering! Those who were present on the occasion were only tickled for a moment, but *I* have always regarded it as a very clear evidence of Ghulam Ali's remarkable capacity to adapt his patterns to suggestions of the moment.

The second instance which I recollect in this context is more revealingly pertinent. It occurred as a memorable incident in the last (*bhairavī*) number of his second recital at the Khadi Exhibition referred to earlier. The artiste, the audience, and the early morning all seemed to be under a spell when suddenly the shriek of a railway engine broke out from somewhere behind the stage and threatened to shatter the magic with its shrill, discordant sound. But how could the sensitive Ghulam

Ali allow the disharmony to persist? He forthwith let his voice fly meteorically to the *taar saptak;* made it merge with, and linger for a moment at the shriek of the engine; and then, using that high note as the point of take-off, he executed a beautiful, fluent *avarohī* pattern which cancelled the otherness of the noise completely, and even made it look integral to the run of the *taan*. There is no greater proof of an artiste's imaginative power than this capacity to transmute a quite unforeseen and utterly alien detail into the material of beauty so readily.

Philosophy does not find it easy, though it often tries to resolve discordances by putting them in a wider context; but creativity in the region of art is in fact seen to accomplish this end quite freely. Ghulam Ali could indeed attain such complete oneness with the spirit of music during the course of singing that, if only occasionally, even deviant particulars yielded to the "plastic stress" of this attunement, becoming an element of musical charm. That explains why, like other great *vocalists*, he could (for a moment) incorporate a *vivādi* or unprescribed (not *varjit*) *svara* in his singing without any detriment to melody, of course after evoking an intense musical spell of the *rāga* being sung.

It is quite evident that such aesthetic ends cannot be attained without a perfect prior mastery over technique. It has not been easy for me to isolate and identify the details of Ghulam Ali's technical prowess, and the reason simply is that, because of their mellifluous quality and meteoric fluency, his recitals had about them a coercive wholeness which made immediate analysis not only difficult but unwelcome. Subsequent analytic attention, however, made it clear to me that he generally preferred to execute those *taan*s which had a free-flowing, expansive movement as against those of the *uljhattī* variety which excel in ornateness and intricacy woven around two or three specific *svara*s, rather than in simplicity and sweep. This does not, however, mean that he was incapable of executing intricate patterns. I remember it clearly that in his *adānā khayāl: Ram charho . . .* at the National Festival of Music in 1955, he executed many complex *taans* with abandon and delightful effect. As a rule, however, his recitals bore out his set view that the real style of good *khayāl*-singing is *ekahrī gāyakī*, that is, patterns which describe a more or less clear ascent-descent order, as distinguished from those which show the voice first rising to a *svara* and then repeatedly reinforcing it with other flourishes that gather themselves up from somewhere below that note. He was also emphatic on the point that *khayāl*-singing should steer clear of *taans* of the *tappā* variety which, though admittedly skilful, are clearly a bit too restless and intricate to present an easily followable look or to chime with the dominant emotive colour of the total singing. What is more, because of their *unexpected* turns and twists, they also deny the *rasika* a very legitimate pleasure, namely, the pleasure of visualizing *successfully* the next melodic step on the basis of what is presently heard.

The character or design of Ghulam Ali's *phirat* never violated the requisite look of a *taan* as an artistic device. As a distinct facet of *khayāl*-singing, a *taan* must possess some essential features. First, at no point of its flowing form should the singer's *akāra* show any waning of its colour, roundness, inner evenness of texture and sweetness. Second, a *taan* must have a distinctive design, or else it is a mere collocation of notes rather than a pattern. What is more, this design should not be too difficult to follow; otherwise it will fail to win wide and ready appeal. *Such* appeal, I may add, is demanded by the very way in which *rāga* is freely defined, that is, as *rañjako janacittānām*. And as for *taans*, their very basic purpose is to embellish and not only to complicate or merely overlay the melodic form. Thirdly, as I have already insisted, it should be able to blend continuity of flow with clarity of constituent notes.

Ghulam Ali's *taans* met all these requirements admirably.

However, there is a particular feature of his *taans* which deserves special mention. In the *adānā* rendering which I have already referred to, I noticed that Ghulam Ali would first execute a very fluent *ārohī taan* in his usual impeccable manner, and would then etherealize it, so to say, at the very last note, into a flowing breath of sweetness, impressively supple but without inner marks, and flashing to the *taar* with remarkable effect. To me this particular detail of his *gāyakī* is a quite singular use of the psychological principle of figure and ground. Though it comes *as a sequel*, the sheer flow which follows the beaded pattern serves as the ground against which the earlier sequence of round, shapely *svaras* appears to be all the more articulate; and, what is more, because of the very quick pace of singing, the listener does not find it difficult to hold on to both the pattern's undivided sweep and its, so to say, multi-beaded filling. The result is that the whole *taan* comes to look like the starlit silvery haze that makes the milky way. It is important to note that in such cases the *taan*'s effect on the mind emerges only when the flow in question too has been duly registered. The pliancy of the voice as it glides, without any break, across the different *rāga-svaras* is itself a specific formal excellence, which has to be cultivated expressly by the *khayāl*-singer. Ghulam Ali also uses it in keeping the *sthāyī* undivided on the inside, but his distinctive employment of it is seen in providing relief to a flowing *taan* with a filling of *svaras* of undimmed *dānā* or discreteness, in the manner I have just indicated.

Sheer excellence of execution, however, does not exhaust the art of Ghulam Ali. His imagination too could work sensitively. I say this because of his ability to utilize the aesthetic principle of sound-sense harmony. Thus, to turn again to his recital at the National Festival to which I have already referred, I recall that in one of the pieces the image of an army's invasion was duly projected through a matching vocal pattern. On the same occasion, during the course of the *ashtapadī* that he sang in *rāga Des*, the word *lalit* was sung exactly as the word's very meaning demanded, that is, in terms of a beautiful vocal phrase. In the *ghazal*, where the threatening heavens were addressed as follows: *abre siyāh tū jhūmtā ātā hai kidhar se*, the thunder of the gathering clouds and the nightingale's warble were both pictured in terms of adroitly adapted *taans*. I was also struck by the way the maestro pictured the image of rain, that is, by means of a fascinating *avaroha taan* which looked as if there was a virtual drizzle from the heavens above. Such moments of singing, we may note, are as much an index of the vocalist's own ability as of the intrinsic aesthetic potential of the art of music.

It would, however, be wrong to suppose that Ghulam Ali was a master of melody alone. Rhythm and what we call *layakārī* also had its due place in his art. However, let me first explain what the second term means in the context of music-making.

As indicated and kept by a drum, *laya* is the even pace of music as it runs through *tāla* (or rhythm) with its ordered emphases of *khālī*, *bharī* and *sama*. *Layakārī* is the musician's skill as seen in making *laya* appear to assert its own vitality, so to say, partly by refusing to conform all along to the set accents of the rhythm(-cycle) and partly in terms of passages, comprising *bol*s or *svaras*, which show that distinctions of *mātrā*s and *bol*s, though admittedly important, do not disrupt the original singleness of *laya* or exhaust the creativity it admits of. Taking the two together, we may say that the major marks of *layakārī* are as follows: emphasis (in the flow of *laya*) on those accents which are different, or appear displaced from the ones which have been identified, fixed and named in the form of a *ṭhekā;* instances of how the *sama* can in fact be arrived at in a shapely manner from almost any moment in the recurrent form of the *ṭhekā*, and not only from its clearly marked sub-divisions, so as to suggest to the thoughtful eye that the distinctions which *tāla* brings in — though undeniably of help — are not quite as necessary as *the mind's self-identification with the manner and speed of laya itself*. An intentional avoidance (by *laya*) of the set moment of the *sama* by pausing a little short of, or by slightly overstepping the *moment*, gives rise to those rare forms of *layakārī* which are known as *anāgat* and *atīt*.

Yet, whatever be the specific form of *layakārī*, *laya* is always felt as retaining, in the minds of both the artiste and *rasikas*, its essential seamless flow; otherwise, the structure of music and our relish of it will both tend to suffer. Now, not all the forms of *layakārī* I have distinguished are visible in Ghulam Ali's singing, although he always took care to see that his handling of rhythm never degenerated into a random and jerky accentuation of any moment within the *ṭhekā*, accompanied — in the case of some *khayāliās* — by that fake look of confidence which serves more to conceal their deficient hold over *laya* as a continuous flow than to work up any likeable effect. Aesthetic coherence is, indeed, the one quality which Ghulam Ali never sacrificed and I have never seen him fumble in his approach to the *sama*. On the other hand, he always displayed a remarkable capacity to attain this pivotal beat from the most unsuspected moment in the rhythm-cycle. By itself, this ability may not be very remarkable, since only a little practice is needed to remember and mark the *sama*-moment. What is noteworthy in the art of Ghulam Ali is a quite different excellence. His *sama* appears as *the self-completion of a shapely passage;* and because of the rapidity and design of the movement the *sama* which brings it to a close appears *as a climax and no mere terminus*. The pace of the passage is so quick that we become clearly aware of it only when it ends *and not when it runs its course*. This surely requires unremitting awareness of the pace and extent of the rhythm-cycle on the musician's part. What is more, Ghulam Ali often reaches the *sama* through deft, little *tiyās* or threefold divisions of a *svara*-pattern, every segment following the earlier one after a very brief pause. The pace at which the segments unfold themselves is so fluent, their sweetness so unremitting and the space between them so little, that they seem to belong to each other in spite of the intervals that in fact separate them. Such adroitly sung bunches of *svaras* clearly show how the Gestalt law of *good contour* or *common destiny* actually works.

It is true that Ghulam Ali rarely sang in such *tāla*s as *jhoomrā* and *tilawāṛā*, and that his favourite measures were *tritāla, jhaptāla* and *ektāla*. Further, he was generally "accompanied" by his own *tablā* player whose manner of playing, though it never looked really polished, was of definite help to the vocalist because it kept the main accents of the *ṭhekā* quite open to view all along. However, no such consideration may be allowed to detract from the truth of what I have said about this vocalist's hold over *laya*. I clearly remember that he never wavered in keeping to rhythm. Above all, in his recitals Ghulam Ali never committed the aesthetic outrage of projecting *layakārī* in isolation from other aspects of music, which is why his singing always appeared intense and undivided on the inside, and possessed of a coereive wholeness of appeal. It is one thing to take different aspects of *gāyakī* one by one, and to dwell upon them alternately; and quite another to deal with them in such a manner that they may all appear complementary to one another. The former appears loose internally and can never throw a spell over the audience; the other is compact and almost irresistible in its effect, provided of course the basic requirement of melody is duly kept. In fact, whatever Ghulam Ali would do on the stage, and I am not talking of what he did *not* do there, appeared beyond reproach. Take his *sargams*, for instance. He never presented them as a mere series of isolated notes: he would rather make them dance and sparkle, in addition to keeping them perfectly tuneful.

Here, again, I cannot help recalling his recital at Ustad Chand Khan's house, to which I have already referred. After we had all snacked on biscuits, some *namkeen* and a cup of tea, and sat keyed up for the music to follow, Ghulam Ali, with the *sur mandal* nestling in his lap, began toying with some *sargams* in *Bhairavī* with such consummate abandon and grace that though the effect was only one of playfulness and not of high seriousness, his tremendous hold over melody and finesse in execution overwhelmed us, even before he began a regular *bandish*. I had never seen him falter in completing a *taan* or in gaining access to the *sama*. *Gamak aṅg* patterns, sung in a perfectly rounded *akāra* and quite without any trace of exertion; a telling employment of what is called the reverse twist of voice; and a pervasive fluency coupled with sweetness, soft and lush — these are some of the other outstanding excellences which made the music of Ghulam Ali memorable.

Mention may also be made of another subtlety of Ghulam Ali's way of singing. His trellis work of *taans* would often be abundant, but it never hid for long the form of the first line or *sthāyī*. A close look at his recorded music shows that he resiles to the first line after two or three quick *taans* have been completed. The device is obviously simple, but not every good vocalist realises its value. Ghulam Ali remembers that if their ground is eclipsed, the *taans* are likely to come to appear as a mere maze and not patterns of beauty. How indeed can anything appear as a figure except as against a background which has to look steadfast, recurrent though it may actually be? I also feel sure that Ghulam Ali had mastered some excellences of *dhruvapad* singing too. Correct intonation of *anunāsika* letters — that is, singing them with due, yet unforced regard to the nasal element of sound — is essential for a *dhruvapad* singer. Now, I have seen Bade Ghulam Ali meeting this demand admirably, say, in the utterance of such words as *gaṅgā* and *laṅkā*. He also seemed to realize that, in such cases, the requisite look of sound is brought out better in *ascending passages than in abidance at individual notes*. Further, such formal excellences as a sudden, sweeping descent from *taar sa* to the ground *sa* — describing a trail (so to say) in the way of a meteor — are a common source of delight in his singing. I have a definite feeling that Ghulam Ali had gained something positive from listening to such *dhruvapad* masters as Ustads Allabande Khan and Nasiruddin Khan. Even when he had risen to the very top of the music world, he appeared keen to listen to the music of Ustad Rahimuddin Khan Dagar.

Ghulam Ali has distinguished himself essentially because of his own excellences, a major one of them being the ability to imbue his singing with feeling, which is true of every vocal form he revelled in: *khayāl, pahāṛī, ṭhumrī* and *bhajan*. I am aware of the charge that a Ghulam Ali *baḍā khayāl* often appears to be deficient in its requisite depth or dignity; and I do not wish to meet it straight away. The pace of dignity is, as a rule, slow. The *net* impression of Ghulam Ali's recitals, on the other hand, would be one of fluency, sweetness and brilliance, rather than one of repose or contemplativeness. However, a semblance of the latter qualities did often appear, particularly when he tarried at a particular note, say, the *taar shadj*. Ghulam Ali's own rejoinder to the protest may be put thus: evocation of an overall look of such effects as dignity, poise, self-possession or sublimity is the function of *ālāpa* of the *dhruvapad* manner and of some *dhruvapad* songs of *ārādhanātmaka* kind, not of *khayāl*. The distinctive marks of *khayāl*, he would add, are imaginative richness and creative freedom. This answer, however, is not likely to silence the sceptics; for *rasika*s today are quite familiar with the art of some *khayāliyā*s whose manner is not marred by the deficiency we have been talking of and whose singing cannot yet be accused of a lack of imaginative richness. The main vocalists I have here in mind are Pandits Bhim Sen Joshi and Ulhas Kashalkar. But I hesitate to say something definite on the matter right now, as it calls for some careful thinking which I propose to do towards the close of the essay.

Presently, let me just say something about Ghulam Ali's

early years, as also about some of his pet views. The maestro was born at Lahore in 1902, his father being none other than the famous Ustad Ali Bux. At the age of seven, the young Ghulam Ali was put under the coaching of his uncle, the late Ustad Kale Khan. The ceremony was attended by such celebrated figures in the field of music as Mian Jan Khan, Khadim Hussain, Chajjoo Khan and Nazeer Khan. After learning for ten long years under his uncle, Ghulam Ali chose to sit at the feet of his father, about whom he would frankly and lovingly say that no other man had impressed him more as a connoisseur of *khayāl-gāyakī*. Ali Bux also trained his son in the technique of *ṭhumrī* and *dhruvapad* singing. These two teachers of Ghulam Ali — Kale Khan and Ali Bux — were themselves direct pupils of such eminent Ustads as Mehram Khan, Mubarak Ali and Tanras Khan. These details should serve to explain the amazing richness of Ghulam Ali's own singing.

As for his views on the art he so dearly cherished, though he surely admired the growing popularity of classical music in India, Ghulam Ali would at the same time deplore the present tendency to lay too much emphasis on mere theory. Insofar as music is essentially a practical art, he would argue, we should be more particular about rigorous practice than about mere abstract understanding. That actual learning under the immediate presence of a master, and not his mere imitation from a distance, is the real secret of ultimate success; that preferring mere fluency to sweetness is a positive defect; that, instead of singing the full *sthāyī-antarā* twosome, some present-day *khayāliyā*s show a lamentable tendency to let a mere *bol* or two serve as (an apology for) *sthāyī*; and that, on the whole, the quality of *khayāl*-singing is slowly declining, — these are some of the more important views of Ustad Bade Ghulam Ali Khan.

His own emphasis, he would add, had always been on regular *riyāz* and effective singing on the stage.

This is surely borne out by the remarkably consistent quality of his public concerts. Yet, in casual talk, he would occasionally pick the following two of them for special mention: one that he gave in the presence of the Prince of Wales on his first visit to India, and the other at the 1921 Lucknow Conference in the presence of the famous *ālāpiyā*, the late Ustad Allabande Khan. In later years, of course, Ghulam Ali had come to win a reputation which, in respect of both extent and genuineness, could be the envy of the best of our musicians. He never claimed that he was greater than the famous old masters of the Patiala Gharānā, Ali Bux and Fateh Ali. Yet it is unquestionable that he has kept up the glorious traditions of his *gharānā*, and is bound to go down in history not only as the most extensively admired vocalist of his day, but as one of the all-time greats.

However, it would not be fair if I closed this essay without giving thought to some such criticisms of Ghulam Ali's art as have not been addressed so far.

a. First, is it not a fact that Ghulam Ali scored mostly through *rāga*s like *Mālkaus, Bhūpālī, Bhairavī, Jogiyā* and *Deśa,* and not by singing, say, *Āsāvrī, Jaitśrī* and *Lalit Pañcham?* I say, yes, at once; but does the admission prove that the maestro could not properly sing the last three *rāga*s listed? Maybe he avoided the *rāga*s in question simply because he had his own reasons for avoiding them. Which of the two, he could ask, is more binding on a musician — showing off how skilfully he can handle a difficult *rāga,* or how abounding in ever new beauty even a popular *rāga* can look in his hands? Logically, I may add, what one *does not* do is not a sure index of what one *cannot* do.

b. Second, is it not unchallengeable that the *vilambit sthāyī*s of Ghulam Ali are not quite as tranquil as they should

> be? And is it not a fact that the net and overall look of his singing has always been one of nimbleness and tonal dynamics, rather than that of self-possessed, reposeful singing which is an obvious demand of the *vilambit* idiom in our music?

To this I may rejoin as follows:

If Ghulam Ali is (allegedly) inferior to one or two vocalists in this one respect, is he not clearly very superior to the generality of top class singers in at least two respects, namely, fluency and unflagging sweetness of tone? And those who are credited with a more reposeful manner of *sthāyī*-singing, are they really able to make the first line appear as a *bandish* (or composition) in the true sense, that is, as not just completing itself somehow and ultimately at the *sama*, but also as appearing undivided on the inside? Further, where the *ṭhekā* has been set at a very slow pace, and the singer completes the first line in mere tonal snatches, separated by pretty long intervals of silence, is it *vilambit* of singing *or* only of the rhythm? Here, as apprehended in idea, only the flow of *laya* remains undivided, not the singing, not even as a semblance. Above all, if being-in-*sur* is the most fundamental requirement of every form of our classical music, should not Ghulam Ali be given a place of pre-eminence?

Personally, considering the whole range of Hindustānī classical vocal music, and bearing in mind the traditional Indian view of the paramount aim of music, I cannot rank the *khayāl*-form as aesthetically superior to *ālāpa* at its best, or to such *dhruvapad*s of *ārādhanā* as permit very little *upaj* or rhythmic variations. But if individual vocalists be ranked from the comprehensive viewpoint of tonal sweetness, power, fluency, extent of appeal, along with fidelity to grammatical norms, I cannot help venturing the view that, after Ustad Faiyāz Khan, Hindustānī music has not produced any *gāyak* who could be said to be unquestionably superior to Ghulam Ali. The mellifluous fluency of his *taan*s would often leave the *rasika* somewhat awestruck; and I wonder if this could be regarded as perhaps the clearest instance, in our music, of what Kant spoke of as dynamical sublimity. What, however, can be said more intelligibly and acceptably about the maestro's surpassing excellence has been put as follows, with admirable brevity, by *The Hindu*'s well-known music critic and my good friend, the late Prakash Wadhera:

> He (Ghulam Ali) weighed everything in the balance of aesthetical beauty, rejecting all that was harsh and clumsy.[6]

6. Prakash Wadhera, "The Phenomenon that was Bade Ghulam Ali."

12

The Mind and Art of Ustad A. Rahimuddin Khan Dagar[1]

"I DO NOT claim ability to unravel the ultimate mysteries of music, Professor Sahib; but, God willing, I can surely try to take you to a point from where you may well be able to have a *darshan* (worshipful vision) of *sangeet*." These are the words with which Ustad Rahimuddin Khan greeted me when I first met him at a hotel in the Jama Masjid area of old Delhi. If I remember aright, the year was 1952; the month, a summer one definitely, for I can still clearly recall that on seeing me, then an utter stranger, the maestro hurriedly shoved into his crumpled *kurtā* lying alongside his *pāndān*; and that my escort was his own only son, Fahimuddin, today the eldest living member of the famed Dagar family, and winner of almost every prestigious award accessible to India's top musicians. Years of happy fellowship rolled by thereafter; the "professor" became an endearing *bhaiyā*; and whereas the artist, with his music yet burgeoning in spite of long and unrelieved adversity, gained an avid and tireless one-man audience, the college teacher of

---

1. 'A' here stands for *Allahbande*, the first name of Ustad Rahimuddin Khan's father. This practice of prefacing one's own name with the first letter of father's name is typical of the entire Dagar family. Rahimuddin Khan would also insist on spelling his surname as *Dagur*. But the reason why I have preferred to spell the word as *Dagar* simply is that this is how other members of the family spell their surname and also how the family is known all over.

philosophy found himself sucked into a growing magic circle of melodic airs and phrases — and, at times, whole compositions — of ethereal charm, and so just could not help feeling obsessed with the thought that life had somehow to be made a little less difficult for this singer of an old-world yet irresistible appeal, so that he could be enabled to produce his best music not only in the presence of small gatherings at some friends' residences, but in well attended concert halls too.

Whatever now follows in the present chapter is a sequel to this providential but very tight bonding which I cherish to this day because it has not only provided to me numberless moments of sheer aesthetic rapture, but has so quickened my musical imagination that now I can at least try to catch in words some glimmer of that ethico-religious ambience which our music had yet to break through for settling itself, so to say, in an essentially secular terrain, abjuring its primal metaphysical goal for the sake of readier, wider entertainment (*lokarañjan*). This brief article is therefore partly a venture; and so, to make for clarity, I have to get on with the task step by step. Wherever, in the following, I turn to make a definite point, my thinking will either be simply an appeal to some assertion of the maestro himself *or* also a watchful construction thereon by me, but strictly in accord with the general look of his own music, as also with the dominant slant of his thinking on the art.

Ālāpa and the Maestro

What is *ālāpa*? A ready answer here would obviously be: it is effective singing without the aid of language and (beat-measured) rhythm. To say so, however, is hardly enough. Khan Sahib would often refer to what may be called the *mool mantra* of *ālāpa*,[2] which runs thus: *aum antartam tvam tāran taraṇī tvam*

---

2. For my knowledge of this *mantra* I am indebted not only to Ustad Rahimuddin Khan but also to his son, Ustad R. Fahimuddin Dagar.

anant hari nārāyaṇa Aum; and a little close reflection on this text throws up quite a few such ideas of value as are so far unsuspected, besides accounting for the maestro's own attitude during the course of doing *ālāpa*. Let me bring out the point at some length:

The sacred syllable *Aum*, which not only opens but also closes the *mantra* in question, is set forth in the Upaniṣads as an object of profound religious meditation, the highest spiritual efficacy being attributed not only to the whole word, but to its constituent letters. So, as it quietly prefaces *ālāpa*, it is on the one hand likely to remind a thoughtful and traditional *ālāpiyā* of our time-honoured view that music is a way to spiritual liberation (not a matter of mere entertainment);[3] and is, on the other hand, expected to evoke in him an attitude of reverence and humility towards what he is going to do, that is, music-making. (This, incidentally, would be visibly so during the greater part of Khan Sahib's own *ālāpa*-singing.) The point becomes clearer as we turn to see what the other words of the *mantra* signify. *Antartam* means the surpassing immanence (or immediacy, intimateness) of God (addressed as *tvam*); *ananta*, His infinity; and *tāran* and *taraṇī*, His being both the vehicle and agent of liberation from the birth-death cycle, and generally benevolent. The thought of His being benevolent is reinforced by the word *Hari* which not only means the One who relieves us from suffering and sinfulness, but, as taken along with *Nārāyaṇa*, also signifies the Hindu triad of Brahmā, Viṣṇu, and Mahesh. All in all, the *mantra* (I repeat) is expected to quicken a vocalist's mind with the thought that what he is going to do is not only a kind of offering to God, but is at once a drawing on His grace. This, I believe, is one key reason why *ālāpa* of the truly traditional kind has to open very reposefully and to proceed step by step, even as one approaches the centre of the

3. I have here in mind the following words of *Sangeet Ratnākar*: *muktidāyakama na tu rañjkama.*

temple, the sanctuary (or the seat of the deity), with measured steps and reverently — with unshod feet, as it were.

Literally, of course, the word *ālāpa* means: *addressing, speaking to, communication;* and the vocalist here certainly addresses the audience. But insofar as the orientation of his attention (as already pointed out) is not supposed to be merely secular, *ālāpa* (as a kind of address) is not the same in its purpose as, say, the *peshkār* or *farshbandi* of the solo *tablā*-player. Yet, just as the opening pattern, *peshkār* — as played by the maestros of Delhi and *ajrāḍā gharānā*s of *tablā* — comprises almost all the basic mnemonics of *tablā*-rhythm, so the *mool mantra* we have been talking of provides most of the letters that *ālāpa* utilizes. The more important of these are त, र, न and म (besides, of course, the basic letter अ). It is noteworthy that it is only these letters which the word अन्तरतम (in the *mool mantra*) comprises. For proper musical utterance and modulation of *akāra*, however, they need the help of those Hindi *mātrā*s that make for the आ, ई, ऐ sounds.

Our essential concern, however, is not with *ālāpa* taken generally, but with what Rahimuddin Khan thought of *ālāpa* and how he himself did it. Now, one particular remark that he would often attribute to his father, Ustad Allabande Khan, with obvious approval and relish — and which may be taken as some argument for the aesthetic necessity of *ālāpa* — runs thus: "*Svara* is something so delicate that it cannot bear the weight of words."[4] Now, it is obvious, this cannot be accepted in respect of the wholeness of *ālāpa*, for it simply misses the moments of power and majesty that can easily distinguish this genre of wordless music, and for which the *ālāpa* of Rahimuddin Khan's own uncle, Ustad Zakiruddin Khan, was so well known. But a dominant quality of the former's (that is, Allabande

4. This is a literal translation of the following vernacular text: "सुर वो नाज़ुक चीज़ है जो अल्फ़ाज़ का बोझ नहीं बरदाश्त कर सकती."

Khan's) own singing — I mean, its quintessential fineness — is quite well covered by the remark in question. How this particular quality figured in Rahimuddin Khan's singing, and how it blended with some other excellences to produce the remarkable effect that his *ālāpa* generally did, may now be brought out by recalling some of his better recitals, the memory of which still occasionally serves as the bliss of my solitude.[5]

Memorable Recitals

At my residence in 1953 he once sang so brilliantly in the presence of Ustad Chand Khan, his proteges Hilal Ahmed and Nasir Ahmed, and the *tablā* wizard, the late Ustad Habeebuddin Khan — who also provided "accompaniment" on this occasion — that we were all transported with sheer aesthetic rapture. Ustad Chand Khan remarked that the *ālāpa* was a kind of education for them all; and Habeebuddin Khan sighed that whereas in respect of other singers he thought he could well emulate them with a little serious *riyāz*, Rahimuddin Khan seemed unapproachable for ever.

In 1954 he gave two very competent recitals in the Music Conference organized by me as an adjunct of the All India Khadi & Village Industries Exhibition. Later in the year, in a programme presented by me at the Old Convocation Hall of University of Delhi — and attended by such masterly musicians within living memory as Ustads Hafiz Ali Khan (*sarod*), Sadiq Ali Khan (*veeṇā*), and Habeebuddin Khan (*tablā*), all of whom also performed on the occasion — Rahimuddin Khan astounded the (then) Speaker of the Lok Sabha, Sri Ananthasayanam Ayyangar, with his immaculate chanting of a Sanskrit *ashtapadī* as a preface to his bewitching *ālāpa*.

---

5. I borrow this image from Wordsworth's poem on daffodils, titled as "I wandered lonely as a cloud." See here the poem's closing lines.

It was, however, only in 1955 that his art got the notice it deserved. I refer here to his singing in the Music Festival organized (in March) by Bharatiya Kala Kendra, New Delhi, on the lawns of the Constitution Club. The fact that he was required to perform after the seductive *ghazal*s of Mubarak Hussain (and party) did nothing to ruffle him; and he opened with such a wondrous *ālāpa* in *rāga Hindol* that the *quawwāl* himself, sitting next to me, literally gasped in wonder. I think it here needful to recall what I wrote thereon in *The Hindustan Times* of 30 March, partly with a view to explaining how the very *number* of notes in a *rāga* may determine the distinctive structural look of a *bandish*:

> A *Hindol* of only four clear *svaras* (*sa, ga, ma, dha*) with the merest suggestion of *nishad* appears truly majestic. The very sparseness of the filling makes for a form of austere beauty, exactly as a few remote and lean columns can make a vaulted roof appear awesome. This explains the grandeur of the [maestro's] *dhruvapad* [that opened with the words: *nāda Brahma ko ādhār*. In the *Sohnī bhajan* that followed, the far-away look of *rishabh* (in the *taar*) which [looked like a stender and lumious beam], suggesting some detachedness [to me] moved even . . . Bade Ghulam Ali Khan (sitting in the audience) into open admiration.[6]

In a retrospective review, *The Tribune* highlighted an extra feature of the selfsame recital:

> In respect of sheer majesty of execution and consistent sweetness, Rahimuddin Khan's singing is hard to equal. Elizabeth Zuppinger, who gave a piano performance at the National Sports Club last month, was admired for the skilful way in which she conjured up a suggestion of the tinkling of bells. Rahimuddin Khan was seen accomplishing the more difficult task of giving the same suggestion vocally, by

6. As cited here, the extract is slightly different from its original form in the paper.

> articulating the *taar shadj* in the *anuraṇātmaka* way. Here, in fact, we had the additional suggestion that the tinkling was now approaching, now receding, exactly like the one that is produced by the swinging temple-bells.[7]

At Bombay, in the Haridas Sangeet Sammelan of 1956 Khan Sahib sang with such irresistibleness that the listeners clamoured for letting him continue as long as he wanted to. The clock on the stage, indicating the total time allowed for a performance, was taken away forthwith!

In the Radio Sangeet Sammelan of the same year, Khan Sahib sang *rāga Darbārī*. Commenting thereon, the music critic of *The Statesman* acclaimed the "sense of space and repose" that distinguished the *ālāpa*, and *The Times of India* reacted as follows:

> Then came a sensitive, highly tranquillising vocal recital — that of Ustad Rahim-ud-din Khan Dagar. His *rāga* was *Darabarī kanhra*. The treatment of *ālāpa* was eloquent. Khan Sahib displayed an uncanny feeling for correct intonations particularly in his tender approaches to *gandhār* and *dhaivat*. He constructed a sound base on *shadj* upon which he laid the super-structure of a sombre edifice of melody.[8]

In *The Hindustan Times* I wrote the following on this *Darbārī*:

> Two or three renderings of *gandhāra* were immaculate. The note here appeared . . . an aesthetic gem. Moveless in being, it suggested oscillation, even like a prospect which both is and has yet to actualize itself.[9]

In 1958 Rahimuddin Khan gave his second "national programme" from the All India Radio. Here, again, a "critical"

---

7. *The Tribune* of Ambala, 24.4.1955.
8. *The Times of India*, Delhi, 21.10.1957.
9. *The Hindustan Times*, 21.10.1957.

notice may be quoted specially because it makes comments of value on the essential nature and aesthetic necessity of *ālāpa*:

> The opening *ālāpa* in *rāga Mālkaus* was . . . a passionate vindication of its aesthetic necessity. The warrant of *ālāpa* as a distinct form of singing is its ability to accommodate those formal excellences which textual singing can only blur, broaden or blight. Rahimuddin Khan's *ālāpa* used some of these with commendable effect: chiefly *lahak, mīṇḍ, gamak, vedāng, dyut* and *anuraṇātamaka.* It is excellences such as these which make *ālāpa* a perfect identity of form and content. The singing in question (I may add) rebutted the myth that the appeal of *ālāpa* is purely perceptual. *Ālāpa* is pure music, to be sure; but it is pure, not in the sense of having no ideal significance, but [negatively, in that of being quite without any non-melodic accretion, and positively] in virtue of being, in principle, unremittingly and exactly in tune. True *ālāpa* enables us to visualize not indirectly through the meaning of words — which it obviously eschews — but directly through the breath of its being, that is, as sheer sound, even as a tear may at once look sad; or a shady nook, cool.[10]

It would, however, be wrong to think that Rahimuddin Khan could cater only for classically trained listeners. In response to my humble requests, he sang freely for motley audiences of students and teachers on the campus of Delhi University, and always most effectively. The listeners, I distinctly remember, would feel very deeply touched and *look* visibly so; and such of them as really knew classical music would marvel at the way Rahimuddin Khan would appear to transcend the best that we find in the region of this art. One of these recitals, presented at Vivekanand Hall of the Delhi School of Economics by the Delhi University Music Society in August 1958, elicited the following thoughtful comment from a critic:

---

10. From *The Hindustan Times* of 28.4. 1958. Rahimuddin Khan's first National Programme (A.I.R.) was broadcast on 8.3.1955.

> In respect of bringing out the inherent . . . richness of a single *svara* (or of a tiny tuft of *svaras*), Rahimuddin Khan's *ālāpa* in *rāga Pūriyā* was remarkably effective. Whether in the lingering rendering of a single note, or (in) a simple, unconstrained, descending *taan*, music here was always sweet and chaste. The aesthetic effects conjured up were at places bewildering because of the simple, apparently artless way in which they stole into us. Sparkle, yearning tenderness, piercing the *svara* at the very centre of its luminous halo, — these were some of the more important effects worked up.[11]

My own impression of this recital is that of a luminous *ni* (in the *madya*) which just seemed disembodied, a sweet omnipresence, a free and intense diffusion. In about fifty years of my experience as a listener at classical concerts I have not been blessed with a more satisfying feel of the power of a single *svara*. To *speak* of infinity as implicit in a note or in the compass of some *mātrās* is one thing; to show it up in practice, is quite another.

The master I speak of was indeed very mindful of the proper *musical utterance* of the single note, as against merely *naming or identifying* it. I am here reminded of a Seminar organized by the Gandharva Mahavidyalaya, New Delhi, on the occasion of their 1957 Vishnudigambar Jayanti. Participants included such scholars as Thakur Jaideo Singh, Ustad Vilayat Hussain Khan and Principal S.N. Ratanjankar. When the talk turned to the *dhevat* of *rāga Lalit*, Rahimuddin Khan insisted on *showing* what it was rather than merely *naming* it; and, quite without the aid of a *tānpūrā*, he sang it so many times as the mere disappearing accent of an *avaroha taan*, and with such immaculate sweetness that the merest hint, as against a steadfast singing of the note, won immediate applause even from lay listeners. Another such instance of extempore illustration that I am here reminded of is the Seminar organized, a few years

11. *The Hindustan Times*, 24.8. 1958.

later,[12] by the Music Faculty of Delhi University. The place was the hall of the Faculty of Arts. Here, the Ustad astounded and delighted everyone by analysing lines of a popular film song[13] and showing how their accents of melodic appeal have been consciously cultivated and built upon by *ālāpa* of the *dhruvapad* kind, all in terms of actual singing; and once again without the help of any "accompaniment."

To turn again to the maestro's full length concerts, the one that is unforgettable to me relates to the Radio Sangeet Sammelan of 1956. It elicited from *The Times of India*'s music critic the following very apt comment:

> The finest recital of the day came from Rahim-ud-din Khan Dagar whose treatment of *toḍī* was *an embodiment of repose and tranquillity.*[14]

My own detailed write-up on the same may here be cited (with some changes) by way of explaining not merely this vocalist's attitude to single *svara*s, but also how his *ālāpa* was distinguished by quite a few delightful formal graces:

> His attitude to a note is profoundly different from that of the average singer. It is throughout gentle, at times even reverent. Often, with a view to injecting *ālāpa* with a little sparkle he sings a *svara* [as just a throb]. Or, he may make it tarry as a fount of luminous feeling! It is this manner of lavishing love on details which gave to his *rishabh* in the *taar* a far-away look at some places, making it seem detached or *sannyastha* [as the maestro himself would prefer to call it].
>
> Above all, a *svara* in his *ālāpa* at times appears as a halo of light that is not only to be noticed but (so to say) lived from

12. In 1966, from 14 to 17 March, to be precise.
13. From the film *Nagin*. The song opens thus:

    "मेरा दिल ये पुकारे आजा"
14. My italics.

> within. This . . . allows contemplation in the midst of creation and makes us *see* the meaning of the view that the singer's best moments are those of self-absorption in the constancy of a [single] *svara* ('अचल सुर में लीन होत').
>
> Thus alone does the treatment of *svara* answer its definition as *svyameva rājate*, or as that which is not merely self-existent, but self-luminous. It is such a manifold and detailed treatment of a *svara* that purifies feeling, sharpens the intellect, and moves us beyond words.
>
> Fineness, animation, sweep and sparkle — these were the four essential graces of his *ālāpa*. The suggestion of vigour was provided by subtlaties known as *hudak* and *sphūrt*; of fineness in movement by *lahak* and *anunāsika*; and of sparkle and resonance by *vedāṅg* and *anuraṇātmaka* . . . Sometimes the last of these was used to work up a halo of woolly glow around *taar sa*. The articulation of *sargam*s (or note-names) never seemed a mere arrangement of inert points . . . , the *svara*s, in fact, would seem to twinkle in a liquid radiance.[15]

By this *ālāpa*, I still clearly remember, Thakur Jaideo Singh[16] was moved into a very feeling compliment: "*This* was, to be sure, a parallel of the music of *gandharva*s. Where else has it been heard, Khan Sahib, in our mundane experience?"

Some Aesthetic Analysis

A little more analysis may here be permitted, for it was in *ālāpa* that Rahimuddin Khan revelled. It would, as a rule, be exceptionally sweet; and look *sāttvik* too, unlike the usual kind of likeable singing. The suggestion of depth was here produced

---

15. This, Khan Sahib assured me, was a distinguishing feature of the singing of his father, Ustad Allabande Khan.

16. In the period to which this concert relates, Thakur Sahib, I may add, was not only the Chief Music Producer at A.I.R. (Delhi) but was widely regarded as an authentic *rasika* and musicologist.

not directly by the quality of his voice — which seemed a little deficient in volume — nor even by curvilinear *passages* from one note to another, as has always distinguished the Dagar Brothers' singing; but by the steady, contemplative utterance of individual notes. A *rasika* would here be struck also by an effective employment of *diverse* formal graces like *dyut, vedāṅg* and the *anuraṇātmaka* way of singing. All this made his *ālāpa* appear unmistakably "vocal," and utterly distinct from *ālāpa* on the *veeṇā*. At quite a few places it would seem just daintily linear. Fineness, repose, a certain ethereality, and a woolly, regulated (*anuraṇātmaka*) glow, in addition to consistent sweetness, were indeed the major effects of Rahimuddin Khan's *ālāpa. Occasionally, depth was here manifest in the manner of a sigh, as a reflex of inwardness, not of physical bulk; and what led to the overall purity of effect, in the absence of words, was a daintiness of manner that spoke to the spirit, instead of titillating sense or amorous fancy.*

However, I do not wish to underrate *ālāpa* of the *veeṇā* way. In fact, I have not yet forgotten the overwhelming effect of *such ālāpa* as once *sung* by the maestro in the presence of his son and the late Ustad Sadiq Ali Khan, a recognized *veeṇā* player. The occasion was an informal get-together at my residence.[17] Asad Ali, the instrumentalist's own son,[18] began playing *Bhīmpalāsī*; and something in the rendering so touched Rahimuddin Khan that he began *singing in the idiom of the instrument*. It was a lively, ceaseless, up-and-down flow of the *rāga* as disembodied, so to say, from its constituent *svara*s where the voice rarely tarried; and the impact was such that I soon found it unbearable, and had in fact to pray for its immediate closure. Ustad Sadiq Ali Khan, on the other hand, was literally in tears, averring that the unusual singing by the masterly *ālāpiyā*

17. In the winter of 1954-55.

18. And today, one of the country's top *veeṇā* players.

was a cruel reminder of what *veeṇā*-playing *used to be* in olden days.

It would, however, be wrong to believe that the art of Rahimuddin Khan was simply an extension of tradition. His own imagination was pretty lively, and I may here cite what I wrote more than fifty years back:

> I have seen Ustad Rahimuddin Khan Dagar delighting an audience of university teachers with an evocation, through *ālāpa*, of the image of a flower opening up gently to the rays of the sun. In such cases the audience has, of course, to be notified in advance. But the interruption . . . is more than set off by the completeness of delight which follows.[19]

Here a *visual* effect is worked up through the medium of *sound*. So it is not imitation, but a clear case of what Susanne K. Langer calls *transformation*, that is,

> the rendering of a desired appearance without any actual representation of it, by the production of an *equivalent* sense-impression, rather than a literally similar one, in terms of the limited, legitimate material which cannot naively copy the desired property of the model.[20]

Rarities of Structure, Execution

Specific aesthetic *effects*, however, are not everything about the art of Rahimuddin Khan. He had a rich repertoire of *compositions* as well. Some of these which the maestro often sang to me on request, but hardly ever presented to regular audiences, may be mentioned here in brief, primarily for the purpose of showing how a *bandish* may be distinguished by its adroit

---

19. See my essay, *Ustad A. Rahimuddin Khan Dagar*, in *Sangeet Natak*, 39, January–March 1976, pp. 8-9.

20. S.K. Langer, *Problems of Art*, London: Routledge & Kegan Paul, 1957, p. 98.

employment of the principle of sound-sense harmony. I recall, to begin with, a (*gurjarī*) *toḍī dhruvapad* set to *sool tala*:

कीन्हीं सकल सृष्टि इक छिन में,
उन साहब करतार

Here, the word छिन (in *sthāyī*) would be sung by Khan Sahib in such a manner that it not merely *conveyed* its meaning, but in fact *looked* briefer than the merest point of time, and yet a clear accent of *springiness*, which was only demanded by the thought of *bringing the universe* (सकल सृष्टि) *into being* quite abruptly, and not by any laboured process. And a little later, in the same composition, the word *sapnā*, suggesting the transitoriness of whatever the world presents, would be so skilfully sung — by means of a निधमगरे *anudātta* glide which would seem *to fade in colour, without becoming unmusical* — that evanescence itself would seem *held up to view*, and not merely *meant* by the word. I can only wonder how challenging it must have been for the composer to create a tonal analogue of such a concept as that of transitoriness.[21]

The working of the principle in question, I recall, would be *more clearly manifest* in Khan Sahib's *dhruvapads* of *ārādhanā* which aim, in the main, at saturating the singer himself with devout feeling, and not at entertaining an audience. Here, *upaj* (as creative variations) has to be minimal, if not totally absent; and the basic requirement is adaptation of the run of music *not to the meanings of individual words, but to the general feeling permeating the text*. Some of such compositions which the maestro could sing not only to a nicety but with remarkable effect are as follows: "आज आयो आनन्द" in *rāga Jogiā Āsāvari;* "जय जय जग जननी देवी" in *Durgā;* "तू ही है सुमिरन जोग मोरे दाता" in *Kanakāṅgī;* and that soul-elevating composition in *rāga Sivamat Bhairava*, "प्रथम उठ भोर" the manner of which would be so consistently

---

21. I hasten to add that the composer in this case is *not* the maestro I am writing about.

soft, serene, and ennobling that the whole singing would look like a leisurely ascent, so to say, of the very incense of devotion to regions ethereal.

Of Aesthetic Discourse

Yet this wondrous fineness of the compositions that made his repertoire is not the only thing that distinguished Rahimuddin Khan. The way he *talked* about music is also noteworthy.

How do we distinguish the shades of a single *svara* today? The answer is: as *shuddha-komal,* or *ati komal, āndolit*. But is such talk adequate to the fabric of music, so rich and varied in design and appearance? One can hardly say, yes. This should become clear as we turn to consider the following brief account of Rahimuddin Khan's way of (thinking and) talking about some *svaras*:

The (*komal*) *rishabh* of *Puriyā* is *lajjit* or coy, the (aesthetic) meaning here being that the note is to be sung not self-assertively, but as a mere gentle accent in a phrase[22] that evokes, by the very manner of its flow, the image of a dainty blushing droop. In a rendering of *hindol* the *gandhār* should be *prajjvalit*; that is, it should look steadily luminous. The *pañcham* of *rāga Śrī* is *kamalvat;* which means that, rising from the *rishabh* slimly as a stem, the voice should open up at *pa*, so that the *pañcham* may seem to bloom, like a lotus. The way *we* commonly speak of such notes is, by contrast, the following prosaic one: the *rishabh* in *Pūriyā* is but a *zarrā* or *kaṇ* (dot or particle); *hindol* gives prominence to *ga-dha* concordance (*samvāda*) and in singing *rāga Śrī*, one has to highlight the *rishabh-pañcham* passage. I fail to see why we should confine ourselves to this latter kind of (merely grammatical) talk when in the context of other arts we speak freely of colours as *vibrant* or *recessive;* of vaulted roofs and pillars that seem *strained* in holding the beams aloft; and of

22. Say, the *ni, re, ni* phrase.

phrases that appear to clang or caress. It is noteworthy that all these adjectives (put in italics) relate to appearance or semblances, not to literal fact.

The matter is important because it relates to the very choice of taking a merely grammatical *or* truly aesthetic view of the look of music as it presents itself. So I feel impelled to expatiate it, as follows:

a. The notes in actual music *appear in a setting.*[23] So the way we talk about *svara*s should square with how they *seem* and relate to the context. In other words, our viewpoint should be mainly *phenomenological.* At present, however, it is not at all so. Our books on music of course speak of *svara*s to be used *in* a *rāga* — like bricks in building, as mere aggregation — though with inequal individual prominence. But they rarely link any effect or image with their use. And though the concept of *saṁvāda* is freely bandied about, nothing is said as to what the notes thus related are to look like. *The result is a chasm between our pedagogic talk about music and our actual experience of the art.*

b. This gap can be bridged only by the kind of discourse I have emphasized, following Khan Sahib. Such talk, I may add, has classified musical utterance itself — as against *svara*s and their groupings — from the viewpoint of manner and effect. The master indeed often brought out in singing five of such *vākya*s: *shuddha mudrā sādhāraṇa, tertik, vajravāk, sampūraṇa,* and *sāṁkhrā* (or *saṅkīrṇa*). To illustrate the first, a *bhairavi dhruvapad* — itself beginning with the words: *shuddha mudrā sādhāraṇa*

23. This setting may even be just an instant of quiet. As for the relation of music to silence taken generally, see my essay, "Music and Silence", in *Journal of Indian Council of Philosophical Research*, New Delhi, vol. XX, no. 3, July–September, 2003, pp. 224-34.

— would be sung. *Tertik*, I could see, means a tender, yearning manner of calling some one far away. *Vajravāk* is the opposite manner: stiff, regal, egotistical. The former, (that is, *tertik*) Rahimuddin Khan would add, distinguished the singing of his father; and the latter, that of his uncle, Zakiruddin Khan. The lesson for theory here is that (what is grammatically) the same *svara* or *svara-samooha* may be sung in ways which are *identifiably different in respect of seeming*. To be sure, a note may appear to be gently whispered or assertively thrust into silence. Unless these details are duly heeded, I ask, how is our concern with (and talk about) music *aesthetic* at all?

c. A more basic point may be made here. The Ustad would often insist that the *dhruvapad* word for cultivation of music is *sādhnā*, not *riyāz* or practice. *Riyāz* aims at better presentation — to the outside world; *sādhnā*, at a reverent probing into the mysteries of song, *and* at a concurrent imbuing of oneself with attitudes that make for self-improvement, and ultimately for the crowning goal of music: liberation. All this should become a little intelligible, if not readily acceptable, in the light of the following *dhruvapad* of *nād sādhnā* in *Rāga Bihāg*:

सुर तत्व ज्ञान, जीवन मुक्ति को रूप साधे, तब पावे
ज्ञान को मरम, गुनि जन सुनो प्रमान
जीव चित्त फिरे, तब चित्त पावक में प्रवेश करे
देह वायु को ले जाय, बह्म ग्रन्थि करके समान

But, one may ask, how does the idiom of our talk about music actually relate to the cultivation of *attitudes*, or, say, to orientation of being? I may here reproduce what I wrote long ago, as a mere summary of Khan Sahib's own comments that he would freely make while singing to his friends:

> Imagine a devotee hallowing the morning with *svaras* of the *bhairava* mode. Steadying himself with the basic *sa* (tonic), he sings to saturate himself with images and attitudes that suit the hour — the rising sun, yearning in prayer and chastening of self, pouring *arghya* (holy water) on the Deity, and non-attachment towards things of the world. A brief but sure touch at the tonic, followed by *komal rishabh* prolonged firmly and sweetly, at once blends the mind with the sunrise outside by suggesting effulgence, *the identification being helped by the fact that he has learnt to think of a "re" so sung as "tejasi"* or luminous. The same note, *komal re*, touched while descending from *ga*, provides, in manner, a musical transcript of the downward slant of pouring *arghya* on the idol; and this quite acceptably, because the singer has been trained *to call this rishabh "arghi."* As attunement grows through the aid of the *svaras*, detachment deepens and the devotee co-operates by holding on to the *sa* merely in idea and lingering repeatedly at the *re*, now softly, though sweetly — the note suggesting transcendence [of what is merely mundane]. The *re* thus becomes a symbol of devotion and elevation of the self.[24]

The Maestro as a Person

Yet, as a human being, Rahimuddin Khan was in no way exceptional. It was never easy to win his approval in respect of things which he did not already like, and what he always loved to do was singing to his friends, talking on music, rich tasty food and his five daily prayers. Only in respect of one of these I sometimes had to bend his will; and that was food. In spite of having a fairly robust constitution, he sometimes suffered from moderate attacks of piles, diabetes and tremor of the heart. On such days, though he would agree to do what I

24. This whole passage is an extract from my essay, "Essentials of Hindustānī Music", *Diogene*, 45, Paris, January–March, 1964, pp. 20-21.

wanted him to — that is, taking simple food, some biochemic remedies or a brief walk — he would, while eating what I offered, look pathetically glum. Once, when I had for a while extolled the virtues of boiled, vegeterian food, he angrily protested that he was not born to become a wash-cloth, like me, to be hung on a string.

He was indeed, in some select matters, headstrong. At the same time, one could not help acknowledging his keen sense of self-respect. Once he spurned the offer of a job, when (I knew) he needed it most, just because the "patron" who made the offer had, a few days earlier, branded "the whole tribe" of musicians as being "undependable." The late Acharya K.C.D. Brihaspati and I were two of his best friends; but both of us had also been, at times, the objects of his ire which, however, would be merely momentary. At the same time he was deeply responsive to sheer human love and concern; and my most moving image of the man is *his appearing quite honoured, and delighted like a child* when once, with my family, I visited his sparsely furnished residence.

He was indeed a simple man at heart. And the honours he won did nothing to change him. Yet, these were many and exalted: Sangeet Natak Akademi Award for Hindustānī Music in 1964; *Sangeet Ratnākar* from Bharat Dharma Maha Mandal Dharma Sabha, Varanasi; *Sangeet Martand* from Lalit Kala Akademi, Kanpur; and honorary doctorate in music from Sur Singar Samsad, Bombay; and, above all, the coveted *Padma Bhushan.*[25]

This, however, was hardly the kind of attention he *needed,* though he richly *deserved* it all. His finances were generally so

25. What is, however, a surer index of Rahimuddin Khan's quality as a musician is the fact that he was held in high regard by vocalists like Ustads Bade Ghulam Ali Khan and Amir Khan, and the sitar wizard, Ustad Wilayat Khan.

bad that even a hand-to-mouth living appeared to satisfy him. The last thing he did with my help was to fill an "application for financial assistance" from the Department of Culture (Government of India) under the "reactivated" 1961 scheme for help to distinguished artists. And he was visibly relieved when he saw that he *could* apply; for, as per conditions, his monthly income did not exceed the sum of two hundred and fifty rupees — his Radio fee for one day's singing!

His closing days, however, were by no means forlorn. At Jaipur, where he suffered his first heart attack in January 1975, the doctors and Saiduddin, his son-in-law, did all that they could. When (after summer) he had shifted to Delhi, he would often make a grateful mention of this fact. Here, in the capital, he was scheduled to sing for the last time in his life, on 9 November, in the Tansen Festival. But the strain of sitting through Ustad Bismillah Khan's recital on November 7 quite incapacitated him. He now looked exhausted and in distress; and had therefore to be hospitalized.[26] Here, intensive medical care, the presence of his son and the soliticitous visits of Dagar Brothers, Asad Ali, Smt. Saira and other friends seemed to enliven him for a while. But he passed away on November 20, 1975, a little after midday. His last wish was to offer *namāz*; and it was, in fact, during the preparatory ablutions that he sank into lifelessness, in the lap of his son.

Rahimuddin Khan Dagar was not just one vocalist, but a significant link with our hoary past. Yet what makes him an object of abiding reverence to me is the general look of his music. It would be unmistakably *sāttvik*. But let me explain. Times without number, I would be raised by the power of his music to a kind of deep, emancipated feeling, produced not by mere melodic sweetness but by evocation of thoughts and

26. That is, at the All India Institute of Medical Sciences, New Delhi.

images of sheer unboundedness. I would experience, in addition, that rarefaction of the self where the *rasika* does not only listen, but (so to say) inhales a melodic ambience which also encompasses him and makes him feel better and purer, and not merely sweeter after the recital.

Plotinus has characterized art as a kind of "metaphysical homesickness." More or less similarly, Tagore speaks of the "lonely region of renunciation" to which our music tends to lift us. If utterances such as these make sense, and I am sure they do, it is only in the light of the art of musicians like Rahimuddin Khan Dagar.

Bibliography

Anantapadmanabhan, S.C., *The Veeṇā — Its Technique, Theory and Practice*, Delhi: Gana Vidya Bharati, 1954.

Bandra, St. Paul, *The Return of the Prodigal Son — A Story of Homecoming*, Mumbai, 1998, Delhi: Vidya Jyoti.

Barfield, Owen, *What Coleridge Thought*, London: OUP, 1972.

Beardsley, Monroe C., "The Aesthetic Point of View" in *Metaphilosophy*, vol. I, no. 1, January 1970.

Bradley, A.C., *Oxford Lectures on Poetry*, MacMillan, 1965.

Brelet, Gisele, "Music and Silence", in *Reflections on Art*, ed. S.K. Langer, Baltimore: The John Hopkins Press, 2nd printing.

Budd, Malcolm, "Motion and Emotion in Music: How Music Sounds" in *BJA*, Summer 1983.

Coleman, Francis Jerome, *Contemporary Studies in Aesthetics*, New York: Mc Graw-Hill Book Company, 1968.

Croce, B., *Aesthetic — As Science of Expression and General Linguistic*, London: Vision Press, 1962 rpt.

Davies, Stephen, "Is Music a Language of the Emotions?" in *BJA*, Summer 1983.

Dewey, John, *Art as Experience*, New York: Capricorn Books, 1958. (7th Impression).

Gatt, Giuseppe, *Turner*, A Dolphin Art Book, Thames and Hudson 1968.

Greco, El, "Resurrection", in C. Bazin's *A Concise History of Art*, London: Thames and Hudson, Second Impression, Part II, 1964.

Hahn, L.E., *The Philosophy of Charles Hartshorne* (vol. XX in The Library of Living Philosophers), La Salle, Illinois, Open Court, 1991.

Havell, H.L., "The fifth cause of sublimity, which embraces all those preceding, is majesty and elevation of *structure*", "On the Sublime", tr. of *Peri Hupsous* of Longinus, Everyman's Library, 1963, p. 144.

Hegel, *The Philosophy of Fine Art*, tr. F.P.B. Osmaston, London: G. Bell & Sons, 1920, vol. II.

Johnson, M.L., "Kant's Unified Theory of Beauty" in *The Journal of Aesthetics and Art Criticism*, Winter 1979.

Kant, on "empirical form", in T.E. Uehling's *The Notion of Form in Kant's Critique of Aesthetic Judgement*, The Hague: Mounton, 1971.

Kant, *The Critique of Judgement*, tr. J.C. Meredith, Oxford: Clarendon Press, 1969 Reprint, 68/Academy Edition.

Kivy, Peter, *Music Alone — Philosophical Reflections on the Purely Musical Experience*, Cornell University Press, 1990.

Kunhan Raja C., *Sangeet Ratnākar*, English tr., The Adyar Library, 1945, vol. I.

Langer, Susanne K., *Feeling and Form*, Routledge and Kegan Paul, 3rd Impression, 1963.

———, *Mind: An Essay on Human Feeling*, vol. I, John Hopkins University Press, 2nd printing, 1975.

———, *Problems of Art*, London: Routledge & Kegan Paul, 1957.

LeFevre, Perry D., *The Prayers of Kierkegaard*, Chicago and London: The University of Chicago Press, 1963.

Lippi, Filippo, "Adoration in the Forest", in C. Bazin, *A Concise History of Art*, London: Thames and Hudson, Second Impression, Part I, 1964.

Lowe, Benjamin, *The Beauty of Sport*, New Jersey: Prentice-Hall, Inc., 1977.

Lucie Smith, Edward, *Movements in Art since 1945*, London: Thames and Hudson, 1969.

Martin, F. David, "Architecture and Sublimity" in *Art and the Religious Experience: The "Language" of the Sacred*, Lewisburg: Bucknell University Press, 1972.

Mcadoo, Nick, "Can Art Ever be Just About Itself?" in *JAAC*, Spring 1992.

Mitias, Michael H., "What makes an Experience Aesthetic", in *Journal of Aesthetics and Art Criticism*, Winter 1982.

Mittal, Anjali, *Hindustānī Music and the Aesthetic Concept of Form*, D.K. Printworld, 2001.

Monier-Williams, M., *A Sanskrit–English Dictionary*, p. 1120, New improved edition, Motilal Banarsidass, Delhi, 2002.

Osborne, Harold, *The Art of Appreciation*, OUP, 1970.

Popley, H.A., *The Music of India*, The Heritage of India Press, 1950.

Pyarelal, *The Last Phase*, Ahmedabad: Navajivan Publishing House, 1958.

Reid, L.A., *Meaning in the Arts*, London: George Allen and Unwin, 1969.

Reid, L.A., "Art: Knowledge-That and Knowing-This", in *BJA*, Autmn 1980.

Saxena, Sushil Kumar, *Avenues to Beauty*, New Delhi: Sangeet Natak Akademi and D.K. Printworld, 2009.

———, "Aesthetics of Hindustānī Music" in *Aesthetical Essays*, Delhi: Chanakya Publications, 1981.

———, "Aesthetics of Hindustānī Music", *Sangeet Natak*, no. 28, April–June, 1973.

———, "Altaf Hussain Khan", *Sangeet Natak*, no. 2, April 1966.

———, "Essentials of Hindustānī Music", *Diogene*, 45, Paris, January–March, 1964.

———, "Hegel on the Sublime" published in *Religious Studies*, England, no. 10.

———, "Kant, Aesthetical Theory and some Indian Art" in *Kant Studien*, vol. II, 1978, Berlin and New York: Walter de Gruyter.

———, "A Master of Melody — Ustad Bade Ghulam Ali Khan", in Malti Gilani and Quaratulain Hyder, *Ustad Bade Ghulam Ali Khan — His Life and Music*, New Delhi: Harman Publishing House, 2003.

———, "Music and Silence", in *Journal of Indian Council of Philosophical Research*, New Delhi, vol. XX, no. 3, July–September, 2003.

———, "The Aesthetic Attitude", *Philosophy East and West (PEW)*, 28, no. 1, January 1978; "Reply to My Critics" (*PEW*, 29, no. 2, April 1979), and "The Aesthetic Attitude: Reply to some New Criticisms" (*PEW*, April 1980).

———, "The Fabric of Amad: A study of Form and Flow in Hindustānī Music", *Sangeet Natak*, no. 16, April–June 1970.

———, "Ustad Amir Khan: The Man and His Art", *Sangeet Natak*, Jan–March, 1974.

———, *The Winged Form — Aesthetical Essays on Hindustani Rhythm*, Sangeet Natak Akademi, New Delhi, 1979.

———, Ustad A. Rahimuddin Khan Dagar, *Sangeet Natak*, 39, January–March 1976.

Schneider, H.W., *A History of American Philosophy*, New York: The Liberal Arts Press, 1946.

Shakespeare *Hamlet*, Act III, Scene I.

Shelley, P.B., *Epipsychidion*.

Smith, Edward Lucie, *Movements in Art Since 1945*, London: Thames and Hudson, 1960.

Stolnitz, J.,"The Aesthetic Attitude", in J. Hospers ed., *Introductory Readings in Aesthetics*, The Free Press, 1969.

Uehling, J.E., Jr., *The Notion of Form in Kant's Critique of Judgment*.

Valentine, C.W., *The Experimental Psychology of Beauty*, 1962.

Wadhera, Prakash, "The Phenomenon that was Bade Ghulam Ali Khan", in Malti Gilani and Quaratulain Hyder, *Ustad Bade Ghulam Ali Khan — His Life and Music*, New Delhi: Harman Publishing House, 2003.

Wordsworth, "Lines Composed a Few Miles Above Tintern Abbey", lines 95-104.

Index
(Names)